WHERE ARE ALL THE GOOD JOBS GOING?

WHERE ARE ALL THE GOOD JOBS GOING?

What National and Local Job Quality and Dynamics Mean for U.S. Workers

Harry J. Holzer
Julia I. Lane
David B. Rosenblum
Fredrik Andersson

Russell Sage Foundation
New York

The Russell Sage Foundation

Library of Congress Cataloging-in-Publication Data

Where are all the good jobs going? : what national and local job quality and dynamics mean for U.S. workers / Harry J. Holzer . . . [et al.].
    p. cm.
Includes bibliographical references and index.
    ISBN 978-0-87154-458-2 (alk. paper)
    1. Labor market—United States.   2. Employment forecasting—United States.   3. Quality of work life—United States.   4. Wages—United States.   5. Employment forecasting—United States.   I. Holzer, Harry J., 1957–
    HD5724.W417 2011
    331.10973—dc22   2010040004

Text design by Genna Patacsil.

The opinions expressed are those of the authors and may not represent those of the institutions they represent.

RUSSELL SAGE FOUNDATION
112 East 64th Street, New York, New York 10065
10 9 8 7 6 5 4 3 2 1

Contents

About the Authors |

HARRY J. HOLZER is professor of public policy at Georgetown University and institute fellow at the Urban Institute in Washington, D.C.

JULIA I. LANE is program director of Science of Science and Innovation Policy at the National Science Foundation, research fellow at the Institute of Labor (IZA), Bonn, Germany, and former senior research fellow at the U.S. Bureau of the Census.

DAVID B. ROSENBLUM is senior economic analyst at NORC at the University of Chicago.

FREDRIK ANDERSSON is an economist in the Economics Department of the Office of the Comptroller of the Currency, U.S. Department of the Treasury.

Acknowledgments |

WE ARE GRATEFUL to the Ford and MacArthur Foundations for their generous support of this project, and particularly to Rick McGahey and Erika Poethig for help along the way. Tim Bartik and Howard Wial have given us helpful comments, as have seminar participants at Georgetown University. Suzanne Nichols and Eric Wanner of the Russell Sage Foundation were extremely accommodating in getting the manuscript out in a timely and efficient manner and were generally very supportive of us. And four anonymous referees (two providing reports to the Russell Sage Foundation and two to the Center for Economic Studies at the U.S. Census Bureau) helped enormously as well.

This research uses data from the Census Bureau's Longitudinal Employer-Household Dynamics (LEHD) program, which was partially supported by the following grants: National Science Foundation (NSF) SES-9978093, SES-0339191, and ITR-0427889; National Institute on Aging AG018854; and grants from the Alfred P. Sloan Foundation. The LEHD program data infrastructure was developed by many individuals, including John Abowd, Fredrik Andersson, Matthew Armstrong, Sasan Bakhtiari, Patti Becker, Gary Benedetto, Melissa Bjelland, Chet Bowie, Holly Brown, Hyowook Chiang, Stephen Ciccarella, Cynthia Clark, Rob Creecy, Lisa Dragoset, Chuncui Fan, Colleen Flannery, Lucia Foster, Matthew Freedman, Monica Garcia-Perez, Nancy Gordon, Matthew Graham, Owen Haaga, Hermann Habermann, John Haltiwanger, Heath Hayward, Tomeka Hill, Henry Hyatt, Emily Isenberg, Ron Jarmin, C. Louis Kincannon, Fredrick Knickerbocker, Mark Kutzbach, Walter Kydd, Julia Lane, Paul Lengermann, Tao Li, Cindy Ma, Erika McEntarfer, Kevin McKinney, Thomas Mesenbourg, Bong Mulato, Nicole Nestoriak, Camille Norwood, Ron Prevost, Kenneth Prewitt, George Putnam, Uma Radhakrishnan, Bryan Ricchetti, Marc Roemer, Kristin Sandusky, Ian Schmutte, Liliana Sousa, Bryce Stephens, Martha Stinson, Michael Strain, Stephen Tibbets, J. Preston Waite, Chip Walker, Dan Weinberg, Bill Winkler, Simon Woodcock, Jeremy Wu, Laura Zayatz, Chen Zhao, and Chaoling Zheng. The opinions expressed in this volume are those of the authors and not the U.S. Census Bureau or any of the research sponsors.

We want to acknowledge Beth Shulman, a friend with whom we had a long series of conversations over the past few years on the issue of good jobs and how to fill and create them. Beth, who died quite unexpectedly while this manuscript was under preparation, was a source of great knowledge and inspiration on this issue. We remember her very fondly and miss her very much.

Chapter 1 | Introduction and Background

THE COMBINATION OF inequality and volatility that characterizes the U.S. labor market has clearly generated a great deal of *insecurity*, even among currently employed Americans. They worry about when they might lose their jobs, how they might sustain themselves and their families during a period of joblessness, whether their wages and salaries on their next jobs will be as good as the ones they might lose, and also whether or not they will be covered by health insurance and other benefits.[1] This was true even before the Great Recession of the past few years, and it seems to have become even truer in the period of high joblessness we have experienced recently.

The policy debate on these issues has often focused on the education and skills of American *workers* and the question of whether these skills are sufficient to generate broadly shared prosperity and earnings security in the years to come. There is little doubt that differences in education and skill levels across workers now generate more inequality than in previous years and that the importance of raising worker education and skills at all levels has risen as well.

However, many analysts believe that improving education and skills alone will not be sufficient to generate broadly shared prosperity and security and that we need to focus as well on the *jobs* that our labor market is producing. Of course, in the aftermath of the Great Recession, and with a slow recovery projected by most economists, the *quantity* of jobs available to American workers will be a serious issue for years to come. But, at the same time, we should also focus on the *quality* of these jobs, as measured by pay levels and benefits, and their degree of *permanence* over the longer term. Have these two attributes of jobs in the U.S. labor market been changing over time? Are "good jobs" actually disappearing in the

1

United States, and if so, for whom? Should public policy encourage the creation of more "good jobs" as well as "good workers"? And if the answer to that question is yes, how shall it do so? Will good jobs exist in sufficient quantities to absorb many more workers if they have the appropriate skills? To the extent that there is enormous variation across the United States by state and local areas, is there a role to be played by state and local economic development policies? If so, what constitute cost-effective public interventions in this area, and to what extent must education and training be an integral part of these strategies?

The goal of this book is to shed light on these questions about job quality and volatility over time and what they imply for inequality and insecurity among American workers. We provide evidence on what is happening to the availability of good jobs, over time and for which groups of workers; what kinds of good jobs are now being generated; what happens to dislocated workers who lose good jobs and how their prospects are affected by the availability of good jobs today; and how all of this varies by the time period studied and the local labor markets.

We also look at the dynamics of job creation and destruction within existing firms and within firms that are themselves "dying" or "being born." That examination sheds some light on the possible effectiveness of economic development policies that attempt to generate or attract good jobs and the firms that create them. Finally, we consider what all of this means for public policy.

INEQUALITY AND VOLATILITY

The American labor market is very unequal; by almost any measure, it is the most unequal in the industrialized world. Inequality has increased a great deal over time, and differences in earnings across individuals and skill groups have grown dramatically over the past three decades. Indeed, the real (or inflation-adjusted) earnings of Americans without college diplomas, especially men, have stagnated, while those of the college-educated have grown, creating very high earnings gaps. Most strikingly, in the last decade the earnings of the top 1 percent of earners have skyrocketed relative to those of everyone else.[2]

The American labor market is also volatile. Each year many millions of jobs are destroyed and others are newly created, and American workers often experience both voluntary and involuntary spells of unemployment as they seek new jobs.[3] The forces of technological change and globalization generate the restructuring of industries, the decline of existing businesses, the entry of new businesses, and the reorganization of workplaces in surviving firms. The severe economic downturn of 2008 and beyond certainly exacerbated the effects of these developments for many Americans as the rates of job destruction outpaced those of job creation for more than two years, leading to the net loss of several million jobs.

Furthermore, the institutions that traditionally have protected workers from both inequality and turbulence—like minimum wage laws, collective bargaining, and other government regulations, as well as the human resource policies of companies that created some protections—have weakened over time, rendering workers vulnerable. Fewer workers are covered by unemployment insurance, at least in good times, than at any time in recent decades, and those who are covered are more likely to see their benefits expire while they remain jobless (Burtless 2007). Workers who lose jobs are also more vulnerable to the loss of employer-provided health benefits, as these have become scarcer over time as well.

But a broad evaluation of the trends in the U.S. job market over time does not paint a completely negative picture. Although inequality has increased, a rising tide has lifted most boats: the majority of American workers have enjoyed at least some real earnings growth (when correctly measured) in the past three decades, and highly educated workers, especially women, have enjoyed strong earnings gains over time.[4] There is no consensus that, aside from the huge rate of job destruction in the recent recession, job volatility has been rising over time. Although some popular accounts, such as those written by Jacob Hacker (2006) and Peter Gosselin (2008), show evidence of rising income volatility—which they attribute to rising volatility in the job market—other analyses suggest that this is far from certain. And the effects of volatility on workers in some cases are more positive than news accounts suggest, with many workers taking advantage of the opportunities for earnings growth that appear in many newly created jobs.[5]

THE IMPORTANCE OF JOBS AND JOB QUALITY

From an economist's point of view, jobs are generated on the demand side of the labor market, while workers reflect the supply side. In the market, the two sides interact to generate the wage and employment outcomes we observe for different groups of workers in different kinds of jobs. Indeed, wages fluctuate up or down to "equilibrate" the market—that is, to make sure that, in most cases, the available jobs can be filled by the workers who seek them. If the number of jobs grow more rapidly than the number of workers to fill them in some occupations or sectors, wages there will rise to attract more workers and limit job growth; the opposite occurs when too few jobs are available relative to workers.

But factors working independently on the demand side of the labor market—such as technological change and globalization—can affect the quality and stability of jobs that workers face in the market. If new technologies enable employers to reorganize the workplace in ways that use fewer less-educated or lower-skilled workers, then their wages might be driven downward relative to those of other groups, and some of the jobs will disappear entirely. The same is true if imports generate competition for these workers from lower-paid producers overseas or if more work in the United States can be outsourced abroad. These forces have no doubt contributed importantly to the steep relative decline in earnings experienced by less-educated or less-skilled American workers in recent years and the disappearance of many of the well-paid jobs that they held.[6]

Of course, markets do not always clear, and institutions can play some role in affecting these market outcomes. Labor unions, in particular, are an institution that historically has played an important role in raising workers' wages and benefits. Government regulations, especially in the form of minimum wage statutes as well as overtime premia, can affect pay as well, particularly at the bottom of the wage spectrum. Together, these forces affect the pay available on some jobs and in some firms relative to others, even for workers of a given skill level. The weakening of these laws and institutions over time has no doubt also contributed to the declining relative earnings of less-educated workers in the United States.[7]

But wages also vary systematically with other demand-side characteristics, such as industry and firm size, even after adjusting for the skills of workers in these firms and sectors. Industries such as construction, durable manufacturing, transportation, utilities, and wholesale trade have traditionally paid well, even for workers with relatively less education. These wage premia across industries might be partly accounted for by factors like the capital-labor ratios of the firms in those industries, but not fully. And large firms have long paid more than small ones, even when hiring the same kind of labor. For instance, it is clear that major hospitals pay more than nursing homes for workers at low levels of education or skill. A variety of hypotheses have been put forward to explain the "size-wage premium," though none has done so very completely.[8]

The average differences in pay by industry and size category suggest that employers are not perfectly passive players in a labor market completely determined by technological and global forces. In the face of competitive forces, employers choose how to organize the workplace, how to recruit and screen their workers, how to train them, when and whom to promote or discharge, and how to compensate workers, in terms of wages as well as benefits. These are broadly referred to as *human resource* practices, and all reflect important degrees of employer choice—even within the same narrowly defined industry and geographic location.

For example, some employers choose to compete on the basis of low costs and therefore pay the lowest possible wages and benefits needed to attract workers and fill available jobs. They are willing to live with lower productivity among their workers and the higher costs associated with rapid turnover. Other employers who choose to compete more on the basis of higher productivity and lower turnover pay more for their workers because that enables them to attract more productive workers and to retain them for longer. Some of these employers pay more because they find it economically worthwhile to do so, as the labor market research on "efficiency wages" suggests.[9] Others might do so because of union requirements or because of their own preferences and sense of fairness, especially if human resource decisions are made by managers in relatively less competitive industries who are not under a great deal of pressure to generate higher profits. The lowest-paying ones are often referred to as "low road" employers and the better-paying ones as "high road" employers, though the choices they make are often less dichotomous and more varied than these terms might suggest.

Thus, the "quality" of American jobs can reflect many factors, sometimes independently (at least to some extent) of the quality of workers available to fill them. An important corollary of this view is the notion that good jobs can come in at least two varieties: some pay well directly because they require personal skills and credentials that are highly rewarded in the market; others pay well because employers have chosen (or are forced by laws or unions) to pay more, independently of these required skills and credentials. Later in the chapter we consider whether trends over time in the quality and stability of good jobs vary according to which definition we use.

But these definitions raise a conundrum: if high-road firms in competitive industries need more productive workers to offset their higher wages, to what extent are the wages they pay really independent of the personal characteristics of their workers? And in this case, won't firms need to be choosier about the underlying skills and productivity of the workers they hire?

High-road firms might hire fewer workers who will remain unskilled and unproductive, regardless of the firm's human resource policies. But it is also likely that the productivity of many workers rises when they are hired at a high-road firm, because the firm invests more in training them or in retaining them over time (in which case they acquire skills informally through on-the-job training), in motivating them to work harder, or in organizing a workplace that effectively harnesses workers' potential productivity. In this case, the wage effects attributed to a firm correctly capture its contribution to worker earnings, especially if that higher productivity is not perfectly transferable to other jobs later held by its workers.

Finally, it is also clear from previous analysis of worker and firm effects that the quality of jobs and the firms that provide them have important effects on worker outcomes, such as earnings levels and advancement over time, controlling for underlying worker characteristics. To the extent that some workers systematically have more access to some kinds of firms and jobs than do other workers independently of their skills—perhaps owing to discrimination, geographic location, or informal networks—then important wage differences across groups can persist over time for reasons other than skills.[10] Encouraging more employers to create good jobs and ensuring their availability to a wider range of workers might then become important components of strategies to reduce poverty and earnings gaps between specific demographic groups.

GOOD JOBS: LESS AVAILABLE OVER TIME?

The evidence that good jobs can exist for a variety of different reasons leads to a very salient question: have good jobs become less available over the long term? This question has appeared in many contexts and been asked by many public commentators in recent years. In particular, those opposed to expansions of trade and offshoring—like Lou Dobbs, Ross Perot, and many others[11]—have argued that competition from low-wage workers abroad tends to eliminate good jobs here at home. Others on the leftward side of the American political spectrum—for example, the Washington Post columnist Harold Meyerson (2009)—have made similar arguments.

Is there much basis to these claims? Perhaps the answer depends on which definition of "good jobs" we are using. To the extent that good jobs are those that are filled by "good workers" (whether the higher worker productivity is due to the worker's characteristics or those of the firm), it is not obvious why they should be threatened by foreign trade and offshoring—unless competition from highly skilled workers earning much lower wages elsewhere than the United States increases competitive pressures on these workers, as the Harvard economist Richard Freeman and others have argued.[12] To the extent that new technology could replace highly skilled workers, their jobs could also be threatened—though most of the empirical evidence suggests that much of the technological change of recent years has been "skill-biased" in favor of those with more education and against those with less.[13] Perhaps these forces reduce the ability of relatively less-productive workers within each observed educational or training category to fill good jobs over time, so that only those within each education group with the best analytical or social skills are productive enough to survive the technological or global shifts in production.[14]

Clearly, technological change and import competition have reduced the availability of well-paid jobs in the traditional goods-producing sectors, like durable manufacturing, that have traditionally paid good wages to millions of less-educated workers (those with high school diplomas or less). In fact, the share of U.S. workers employed in durable manufacturing has fallen from about 12 percent in 1970 to 6 percent in 2008 as both technology and globalization reduced the demand for domestic labor in these jobs.[15]

And the dramatic declines of collective bargaining and union membership over time, at least in the private sector, suggest a similar decline in high-wage job availability; the share of workers in unions overall has fallen from about 35 percent in 1955 to roughly 12 percent overall and 7 percent in the private sector in 2008.[16] Federal minimum wage levels have also tended to fall over time, relative to median wages in the private sector.[17] All of these forces tend to reduce the quality of jobs available to those with relatively lower levels of education (such as a high school diploma or less). And these developments to some extent reflect legal and institutional choices made by American policymakers—especially to be more relaxed about enforcing labor laws governing collective bargaining and to be more protective of management prerogatives (Freeman 2007a).

But the declines in employment in high-wage jobs apparently go well beyond those in durable manufacturing and those workers directly affected by unions or the minimum wage.[18] Why else, then, might good jobs more broadly be disappearing, especially for less-educated workers? In general, it is likely that new technologies and globalization have made a range of markets more competitive than before. Product markets become more competitive when consumers have more choices available to them as a result of rising imports or Internet-based competition domestically; capital markets become more competitive if firms face more pressure from the suppliers of capital (like major pension funds) to raise profits; and labor markets become more competitive when highly paid workers lose their jobs to their lower-paid counterparts overseas or at home.[19] More competitive product and capital markets make it harder for employers to pass on higher labor costs to consumers in the form of higher prices or to capital owners in the form of lower rates of return. And both new technologies in the workplace and globalization might directly make labor markets more competitive as firms increasingly shift production overseas to lower their costs or rely more heavily on machines than on less-educated workers.

Of course, one can also argue that recent developments in executive and financial market compensation do not reflect well-functioning labor markets at all. Instead, they seem to indicate market imperfections and concentrated power that have not only led to enormous concentrations of earnings at the very top of the distribution but also abetted the development of a debt-driven housing and financial bubble that ultimately collapsed and drove us into the Great Recession (Bebchuk and Fried 2004; Roubini and Mimh 2010). Yet it is also likely that both sets of developments have occurred simultaneously—with more competitive product and labor markets imposing greater constraints on many or most workers, especially those without the strongest educational credentials, while outlandish financial bonuses and CEO pay have created huge windfalls for those at the very top.

If true, then the more competitive forces affecting most workers would be generating labor demand that is more "elastic"—that is, where employment levels are more (negatively) responsive to labor costs. Under these circumstances, there is more pressure on employers to either reduce compensation or ensure that higher compensation is offset by higher productivity.[20] Fewer employers have the luxury often afforded by less competitive markets in the past to pay above-market wages according to "managerial preferences." And in addition to other legal and institutional factors, more elastic labor demand might well contribute to the declining power of unions, which now find it harder to generate wage increases without causing a loss of employment in many private-sector industries.[21]

Furthermore, even those firms that have historically offset higher compensation costs with higher worker productivity may face growing pressure in this new competitive environment. The high-road model may become relatively competitive mostly in the production of "niche" products rather than broadly consumed goods and services. The dramatic success of Wal-Mart as a distributor of low-cost goods produced in China and elsewhere may reflect a new model and a growing competitive advantage for low-cost producers that are now better able to undercut and out-compete some of their higher-road competitors like Kroger or Costco.[22]

If the disappearing higher-wage firms are those that disproportionately benefited less-educated workers in the past, greater labor market inequality would result from these shifts. On the other hand, well-paid jobs in sectors like health care (and especially at larger employers like hospitals) probably face much less of this pressure and therefore continue to grow because of demographic shifts (such as the aging of the U.S. population) that increase the demand for health care services. Since new technologies in health care can substitute for direct worker input only to a limited extent, and since most health care services cannot be imported or easily offshored, demand in this sector will remain quite strong and thus limit the downward trend in the availability of well-paid jobs in this sector.

The notion that some good jobs are more easily replaced by technology or globalization than others appears in claims that the job market is experiencing a "hollowing of the middle": well-paid jobs for less-skilled workers disappear when the work involved is routinized and can be easily done by computers, robots, or non-English-speaking workers (abroad or domestically) who do not need to interact with customers. Those jobs that survive are either highly paid and involve nonroutine analytics (especially for those with bachelor's degrees or higher) or low-paid and based on social interactions with customers or coworkers.

The empirical evidence to date certainly provides some support for the notion that middle-paying or middle-skill jobs declined in magnitude (and in pay levels) more than others, especially during the 1990s.[23] At the same time, it is clear that many well-paid middle-skill jobs, requiring some postsecondary schooling or training but less than a four-year college degree, remain in the U.S. labor market. These jobs remain good jobs for workers with appropriate levels of skill and previous training, even if they do not have college diplomas, and many of them cannot easily be outsourced or replaced by machines.[24]

All of this discussion suggests that good jobs may decline in magnitude and availability in some cases but not in others, and for some workers but not for others. Those jobs that face the greatest changes in the technology of production or that are amenable to being globally provided may be declining the most—or at least may be filled increasingly by workers with greater productive potential. And other legal and institutional developments over time interact with these forces and no doubt reinforce their effects.

THE CONSEQUENCES OF VOLATILITY

If high-compensation producers are now under greater competitive pressure than before, the jobs they provide to workers may not only pay less but also may be less secure over time and more vulnerable to permanent dislocation. Of course, the movement of workers across jobs can lead to major wage gains, especially when such movement is voluntary; this is particularly true of job changes for young workers and those who have been stuck in low-wage jobs.[25] But when workers become involuntarily "displaced" or "dislocated," they tend to suffer major losses in earnings—

which might be related to the quality of the jobs they have held, relative to their own general skills.[26]

For instance, dislocated workers tend to experience some employment losses in the first few years after losing their jobs—until they gain new ones that last—and they frequently experience earnings losses over the longer run, because their new jobs do not pay them as highly as their old ones did. Perhaps they have lost seniority, perhaps the returns to specific skills were more valuable in their older jobs than in the newer ones, or perhaps the new job simply does not pay as well as the old one. Empirically, the long-term earnings losses average 15 percent or higher, as we note later. They are higher for older and less-educated workers than for younger or more-educated ones, who tend to move more easily across economic sectors and, because of their higher general skills and lower family commitments, are more likely to benefit from new opportunities that open up.[27] But the extent to which such losses might be higher for those who lose good jobs, especially when they cannot replace those jobs with ones of comparable quality, remains unclear.

Thus, today's workers might experience growing economic losses due to job market turbulence in a variety of different ways, especially when it comes to the role played by job quality. Even if the average quality of jobs is not changing—in the aggregate or for less-educated workers—new technologies and globalization may make existing jobs more unstable and lead to greater potential losses as workers are faced with the need to find new jobs and endure some loss of seniority or skills specific to their older jobs. This would be true even if *job creation* in high-wage sectors fully offsets *job destruction* in magnitude, leading to little *net* change in the availability of high-wage jobs for different groups of workers.

If jobs are no more unstable than before but fewer employers now offer health insurance or contributions to pension plans, the *incidence* of displacement might be no higher than in earlier years but its *costs* might rise over time, especially along certain important nonwage dimensions. And if higher-wage jobs are, in fact, becoming less available over time, either overall or for less-educated workers, then the wage costs of displacement might also rise, because it becomes more difficult to replace a lost job with one that pays comparable wages.

In this latter case, the distribution of net job creation would be shifting toward lower-wage sectors, at least for some workers. Not only would inequality rise overall in the labor force, especially for newer (or younger) cohorts of workers relative to older ones, but the older cohorts themselves would increasingly experience losses over time, and all might feel greater insecurity in the labor market, even while other groups of workers benefit from the creation of new jobs in the labor market.

THE IMPORTANCE OF LOCAL
LABOR MARKETS

The late Speaker of the House Thomas P. "Tip" O'Neill (D-Mass.) once proclaimed that "all politics is local." In a similar way, all labor markets are local—in the sense that the broad national and international forces described here play out in local labor markets around the country that differ from one another in the demographics of their workers, the concentrations of industries, and their vulnerability to (or ability to profit from) the many changes occurring around the world.

Local labor markets matter for a variety of reasons. For instance, worker mobility across local areas is often costly and somewhat limited—so that a "shock" to a set of local industries and jobs (like a fall in the prices of imported products that makes it harder for local industries to compete) limits the opportunities of workers in those localities and industries, at least in the short term. If their ability to relocate across industries or local areas is limited over time—by investments in skills specific to those industries, by ownership of local housing, or by non-economic factors (such as close family ties)—their inability to adjust by moving to a new industry or location might last even longer. And policy issues for workers often play out locally as well, with education and training policy for workers heavily determined by a variety of local boards with federal, state, or local funding.[28] Because of all of these factors, local economic forces often have important effects on workers and their well-being.

Local labor markets are primarily based in *metropolitan statistical areas* (MSAs), including the central cities and very diverse suburbs in which both workers and firms are now located.[29] Furthermore, the metropolitan areas in certain *states and regions* tend to follow broad patterns of industrial concentration and of growth or decline, which generate commonalities in their overall labor market experiences and challenges. For instance, certain metropolitan areas—including but not limited to those of the industrial Midwest—have been hard hit by the decline in durable manufacturing employment over the past decade and earlier, and especially in the economic downturn of the past few years.[30] These are often medium-sized areas in which an above-average fraction of the workforce was employed in manufacturing at some point in the recent past and where the loss of these and other jobs has hit disproportionately large numbers of people. Furthermore, some of these metro areas have no doubt been more successful than others in attracting or developing new industries and good jobs to offset the losses experienced in manufacturing.

These developments raise a number of important questions. To the extent that the areas that have lost large numbers of manufacturing jobs have been successful in replacing them, what has happened to job quality and volatility there? In other words, are the new jobs as high in quality as the old ones, and do they require similar or different (and higher) skills, thereby benefiting a different group of workers than those displaced? Do the areas that attract more highly educated workers also provide more growth and better opportunities for the less-educated? Are there systematic differences between larger and smaller MSAs in this regard, or between those in the South or Midwest relative to those on the two coasts? Has inequality grown more dramatically in some of these areas, and have older and less-educated workers been hurt worse in some places than in others?

To fully understand what has happened at these local levels, we also need to know more about the *dynamics of firms and jobs* as well as workers. For instance, to what extent is local job growth driven more by the creation of new jobs or more by the preservation of older ones, and who benefits in each case? Are new firms (or establishments) the primary generators of new jobs, or are new jobs more likely to grow in existing firms? How important is it to offset firm deaths with births, and how does this vary across industry and local labor markets as well as by job quality?

The answers to these questions have important implications for the appropriate policy responses to the developments we have described. We now turn to a discussion of these potential responses.

POLICY RESPONSES

All of these issues raise important questions for public policy. There is little doubt that differences in education and skill levels across workers are generating more inequality than in previous years and that the importance of raising worker education and skills at all levels has risen as well.

But should public policy encourage the creation of more good jobs as well as "good workers"? And if the answer is yes, how shall it do so? Increases in minimum wage laws and other regulations, especially mandates on benefit provision or training, can improve job quality, but perhaps at the cost of some further job loss as labor costs rise. Legislative or regulatory changes that make it easier for workers to choose union membership and collective bargaining might have a similar effect, depending on the extent to which wage and benefit increases can be offset by higher productivity.

These, indeed, are the preferred policies of many commentators who bemoan the loss of good jobs in our economy. Alternatively, the government might also use "carrots" as well as "sticks" in its efforts to improve job quality—perhaps by providing tax credits or subsidies for on-the-job training or technical assistance for firms seeking to build more career ladders into their workplaces. These kinds of policies might generate fewer losses due to rising labor costs, though they might also make it harder to generate large-scale labor market changes.

Furthermore, if good jobs increasingly must be filled by "good workers," then perhaps the traditional distinction between these two sources of higher earnings has diminished with time. Good jobs might exist in sufficient quantities to absorb many more workers if the latter have the appropriate skills, even without college diplomas, but these skills might require sector- or industry-specific training and work experience rather than just general education and credentials. These workers might also require more involvement by employers in the training process and by labor market intermediaries who can assess local demand and help workers gain access to jobs as well as to training providers.

The need to link training and jobs more effectively might also arise for dislocated workers as well as for the disadvantaged. Indeed, the former are more likely to have the basic skills and general education it took to attain good jobs in the past, but now must be retrained for available work. These workers might need guidance on the available jobs and their training requirements, and stipends as well as tuition assistance might be necessary during periods of training. Alternatively, if many older and less-educated workers lost formerly well-paid jobs, and if those jobs now available simply require more education than most of these workers can obtain, what kinds of other supports (like health insurance and wage insurance) are needed to persuade them to take lower-paying jobs?

To the extent that the disappearance of good jobs varies by locality, state and local economic development policies may have a role to play. If so, what constitute cost-effective public interventions in this area, and to what extent must education and training be an integral part of these strategies?

Finally, though we don't have data directly for this period, how might the labor market in the aftermath of the Great Recession—with growing numbers of long-term jobless workers who might not meet the skill needs of employers trying to fill good jobs (Elsby, Hobijn, and Sahin 2010)—affect the skill-building and job creation policies that would be most effective?[31]

THE DATA USED IN THIS BOOK

Of course, what we describe here is primarily an empirical exercise, and our work is heavily data-driven. But our ability to test these hypotheses empirically and to distinguish between these different scenarios requires us to be able to distinguish between jobs that pay high wages owing to the high skills of the workers who hold them from those that pay high wages regardless of workers' observed skill level. To make this distinction, we must also be able to distinguish the characteristics of jobs and firms from those of workers, with sufficient detail over time to be able to generate patterns across areas and years. Unfortunately, most of the standard data sources on labor do not allow us to do this, either because they tell us nothing about the characteristics of firms and jobs or because they do not exist in large enough samples and over long enough time periods to enable us to answer the questions posed here.[32]

To our knowledge, only one data set is available that meets all these needs: the Longitudinal Employer-Household Dynamics (LEHD) file at the U.S. Census Bureau.[33] The LEHD data begin with the universe of state-level unemployment insurance (UI) wage records for a sample of states over most of the 1990s and extend beyond the year 2000. The UI wage records are *longitudinal data on all individual workers and their employers* in the sectors of the economy that are covered by UI in each state. These individual records are then matched, wherever possible, with micro survey data on individuals—such as the Census of Population, the Current Population Survey (CPS), and the Survey of Income and Program Participation (SIPP). The data are also linked on the firm side to the various economic censuses that are available. They are also matched with universe demographic data from the Social Security Administration and other sources of administrative data.

The results are large-scale datasets with data on workers linked to firms over periods of several years. The data combine administrative with survey data on both sides of the market, thus generating rich information on workers and firms and the matches between them. In an ongoing process, the data have been painstakingly constructed over several years by the LEHD staff at the U.S. Census Bureau.

What we present here is based on a subsample of twelve states for which the LEHD micro data are available over the period of 1992 to 2003. Furthermore, we supplement this analysis in some cases by considering a subsample of the LEHD that has been linked to the Decennial Census of Population in 2000, which contains much more extensive personal demographics on workers.

By being able to follow the same workers over time, across different jobs in different firms and industries, we can measure the extent of earnings loss associated with job change for different groups of workers. And by being able to follow employment at firms over time and the extent to which firms are themselves created and destroyed, we can test the extent to which gross or net job creation and destruction in different sectors contributes to these processes. And most importantly, having longitudinal data in both workers and firms enables us to calculate worker effects and firm effects on earnings that separately reflect the quality of workers and jobs, thus making it possible to analyze the extent to which job and worker quality are related to or independent of one another. We use these data to measure trends in job quality over time, in the quality of workers who fill jobs, and in the losses suffered by workers who lose jobs of different quality levels.

SUMMARY AND FINDINGS

After describing the data in somewhat greater detail in the next chapter, we proceed to our analysis of job quality and volatility and how they have evolved over time. The rest of the book presents these results.

Chapter 2 presents data on what constitutes good jobs today—that is, the industries in which they are located and the categories of firms (by size, turnover rate, and so on) in which they appear. The chapter concludes that, contrary to popular perception, relatively good jobs are not disappearing, but they are less available in the industries where they were traditionally found (in durable manufacturing) and increasingly require higher levels of worker education and skill. So the distinction between the two categories of good jobs is diminishing somewhat, as is the difference between policies that focus on creating better jobs and those that aim to create better workers with more skills. Our presentation of the "good jobs" issue thus may seem to run somewhat contrary to the arguments often espoused by some commentators, especially those on the political left, but in fact we simply take a more nuanced view: we need to generate both better jobs *and* better workers to fill them.

Chapter 3 looks at levels of volatility for different groups of workers and firms and examines trends in these rates over time. We also look at what happens to workers in a volatile environment. In the past (see, for example, Andersson, Holzer, and Lane 2005), we have argued that changing jobs, especially when young and less-skilled workers do so voluntarily, can have positive effects on worker earnings and is more frequently associated with wage growth rather than decline. But involuntary changes—especially those involving older workers and those associated with the downsizing or shutdown of firms—are much more likely to have a negative impact on earnings. In our statistical work, we find that rates of job dislocation rose very modestly over time, especially during the 1990s. Furthermore, these increased rates of dislocation raise an important question: when workers lose good jobs, how likely are they to find other jobs at their skill level? We show that some of the biggest losses in earnings occur when displaced workers cannot find jobs as good as those they have lost, which happens to a significant fraction of displaced workers. The ability of the displaced to avoid losses also seems to depend heavily on the overall health of the job market: these workers experienced less earnings loss during the boom years of the 1990s and more during the recessionary period after 2000, which implies quite serious difficulties for many displaced workers in the aftermath of the Great Recession.

Chapter 4 focuses on labor markets at the metropolitan level. We look at two types of MSAs: the very large ones in the states that we have, plus another group of smaller MSAs that lost a lot of manufacturing jobs in the 1980s and 1990s.[34] We show that these two sets of labor markets experienced quite different labor market trends in the 1990s and beyond. The large labor markets boomed in the late 1990s and paid highly skilled labor very well in expanding technical and professional service jobs. The smaller labor markets that experienced a lot of restructuring boomed less, had less growth at the top of the earnings distribution, and struggled more to replace the good jobs that they lost. And workers who lost good jobs in those smaller MSAs, especially if the earlier jobs were in manufacturing, experienced greater losses in earnings than did those in larger MSAs. This will likely be even more true after the Great Recession for the next several years.

Chapter 5 looks at the dynamics of firms in these markets: how much job growth occurred in new or growing firms (or establishments)—especially within the industries that have been targeted by local economic development policies—and how good have these jobs been? We show that job flows from new and growing firms are important in replacing those lost in declining and dying firms, and so policies that try to affect these flows and the sources of new jobs can matter importantly, regardless of the economic sector in which they appear.

Chapter 6 summarizes and develops some policy recommendations. Besides our needs for more jobs overall after the Great Recession, we argue that we also need policies to generate good jobs—through higher rates of unionization, increases in the minimum wage, or government efforts to motivate or assist firms that create good jobs, especially through economic development policies that target new and growing firms. But we also need policies that create more good (or highly skilled) workers. Such efforts can be implemented for a range of populations through policies that raise general levels of literacy and numeracy as well as general educational attainment in high schools and colleges across the country. Especially needed at these levels of schooling are high-quality career and technical education as well as sectoral training strategies and the building of career pathways in workforce development. These policies seek to train employees for, and place them in, well-paying sectors and firms, and they often involve intermediaries who work closely with employers to make sure they are getting the workers they want for the jobs they have. Our results also suggest a need for policies for displaced workers that similarly combine job training with effective job placement strategies that are tied more closely to the good jobs that exist on the demand side of the labor market.

To the extent that a "mismatch" between worker skills and those needed for available jobs may be growing over time—and also may be exacerbated as we emerge with so much long-term unemployment from the Great Recession—the need for such policies becomes even more pronounced. But we also must recognize that because some older and less-educated workers and some disadvantaged groups will have much more trouble meeting this demand for higher skills, other strategies that support their more meager earnings (like "wage insurance" and universal health care) make more sense for them.

In short, we argue and show evidence that job and worker quality both matter importantly; that good jobs are not disappearing for everyone, but that they are largely disappearing for less-educated workers, especially in certain traditional sectors of the economy (like manufacturing) and smaller local areas; that good job creation depends a great deal on what happens in new and growing firms and establishments; and that labor market policy should target both skills and good job creation in a coordinated and coherent fashion.

Chapter 2 | Good Jobs: Basic Facts and Trends over Time

ARE GOOD JOBS really disappearing in the United States over the long term, as many notable authors and commentators (like Lou Dobbs and Harold Meyerson, among others) frequently suggest?

Any discussion of job quality and volatility must begin with the question of how we measure this quality in the first place. The previous chapter laid out a few different definitions of "good jobs" and suggested a variety of ways in which they might be measured. It also raised important questions about exactly which workers fill these jobs and how the availability and nature of the jobs themselves (as well as the workers hired into them) might be evolving over time.

This chapter seeks to shed some light on these questions. We begin with a more complete discussion of the data that we use to answer them—including how the data were constructed and their strengths and limitations. We present our own definition of good jobs and the indicators by which we measure them. We then present the characteristics of the firms in which these and other jobs appear (industry, size, and other measures of firm performance such as worker turnover) and the characteristics of the workers who are hired into these different kinds of jobs (age, race and gender, education, earnings capacity).

Having established the average characteristics of good jobs and the workers who fill them, we address the key question of how these jobs and workers are changing over time. We show the extent to which good jobs are growing over time, relative to other jobs in the labor market. We show how the characteristics of these jobs are changing—especially the industries in which they appear. We consider whether the ability of less-skilled workers to obtain these jobs is diminishing, as well as also how wage premia and pay structures within these firms are evolving.

In the end, we show that *good jobs remain quite plentiful in the United*

States—but they are becoming harder for workers with limited skills and education to obtain. This trend, without any narrowing in the skill gaps between workers, no doubt contributes to growing earnings inequality over time. Levels and trends in job volatility (as opposed to quality) and how they play out in local labor markets are discussed in succeeding chapters. All of these findings have important implications for policies that aim to affect the job structure as well as the skills of workers, which we flesh out more fully in the final chapter.

THE LEHD DATA: WORKER AND FIRM EFFECTS OVER TIME

In the previous chapter, we briefly described the LEHD data at the U.S. Census Bureau that we use to measure good jobs and the workers who fill them. Now we take a closer look at these data and how we use them to measure job and worker quality and volatility around the country and over time.

The LEHD program was established at the Census Bureau in 1998 in response to the need to provide more information on economic dynamics. The program draws on already existing survey and administrative data from both the demographic and economics directorates at the Census Bureau and integrates them with unemployment insurance (UI) wage record data from our partner states. With many joining on a rolling basis throughout the 1990s and into the 2000s, our partner states now include over forty states nationwide. This integration, which takes place under strict confidentiality protection protocols, appears in figure 2.1.

Briefly, state UI wage records sit at the core of these data. These records, which consist of quarterly reports filed by employers every quarter for each individual in covered employment, permit the construction of a database that provides longitudinal information on workers, firms, and the match between the two. The coverage is roughly 96 percent of private nonfarm wage and salary employment; the coverage of agricultural and federal government employment is less comprehensive. Self-employed individuals and independent contractors are also not covered, while certain categories of very-low-wage workers (especially those working sporadically, part-time, or "off the books") are likely to be underrepresented here as well. Although the administrative records themselves are subject to some error, staff at the LEHD program have invested substantial resources in cleaning the records and making them internally consistent.[1]

The Census Bureau information used in this study consists primarily of basic demographic information derived from the Social Security Administration: date of birth, place of birth, sex, and a constructed measure of race

Figure 2.1   The Longitudinal Employer-Household Dynamics Program

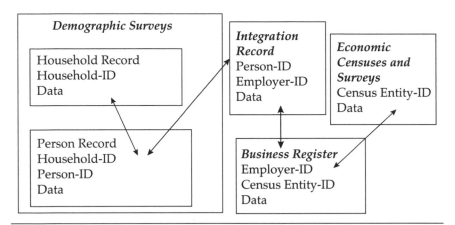

Source: Authors' illustration.

and ethnicity. These are available for almost all workers in the data set—the nonmatch rate is about 4 percent. The UI wage records have also been matched with the Decennial Census of Population and other household and employer surveys at the Census Bureau, but since these other data are purely cross-sectional, we use them mostly to supplement our analysis based on the more extensive LEHD longitudinal data.

There are clearly many advantages associated with this integrated database, including an enormous sample size, a longitudinal structure, and information on employer-employee matches. There are also some disadvantages. One is that hours or weeks worked are typically not reported by employers, so that we cannot measure hourly or weekly earnings and cannot easily distinguish between low wages and few hours worked as sources of low quarterly or annual earnings. Another is that it is impossible to identify whether multiple jobs held within a quarter are held sequentially or at the same time. And we have no direct information on why workers leave jobs or on a range of personal characteristics (beyond basic demographics) that the survey data usually capture.

Two additional conceptual issues need to be addressed. Although we typically refer to the employer as a "firm," the actual reporting unit in the data is an administrative rather than an economic entity; in other words, the filing unit reflects the employer identification number (EIN) rather than a specific firm. The distinction is immaterial for the approximately 70 percent of workers who work for a single-establishment employer, but for those who work for a multiple-establishment employer, it is not clear whether they are working for the firm or an establishment. Given that establishments within the same firm sometimes have different EINs, the opening and closing of establishments within firms might cause us to overstate firm births and deaths. We return to this issue when we analyze firm dynamics and their relationship to job growth in table 2.5.

The other conceptual issue is that of earnings. According to the *Bureau of Labor Statistics Handbook of Methods* (BLS 1997), UI wage records measure "gross wages and salaries, bonuses, stock options, tips, and other gratuities, and the value of meals and lodging, where supplied." They do not include employer contributions to Social Security, health insurance, workers' compensation, unemployment insurance, and private pension and welfare funds.

The primary benefit of these data—in addition to the enormous sample sizes and coverage that they provide—is that longitudinal data on both workers and employers enable us to estimate what economists call "fixed effects" for every worker and every firm. It is clear that both who one is and where one works are important determinants of one's earnings. However, because it is so difficult to measure individual and firm characteristics accurately and completely, most previous research has been forced to rely on relatively crude proxies—such as years of education to measure a person's skills, or firm size and industry to measure a firm's ability or willingness to pay. In this book, we take advantage of work done at the LEHD program[2] that explicitly calculates the skills and other permanent characteristics embodied in each individual in the data set, as well as the firm's contribution to pay. We refer to these as the person and firm "fixed effects" in the rest of the book and discuss their construction in more detail here.

The person fixed effects can be thought of as the market value of the portable component of an individual's skills and attitudes. They have two components: an individual or person effect, which does not vary over time, and a component based on labor market experience. The individual effect includes some factors that are often observable to the statistician, such as years of education and sex, and some factors that are often not, such as innate ability, "people" skills, problem-solving skills, perseverance, family background, and educational quality. The experience component is directly calculated from the data and, as such, is left-censored at the start of the data period. This left-censoring is ameliorated by estimating the number of years of labor force experience that an individual accumulates prior to the first appearance in the data.

The intuitive explanation of the person fixed effect is that it captures the average market value that employers assign an individual as he or she moves from firm to firm. Note that this measure is not some arbitrary skill measure, like years of education or occupation, that may or may not be the correct measure of how the market values skills. If, for example, an individual is a highly skilled blacksmith and the market does not value this skill, the person effect is correspondingly low. If the individual is physically extremely strong and this is of decreasing value in the marketplace, this individual also has a relatively low person effect. But if, for example, the individual scores highly on problem-solving skills and this is valued in the market place, then he or she has a high person effect. As such, such tests are likely to be "better" measures of skills in a more complex economy. Indeed, the case study evidence (see, for example, Appelbaum, Bernhardt, and Murnane 2003) suggests that years of education are simply not adequate measures of human capital in a service economy.

The firm fixed effect similarly captures a variety of factors. Most simplistically, it captures the premium or discount that a given firm pays workers on average, controlling for their individual skills and characteristics. This premium might be due to a higher level of capital in the firm, which would clearly increase the productivity of individual workers. Or it might be due to unionization; the transportation equipment industry, for example, has a relatively high average firm fixed effect. It might also be what economists call a "compensating differential" for unattractive working conditions. For instance, the high average firm fixed effect in the mining industry is presumably in order to compensate workers for the riskiness and unpleasantness of mine work. Finally, the firm effects capture a range of human resource policies chosen by the firm, including the effects of training and promotion policies as well as compensation.

Which states and years of the LEHD micro data have been used for this study, and why were they chosen? We were interested in generating a broad and fairly representative sample of states for which data were available over a lengthy period of time, including much or most of the 1990s. Since states joined the LEHD project on a rolling basis throughout that decade, data were not available for many states that would cover this period. And the LEHD micro data have not been fully processed beyond 2003, limiting how recent our analysis of labor market trends can be.

Within the period of time that we are able to study, we also wanted to analyze separately at least three distinct subperiods, reflecting different macroeconomic and labor market environments during that time: (1) the early to mid-1990s, during which time the economy was slowly recovering from the mild recession of 1990; (2) the mid- to late 1990s, a period of extraordinary strength and growth in the U.S. economy (often referred to as "the Roaring Nineties" or "the Great Boom"); and (3) 2000 and beyond, a period when the economy slowed and then entered another recession, from which the labor market did not begin to recover until 2004 and afterward.

In the end, we decided to focus on twelve states for which we have data over the period 1992 to 2003: California, Colorado, Idaho, Illinois, Kansas,

Maryland, Missouri, North Carolina, Oregon, Pennsylvania, Washington, and Wisconsin. These states are distributed across all regions of the country, include both larger and smaller states, have more and fewer major metropolitan areas (as we note in chapter 4), and represent a wide range of economic and industrial characteristics. We also divide the entire period into three subperiods of equal length: 1992 to 1995, 1996 to 1999, and 2000 to 2003, which largely represent the three subperiods described earlier. While our data do not cover the less robust expansion of 2003 to 2007 or the Great Recession after that, we believe they capture important trends in job creation and worker employment that remain relevant over the latter periods and beyond.

For every individual worker and every firm that appear in these states during this time period (and that meet various other sampling criteria) we have estimated person or firm fixed effects; these measures constitute our primary measures of *worker quality* and *job quality*, respectively. The details of our estimation procedures appear in the appendix to this chapter.

Importantly, we calculate firm and worker effects for our entire twelve-year period of study and separately for each of our three four-year subperiods. This method allows for the fact that firms can (and often do) adjust their human resource and compensation policies, especially in response to changing production needs and labor market situations, while workers can also improve their earnings capacity by acquiring more skills. A firm that changes production techniques—by acquiring or relinquishing plants and sites, adopting or removing products or services, adopting new technologies, outsourcing or "offshoring" work to other companies and countries, and reorganizing the workplace in reaction to these choices—may well change its hiring practices and compensation policies in important ways as well. Our measures of firm pay should be able to reflect these changing realities and firm responses to them. Similarly, workers can improve their earnings capabilities by improving their education and training (both formal and informal) and acquiring skills through new or ongoing work experience. Having three different firm effects at different points in time allows us to analyze how pay policies evolve over time and how the "matching" of workers with different ability levels to firms might evolve as well. Finally, we include in our analysis all new firms that were "born" during these periods as well as those that shut down or "died," and we include all workers who either joined the labor force or left it. Thus, the extent to which worker skill and job availability are affected by the dynamics of both are captured here.

At the same time, we note the potential limitations of our measures. As we have already indicated, our measures miss some dimensions to earnings, such as fringe benefits and the effects of other employer practices. As a single measure based on the level of earnings during a fixed number of years, the firm effect does not itself capture promotion possibilities for workers over time; according to the standard economic theory of "human capital," promotion potential might be negatively related to starting wage levels. However, our own earlier work and that of other authors suggest that, if anything, these other dimensions of firm pay are mostly positively correlated with our firm effects.[3] In this chapter, we briefly provide some information on this and other measures of worker compensation (like turnover rates and within-firm inequality) that we think are additional measures of firm and job quality and how they relate to the measure of firm effects on which we focus.

Another more technical limitation should be noted as well. As students of statistics are well aware, estimating fixed effects from panel data depends primarily on workers who change firms (and, similarly, on firms that change their workers). Within the shorter time periods during which we now estimate the separate fixed effects, fewer such workers change jobs, and therefore it might be somewhat more difficult to disentangle firm from worker effects within any distribution of overall earnings for workers.

At the same time, there is no reason why these problems should be growing more serious over time, so any trends that we infer from these data should not be considered statistical artifacts. More importantly, we have conducted a number of diagnostic examinations of the person and firm effects we calculated and how they compare across multiple methods of computation. We found the estimated firm effects (as well as the person effects) to be quite robust across these various methods. The measures we use are also quite highly correlated with each other across the three shorter periods and with the twelve-year measures, and they correlate sensibly with other observable characteristics of firms (and in ways that have been noted in previous studies of firm effects).[4] Thus, we are confident that our estimated person and firm effects are both plausible and informative regarding worker and firm quality.

As we note in the appendix to this chapter, we have used a measure of "annualized" earnings for each individual worker in each year when calculating fixed effects and when analyzing worker earnings.[5] This follows a pattern that has been set in virtually all work to date using the LEHD micro data. Many individuals work at multiple jobs and for multiple firms in any given year, but we can only focus on one job when considering any person-year observation. We use the one we call the "primary" employer for any person in any year—in other words, the employer for whom the individual has the highest earnings in that year. So as not to understate the earnings of job-switchers who work relatively close to full-time and full-year, we transform each person's quarterly earnings into our best estimate of what they would earn if they worked the entire year. On the other hand, this technique might cause us to overstate the annual earnings of those workers who have unstable work histories with frequent periods of non-employment. Accordingly, our estimates come closer to measuring the determinants of annual full-year earnings potential rather than actual annual earnings.[6]

Finally, for computational reasons (especially related to the enormous sizes of our files), we needed to estimate our person and firm effects separately by state as well as time period. As a result, average (mean) firm effects are, by definition, zero in every state and time period. This means that differences in costs of living across states do not influence earnings outcomes; at the same time, real mean differences in firm and job pay premia across states and over time are not captured by our measures. We recognize that this is a limitation of our work that leads us to focus primarily on trends in *relative* pay premia across firms and jobs rather than on their absolute mean levels.[7]

Still, we can learn a lot about how these premia have changed across jobs and over time. Specifically, we draw inferences about important changes over time by focusing on what has happened to the numbers of workers employed and the premia themselves at fixed parts of the premium distribution (for example, at fixed quintiles that are defined in our starting period) and at firms with fixed characteristics (especially industries). We are thus able to infer changes in the variance and overall shape of the distribution of job quality, and where these changes occur, even if mean levels of such quality are held constant over time by our estimation method.

WORKER AND FIRM EFFECTS: SOME FACTS

We begin our analysis with some basic facts about firm and worker effects, including the earnings paid at firms and to workers of varying quality (as measured by their estimated person and firm effects), as well as the observed characteristics of workers and firms with different levels of these effects and of the kinds of workers hired into higher- and lower-quality firms and jobs.[8]

To do so, we array all of the firms and workers during the first three-year period, 1992 to 1995, according to their firm and person effects and then divide each into quintiles from highest to lowest. We show the characteristics of firms and workers from each quintile and how they match to each other. We then use these fixed definitions of quintiles, in terms of fixed-effects magnitudes, when measuring changes in the distribution of firm effects (and therefore in job quality) in the subsequent time periods.

We begin with an illustration of the extent to which individual earnings reflect both worker and job quality, as measured by the person and firm effects we have estimated. Figure 2.2 presents mean average earnings of workers between 1992 and 2003 at each of the five quintiles of the person

Figure 2.2   Mean Annual Earnings by Firm- or Person-Effects Quintile, 1992 to 2003

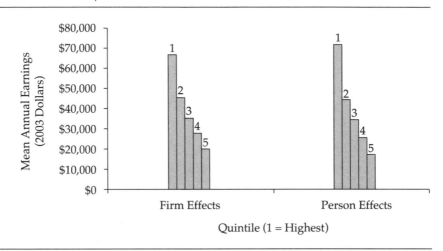

Source: Authors' tabulations using microdata from U.S. Census Bureau (1992–2003; 12 states).

and firm-effects distributions. Firm and worker effects for the three separate subperiods have been averaged together to generate effects quintiles
for the entire twelve-year period, and (as always) earnings are adjusted
for inflation.[9]

The results show that earnings are strongly correlated with both worker
and firm effects. Mean earnings are highest in the highest worker-effects
quintile and decline continuously in all subsequent quintiles; the very
high earnings of workers in the top quintile, relative to the others, is consistent with the very high and rising levels of inequality we have observed
in the past decade or so, especially for those at the very top of the earnings
ladder relative to all others.

But worker earnings are also strongly correlated with our estimated
firm effects that measure the quality of jobs relative to the workers who
hold them. Indeed, mean worker earnings average nearly $68,000 per year
in the top quintile of firms and just over $20,000 in the bottom quintile. At
least in our estimates, job quality thus appears to be strongly related to
(and perhaps a strong determinant of) worker earnings.

THE NATURE OF GOOD FIRMS AND JOBS

What are the characteristics of firms with varying levels of job quality, as
measured by the firm effect? In which industries are they located, and how

large are they? Also, how do observed firm effects correlate with other measures of firm and job quality? How do they correlate, for instance, with worker turnover rates, which are widely regarded as an indicator of job quality for workers, relative to their other labor market prospects?

Table 2.1 shows how employment is distributed across firm-effects quintiles, averaged over the entire twelve-year period, separately by industry and firm size category.[10] Also, we present mean rates of job turnover and churning by firm-effects quintile in this period, where "turnover" measures the sums of the absolute values of all job changes (both accessions to employment within firms and terminations out of such employment), relative to base levels of employment, and "churning" adjusts for levels of net employment growth at these firms to generate a clearer measure of movements in and out of jobs unrelated to firm growth and decline.

A number of important findings regarding firm and job quality appear in table 2.1. For one thing, it is clear that some industries pay much better on average than others, even after adjusting for the quality of workers across industries. Among our more traditional (nonservice) industries, agriculture clearly ranks among the worst in terms of pay, with about two-thirds of employment concentrated in the bottom quintile of firms. In contrast, mining and utilities are high-wage industries, with half to two-thirds of their workers in top-quintile firms. Construction, wholesale trade, and manufacturing (especially durable manufacturing) are high-wage industries as well, with one-third or more workers found in top-quintile firms and 60 percent or more found in the top two quintiles. These are, in fact, the industries where less-educated workers, and especially less-educated men, have traditionally earned relatively high wages. In contrast, retail trade pays low wages, with about 60 percent of jobs in the bottom two quintiles.

All of these findings are consistent with other studies in the past that have found strong differences in pay rates by industry for workers with the same observable skills (see, for example, Krueger and Summers 1987; Dickens and Katz 1987). And even within each of these industries, a range of job qualities can be found. For instance, about 40 percent of all jobs in retail trade are found in the top three quintiles. These jobs are likely to be found in supermarkets, department stores, and other larger establishments, as well as in specialty stores that may require employees to have more specific information or skills.

But, while job quality in these broad sectors largely conforms to past impressions, what job qualities do we find in the service sector? Although many analysts consider this to be a low-paid sector as well, the results indicate a much wider range of job quality than that stereotype suggests. For instance, "accommodations and food" (motels, hotels, and restaurants) is a very low-paying industry, as are, to lesser extents, "entertainment" and

Table 2.1   Distribution of Employment and Turnover Across Firm-Effects Quintiles, 1992 to 2003

	Firm-Effects Quintile (1 = Highest)				
	1	2	3	4	5
Industry					
Agriculture	2.4%	6.5%	10.2%	14.5%	66.4%
Mining	54.3	20.4	11.7	9.6	3.9
Utilities	65.4	25.9	5.3	2.2	1.2
Construction	33.7	26.9	18.0	13.5	8.0
Nondurable manufacturing	28.4	28.7	19.2	12.8	10.9
Durable manufacturing	43.6	24.5	15.5	10.9	5.4
Wholesale trade	34.6	25.3	20.1	11.9	8.2
Retail trade	8.9	8.8	22.8	37.2	22.3
Transportation	14.5	26.3	24.0	20.1	15.0
Services					
Information	52.6	16.8	10.8	10.5	9.3
Finance	29.1	37.2	20.8	10.9	2.0
Real estate	20.6	16.6	20.5	19.3	22.9
Professional	57.5	16.0	8.6	6.6	11.3
Management	43.1	32.1	11.9	7.9	5.1
Administrative	10.6	8.8	14.2	27.3	39.0
Education	0.8	5.9	27.5	42.2	23.6
Health care	7.6	29.1	33.9	16.2	13.1
Entertainment	7.0	10.5	13.1	27.3	42.0
Accommodation and food	2.7	4.1	9.8	28.1	55.3
Other services	16.8	14.5	15.7	20.8	32.2
Public administration	16.6	38.1	27.7	10.9	6.7
Firm size (number of employees)					
25 to 49	19.2	13.3	16.2	18.8	32.4
50 to 99	21.3	14.5	16.8	19.1	28.3
100 to 999	20.9	19.2	20.0	19.7	20.2
1,000 to 9,999	20.6	24.8	22.0	20.7	11.9
10,000 or more	24.6	18.7	23.3	28.0	5.4
Average annual turnover and churning					
Turnover	22.3%	21.5%	23.9%	29.4%	36.6%
Churning	13.8	14.8	17.7	22.8	28.2

Source: Authors' tabulations using microdata from U.S. Bureau of the Census (1992–2003).
Note: For employment distribution, rows sum to 100 percent. Annual turnover of a firm is defined as the number of job accessions and job separations between two consecutive years divided by the total firm employment in those two years. Annual churning is defined as the number of job accessions and job separations minus the absolute change in firm employment divided by the total firm employment. Turnover and churning are calculated for jobs with full-quarter employment only.

"administrative services"; in each case, 40 percent or more of jobs are located in the bottom quintile of firm effects, and thus the low wages paid there cannot be accounted for fully by low worker skills.

On the other hand, professional and information services are high-paying, with over half of all jobs in each located in the top quintile of firm effects. "Management of companies and enterprises," a relatively small sector comprising those firms that own or administer other firms, also pays quite well, with about three-fourths of all jobs found in the top two quintiles of firm effects; similarly, about two-thirds of financial services jobs are in the top two quintiles. No doubt, the education and skills of workers in these sectors are quite high, but even workers who have not been well paid in other jobs in their careers earn good pay in these jobs. Interestingly, real estate jobs are spread almost evenly across the five quintiles, while jobs in health care (about 63 percent) and public administration (about 66 percent) are heavily concentrated in the second and third quintiles of firm effects.

Besides industry, what other characteristics of firms are associated with higher or lower pay, adjusting for skill differences? All else being equal, jobs at large firms have tended to pay more than those at small firms, though the exact reasons for the "firm size–pay premium" have eluded researchers (Brown, Hamilton, and Medoff 1990). Our data show very clearly that this continues to be true today. While firms that range in size from twenty-five to ten thousand have roughly equal chances of being in the top pay quintile, those that are especially large (over ten thousand employees) are more likely than others to be found in the top quintile. And for those in the size categories below the top one, we clearly see higher concentrations in the second and third quintiles for those with one hundred or more employees and in the bottom quintile for those with one hundred or fewer.

Clearly, firm size continues to matter for levels of pay (and presumably benefits), with larger firms still paying significantly more than smaller ones. Past research suggests a number of factors that might account for this, including greater capital intensity, higher rates of unionization, higher profits and "ability to pay," and more professional human resource management activities.

Finally, the measures of turnover and churning that we have calculated are quite strongly related to the firm-earnings premium. Turnover rises modestly between the first and third firm-effects quintile and more substantially as we move to the bottom two quintiles. Churning, which adjusts for firm growth levels over time, shows a similar pattern, but rises even more clearly over the entire range of firm-effects quintiles as we move from the highest- to the lowest-paying firms and jobs.

The fact that job turnover is lower at firms that pay more is perhaps not very surprising. Workers are less likely to quit these jobs and are also motivated to work more productively to avoid being discharged. To the extent that high-paying firms have steeper profiles that associate pay with on-the-job training and worker experience, workers might also be motivated to protect their investments in skill acquisition and seniority at these firms.[11]

In sum, it is clear that there are distinct patterns of pay by industry and firm size categories and that our measures of job quality across firms correlate highly with other measures of worker satisfaction at their jobs, such as turnover out of employment.

THE NATURE OF GOOD (OR HIGHLY PAID) WORKERS

How do the pay premia earned by workers themselves vary, and to what extent do these premia indicate higher levels of skills and earnings capacity? Are workers with particular demographics (age, race, gender, foreign-born versus native-born) more or less likely to be permanently higher earners? And how well does educational attainment (as measured in the 2000 Census of Population for a subsample of our workers) correlate with our worker fixed effects?

Table 2.2 presents the distribution of workers across the five quintiles of worker fixed effects, separately by age group, race, gender, foreign-born versus native-born status, and educational attainment. The table is thus comparable to much of table 2.1, except that it focuses on worker characteristics and effects rather than on those of firms.

We find that, consistent with a lengthy literature in economics on the nature and determinants of differences in pay, the earnings premia of workers do differ quite a bit across demographic groups. For instance, workers in their middle years (ages thirty-five to sixty-four) are more likely to have higher fixed effects than those who are younger (ages eighteen to thirty-four); whites and especially Asians have higher fixed effects than blacks, Native Americans, and especially Hispanics; men are more likely than women to be in the highest-paying quintiles; and the foreign-born are less likely the native-born to be found in the top quintile and more likely to be found in the bottom one.

All of this is consistent, of course, with other findings on pay (Ehrenberg and Smith 2009) and even on person effects (Andersson, Holzer, and Lane 2005). What is less clear is the extent to which differences across these demographic groups reflect real differences in skill and productivity, as opposed to discrimination and other sources of pay difference (such as the quality of networks and information). Recent evidence on pay dis-

Table 2.2   Distribution of Employment Across Person-Effects Quintiles, 1992 to 2003

	Person-Effects Quintile (1 = Highest)				
	1	2	3	4	5
Age					
Eighteen to thirty-four	19.0%	18.4%	20.4%	20.9%	21.3%
Thirty-five to forty-four	22.5	21.2	21.7	19.0	15.6
Forty-five to sixty-four	20.8	20.8	21.8	19.5	17.2
Race					
White	22.0	20.7	21.6	19.6	16.2
Black	15.8	18.4	20.6	21.6	23.6
Hispanic	8.5	13.7	19.8	24.6	33.5
Asian–Pacific Islander	26.4	19.5	18.7	18.3	17.1
Native American	11.2	15.1	23.0	25.9	24.8
Gender					
Female	14.9	16.6	21.7	23.7	23.1
Male	24.9	22.1	20.2	17.0	15.8
Foreign-born					
No	20.5	20.0	21.3	20.0	18.3
Yes	17.6	16.2	18.8	21.7	25.7
Educational attainment					
Less than high school	7.8	14.4	20.7	24.4	32.7
High school	15.6	20.5	22.6	20.7	20.7
Some college	19.8	20.1	21.5	20.0	18.6
Associate's degree	22.0	22.0	23.8	18.4	13.7
Bachelor's degree	32.1	19.3	19.5	18.2	10.9
Master's degree	30.7	15.2	21.3	23.5	9.3
Professional degree	33.4	24.8	20.9	13.2	7.7
Doctoral degree	33.1	25.0	23.8	12.5	5.5

Source: Authors' tabulations using microdata from U.S. Bureau of the Census (1992–2003).
Note: Rows sum to 100 percent. Data on education come from the long form of the 2000 Decennial Census of Population, which includes approximately one-sixth of the workers in our data. Education results are calculated solely for these workers and solely for the year 2000.

parities by gender and race suggests that the role of discrimination has declined somewhat over time and that the disparities that remain are more reflective of gaps in school achievement or language (for differences by race-ethnicity and foreign-born status), as well as gaps in work experience (for differences by gender).[12] On the other hand, evidence from experiments and other data suggest that discrimination has not disappeared and that the skill development and job choices of workers might interact with other forms of stigma and perceived expectations by employers and supervisors.[13] Ongoing pay disparities across these demographic groups probably reflect a range of factors that affect differences in opportunities to develop skills and how such skills are rewarded in the market.

Finally, we see clear differences in worker effects by educational attainment categories. Those without high school diplomas rarely end up with high person effects and are mostly concentrated in the bottom two quintiles of person effects. High school graduates are spread more evenly across these categories, and those with some college (but less than an associate's degree) are only a bit more concentrated in the higher quintiles. But those with associate's and especially bachelor's degrees are substantially more likely to have high earnings premia, while those with professional and doctoral degrees are most likely of all to have high person effects.

On average, then, educational attainment affects earnings capacity substantially. Still, we do find important variation in permanent earnings capacity within each level of education. For instance, about 20 percent of those with a professional or doctoral degree still have earnings premia in the bottom two quintiles, as do about 30 percent of those with bachelor's degrees. Over one-third of high school graduates end up in the top two quintiles of pay premia, as do over one-fifth of high school dropouts. Thus, while the level of educational attainment is certainly important—and has become more so over time—it is far from a perfect predictor of an individual's long-term pay prospects. Variation in educational quality and in cognitive, analytical, and communication skills accounts for large parts of the observed spread in pay, as does the employment sector and the specific skills and experience a worker has developed in that sector.[14] Because of the relatively limited value of educational attainment alone as a measure of personal labor market skill, we focus on the person fixed effects as measures of such skill throughout the book.

THE MATCHING OF WORKERS TO JOBS

If workers from different demographic and educational groups are unevenly distributed across worker-effects categories, how are they distributed across firm-effects categories? In other words, what personal characteristics of workers are associated with the ability to get good jobs? And to what extent does this ability merely reflect their personal skills, as opposed to other factors that also determine such "access," such as discrimination, informal networks, geographic location of residences versus businesses, and so on?

Our earlier work (Andersson, Holzer, and Lane 2005) addresses these questions in detail, but a bit of information appears in table 2.3. This table is structured just like table 2.2, except that now we consider how workers in each category are distributed across firm-effects quintiles rather than worker-effects quintiles. Of course, the person effects of individuals in these groups influence their placement into jobs with various firm effects. So, at the top of the table, we present the distribution of workers across firm-effects quintiles according to the worker-effects quintiles in which they appear. This gives us some sense of the extent to which the skills and earnings capacities of workers drive their distributions across job quality categories. And the distributions of workers by age, race, gender, foreign-born status, and education across jobs can be compared with their distributions across earning capacity groups in the earlier table, so that we can infer how much their access to jobs exists independently of their longer-term skills.

Overall, table 2.3 certainly shows that personal skills and earnings capacity are strongly related to who is hired for good jobs. The top panel of the table shows a strong concentration of workers on the "diagonal" elements of the matrix created by worker- and firm-effects quintiles—in other words, *workers are more likely to be in jobs with roughly similar fixed effects than in jobs with quite different effects.* If correct, this implies that, on average, good workers tend to get good jobs.

On the other hand, the number of workers found in off-diagonal positions in the matrix is also quite substantial. For instance, since 60 to 70 percent of workers in the top or bottom quintiles of person effects end up in the top or bottom firm-effects quintiles, the implication is that 30 to 40 percent are in lower or higher job quintiles than their person effects alone would predict. For those in the second through fourth person quintiles, only 30 to 40 percent are on diagonals—implying that much larger shares of people occupy either better or worse jobs than their person effects alone would predict.[15]

Of course, the strong correlations between person and firm effects might be at least partly statistical artifacts if our data are not strong enough to allow us to fully disentangle these two components of individuals' earnings. In particular, if the four-year time periods in which we estimate these effects are too short, and not enough individuals change jobs within those periods, effects associated with people might be incorrectly attributed to their jobs or vice versa—leading to more diagonal elements than might really be the case.

On the other hand, there is no obvious reason why this should be more (or less) true in some periods than others, so if the matrices change over

Table 2.3   Distribution of Employment Across Firm-Effects
Quintiles, 1992 to 2003

	Firm-Effects Quintile (1 = Highest)				
	1	2	3	4	5
Person-effects quintile					
Quintile 1	66.8%	24.2%	7.0%	1.7%	0.4%
Quintile 2	24.9	37.4	24.7	10.5	2.4
Quintile 3	9.2	24.7	34.5	23.2	8.5
Quintile 4	3.2	9.0	24.4	40.1	23.2
Quintile 5	1.0	2.1	8.7	27.0	61.2
Age					
Eighteen to thirty-four	20.4	18.7	19.7	21.1	20.1
Thirty-five to forty-four	22.7	21.2	20.6	19.3	16.1
Forty-five to sixty-four	20.7	20.2	20.5	20.5	18.0
Race					
White	22.0	20.1	20.5	20.4	17.0
Black	18.0	20.0	20.2	20.6	21.2
Hispanic	14.6	16.1	19.0	23.3	27.0
Asian–Pacific Islander	27.7	20.1	18.3	18.2	15.7
Native American	16.0	19.1	21.3	21.5	22.2
Gender					
Female	15.8	18.5	21.3	23.1	21.3
Male	25.9	20.5	18.9	18.1	16.6
Foreign-born					
No	21.1	19.8	20.3	20.5	18.3
Yes	20.5	17.8	18.7	20.6	22.4
Educational attainment					
Less than high school	12.3	16.3	19.8	23.6	28.0
High school	18.1	20.3	21.0	21.8	18.8
Some college	21.9	20.0	20.3	20.3	17.5
Associate's degree	23.2	22.9	23.0	17.5	13.4
Bachelor's degree	30.6	20.6	19.3	17.6	11.8
Master's degree	28.8	16.2	20.2	22.4	12.3
Professional degree	30.4	23.8	24.7	12.7	8.5
Doctoral degree	26.8	13.4	25.4	22.5	11.9

Source: Authors' tabulations using microdata from U.S. Bureau of the Census (1992–2003).
Note: Rows sum to 100 percent. Data on education come from the long form of the 2000 Decennial Census of Population, which includes approximately one-sixth of the workers in our data. Education results are calculated solely for these workers and solely for the year 2000.

time, this might well indicate systematic changes in how workers of varying skill sets are allocated to jobs over time (an issue we explore later in the chapter). Furthermore, we appear to have sufficient numbers of workers in off-diagonal elements of this matrix to be able to explore the relationship between worker skills and job quality, at least to some extent.

What other characteristics of workers are associated with the tendency to be employed in good (high-firm-effects) jobs? The rest of table 2.3 shows how individuals in different age, race, gender, foreign-born, and education groups are allocated into jobs of different quality. The results largely parallel those of the previous table, which showed how workers in these groups are allocated across personal skill (person-effects) categories. In other words, those workers who are younger or older, black or Hispanic, female, foreign-born, or who have a high school diploma or less are less likely to have good jobs than are those who are middle-aged, white or Asian, male, native-born, or who have a college or graduate degree. That the magnitudes of the differences across these categories for jobs are consistently smaller than for worker skills may imply that relationships between skills and jobs account for some of the differences of these groups, but that beyond skills there are variations in job quality across these groups as well.

A more straightforward way of estimating these differences is to compute the relationship between the job quality of workers, on the one hand, and their skills and demographics, on the other, through multiple regression. We have therefore estimated a regression of the workers' firm effects on their personal effects as well as age, gender, race, and foreign-born status. The results show strong relationships between person and firm effects, as expected, but that some significant race and gender differences in job quality persist as well. For example, women, Hispanics, and the foreign-born have more difficulty being employed at high-paying firms, even controlling for their person effects. The magnitudes of these effects are not enormous; if anything, these estimates are likely to understate the effects of personal demographics, since personal effects might capture these to some extent as well.[16] Nevertheless, *access to good jobs seems determined not only by personal skills but at least partly by other factors*, including discrimination, the quality of networks, and geographic "mismatches" that can influence such access.[17]

Overall, these data indicate that the quality of jobs varies importantly by characteristics of the firm as well as those of workers. But important questions remain about how the availability, characteristics, and accessibility of these jobs for different groups of workers might have changed over time. We now turn to these issues.

JOB QUALITY AND WORKER ACCESS: TRENDS OVER TIME

If we define job quality by the fixed effects that firms pay to workers, adjusting for what they earn on the basis of their own skills, how has job quality (at least in a relative sense) trended over time?[18] The answer to this question appears in figure 2.3, where we plot employment growth during the period of 1992 to 2003 for each quintile of the firm fixed-effects distribution. The data use fixed quintiles, as defined by the distribution of effects in 1992. For each quintile, the bar charts present employment growth for each year during the period between 1993 and 2003, relative to the base year of 1992. The data make use of all firms' employment changes over the entire period—even for newly born firms and those shutting down—as well as any changes that occur in ongoing firms' fixed effects over time.

Overall, figure 2.3 shows that the good jobs are not disappearing. If anything, *jobs in the highest quintile grew more rapidly than did those at any other point of the firm-effects distribution.* But jobs near the bottom in terms of quality—specifically those in the fourth quintile—also grew faster than others. And those in the second quintile—which are good jobs but not the best—grew more slowly than others.

The effects of the business cycle are also apparent in figure 2.3 when comparing jobs in 1999 and 2000 (the fifth and fourth bars from the right) to those in 2002 and 2003 (the last two bars). In each quintile, overall employment peaked in 1999 (or in 2000 in the top quintile) and then hit its trough in 2002, reflecting the job market effects of the recession that began in 2001.[19] The cyclical decline in employment during this recession was strongest in the top quintile, which did not recover as much in 2003 as did employment in lower quintiles. Still, the cycle did not change the fact that employment in the highest and next-to-lowest quintiles grew most rapidly during this entire time period, while in the next-to-highest group it grew most slowly.

This pattern is somewhat consistent with the notion of growing "polarization" in the labor market, though that term is usually applied to workers and their earnings rather than to jobs.[20] The impacts of these job changes on worker earnings depend not only on which jobs grew more or less but also on the impact of job availability on workers of different skill levels, which we consider later in the chapter. Also, the magnitudes of these changes are not quite as large as they seem. Given that each quintile had roughly 6.3 million jobs in 1992, growth rates ranged in magnitude from about 25 percent for the top quintile to just 8 percent in the second quintile for the year 2000, and from 19 percent to 8 percent for the same two quintiles up through 2003. Still, overall employment did not shift dra-

Figure 2.3   Cumulative Net Employment Growth by Firm-Effects
Quintile and by Year, 1992 to 2003

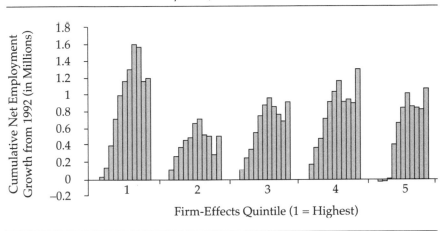

Source: Authors' tabulations using microdata from U.S. Bureau of the Census (1992–2003).
Note: Each bar represents cumulative employment growth within a quintile for a year in the period of 1993 to 2003, relative to 1992.

matically across quintiles over this time period, with employment in the top quintile rising to 21.8 percent of the total in 2000 and 20.5 percent in 2003, while that in the second quintile declined to 18.6 and 18.5 percent, respectively, in those years.

As employment shifted away somewhat from the second quintile toward the first and fourth, exactly which jobs were changing in availability in terms of industry? Did the composition of jobs change within each quintile? And how did these changes translate into the availability of good jobs for different categories of worker by their skill levels?

INDUSTRY EFFECTS

In table 2.4, we begin to analyze these industry effects. The table shows how jobs in each quintile of the firm-effects distribution were distributed across industries in 1992 and in 2003. In the subsequent tables, we then consider who got these jobs and how the ability of less-skilled workers to get good jobs might have changed in this twelve-year period.

A number of findings appear in table 2.4. What is most notable is that jobs in durable and nondurable manufacturing declined in each quintile of job quality, but that the declines were steepest within the highest-qual-

Table 2.4   Distribution of Employment Within Firm-Effects Quintiles, 1992 Versus 2003

| | 1992 | | | | | 2003 | | | | |
| | Firm-Effects Quintile (1 = Highest) | | | | | Firm-Effects Quintile (1 = Highest) | | | | |
Industry	1	2	3	4	5	1	2	3	4	5
Agriculture	0.2%	0.6%	0.8%	1.2%	6.0%	0.2%	0.5%	0.7%	1.1%	5.2%
Mining	0.9	0.3	0.2	0.2	0.1	0.5	0.2	0.1	0.1	0.0
Utilities	3.2	1.4	0.3	0.1	0.0	2.3	1.0	0.2	0.1	0.1
Construction	5.9	4.9	3.1	2.2	1.7	6.7	5.6	3.9	2.7	1.7
Nondurable manufacturing	12.5	13.7	9.4	5.9	6.4	9.2	9.9	6.3	4.1	3.2
Durable manufacturing	24.0	12.6	7.7	5.5	3.4	15.2	9.3	6.0	4.1	2.1
Wholesale trade	7.0	5.6	4.4	2.7	2.1	7.8	5.7	4.8	2.6	2.0
Retail trade	4.3	4.7	12.4	21.4	15.5	5.8	5.8	14.7	21.4	13.6
Transportation	2.4	4.9	4.2	3.3	3.1	2.6	4.5	4.2	3.5	2.8
Services										
Information	7.9	2.4	1.7	1.6	1.6	7.8	3.1	1.4	1.2	1.5
Finance	6.2	9.6	6.3	3.2	0.5	8.1	9.6	4.4	2.4	0.5
Real estate	1.1	0.9	1.1	1.0	1.3	1.4	1.1	1.3	1.2	1.5
Professional services	11.0	3.5	2.1	1.2	2.1	13.5	3.8	2.1	1.5	3.2
Management	1.6	1.1	0.4	0.3	0.2	1.5	1.3	0.5	0.2	0.2
Administrative	2.5	2.2	3.3	6.9	10.3	4.2	3.6	4.8	9.0	13.8
Education	0.2	2.8	12.3	19.7	12.5	0.6	2.7	12.9	21.2	13.4
Health care	2.8	15.8	17.5	8.0	6.8	4.5	16.7	18.4	8.5	7.6
Entertainment	0.4	0.4	0.8	1.8	2.8	0.6	1.0	1.2	2.0	3.6
Accommodation and food	0.6	1.1	3.3	9.4	18.9	1.1	1.6	3.1	8.3	19.0
Other	1.5	1.3	1.4	2.0	3.0	1.5	1.5	1.6	1.8	3.4
Public administration	3.7	10.2	7.1	2.6	1.7	5.0	11.5	7.4	2.8	1.7

Source: Authors' tabulations using microdata from U.S. Bureau of the Census (1992–2003).
Note: Columns sum to 100 percent.

ity quintiles. In particular, jobs in durable manufacturing constituted nearly one-fourth of all jobs in the top quintile in 1992, but only about 15 percent in 2003. Durable and nondurable manufacturing jobs together accounted for about 37 percent of employment in the top quintile in 1992 and only 24 percent in 2003—in other words, the share of the best jobs accounted for by manufacturing declined by over one-third in just over a decade. Comparable shares for jobs in the second quintile were 26 percent in 1992 and 19 percent in 2003, indicating a decline in the manufacturing share of over one-fourth, and with nondurable manufacturing jobs declining by even more than those in durable manufacturing among these.

Where did these good jobs go? That is, which sectors grew the most as a share of jobs in the top quintiles, relative to other quintiles? While the shares of employment in the top quintile rose a bit in construction, wholesale trade, and retail trade, they grew the most in a variety of service jobs—especially in professional services and finance, as well as in health care, administrative services, and public administration. In the second quintile, they grew the most in administrative services, public administration, and retail trade, as well as in health care, construction, and information services. Even within the third quintile, a shift out of manufacturing and toward retail trade, administrative services, and health care is noteworthy.

Thus, the jobs in the top quintiles seem to be shifting away from a sector where less-educated workers have historically filled high-paying jobs and toward those in the service sector (like professional services, health care, and finance) where educational credentials might be stronger determinants of who gets employed and at which firms. Table 2.5 considers the distribution of workers, separately for each person-effects quintile, across these same industries.

What we find is that employment of the most highly skilled workers declined only modestly in manufacturing (both durable and nondurable) and rose in professional services and information. But the declines in manufacturing employment in the other quintiles were larger; indeed, manufacturing jobs fell from about 24 percent to 18 percent of all jobs among second-quintile workers, and from 19 to 15 percent among those in the third quintile. In these two quintiles, health care and public administration mostly made up for the decline in the manufacturing share. But that share fell from 18 to 8 percent among those in the fourth quintile, and from 10 to 4 percent among those in the bottom quintile. Thus, *in the top three quintiles of worker skills, the shares accounted for by manufacturing declined by one-fourth or less; in the bottom two quintiles, they declined by well over half.* Instead, employment in retail trade rose most noticeably for workers in the bottom quintile of skills.

Table 2.5   Distribution of Employment Within Person-Effects Quintiles, 1992 Versus 2003

Industry	1992					2003				
	Person-Effects Quintile (1 = Highest)					Person-Effects Quintile (1 = Highest)				
	1	2	3	4	5	1	2	3	4	5
Agriculture	0.2%	0.2%	0.6%	1.5%	6.2%	0.2%	0.4%	0.6%	1.0%	5.4%
Mining	0.7	0.5	0.3	0.1	0.0	0.6	0.3	0.1	0.0	0.0
Utilities	4.2	0.7	0.2	0.0	0.0	3.2	0.6	0.1	0.0	0.0
Construction	6.5	5.6	3.1	1.6	1.1	8.7	6.1	3.0	1.9	1.5
Nondurable manufacturing	9.0	10.2	10.8	10.3	7.8	8.5	9.0	7.9	4.6	2.8
Durable manufacturing	18.6	14.2	11.1	7.4	2.3	16.3	9.4	7.2	3.7	1.2
Wholesale trade	6.6	6.0	4.8	2.7	1.7	7.7	6.1	4.4	3.2	1.8
Retail trade	3.7	5.8	15.1	18.7	14.9	4.6	6.6	10.7	18.4	20.6
Transportation	4.1	5.9	3.8	2.0	2.0	3.1	6.1	3.9	2.5	1.9
Services										
Information	6.6	3.7	2.1	1.5	1.3	8.5	3.0	1.9	1.1	1.3
Finance	8.7	9.5	4.6	2.5	0.6	9.6	8.5	5.8	1.5	0.4
Real estate	0.9	0.9	1.3	1.4	0.9	1.1	1.2	1.5	1.4	1.3
Professional services	11.8	2.8	2.0	1.4	2.1	14.9	3.6	2.2	2.2	2.5
Management	1.9	0.7	0.5	0.3	0.3	1.7	0.8	0.6	0.5	0.3
Administrative	1.6	2.6	3.0	5.0	12.9	2.9	3.9	4.8	7.7	16.0
Education	2.6	12.0	12.8	12.1	7.7	1.7	5.7	12.6	23.6	4.9
Health care	6.4	8.0	12.7	12.2	11.6	2.9	12.6	17.4	12.2	9.0
Entertainment	0.3	0.4	1.2	2.4	2.0	0.3	0.7	1.5	2.2	3.5
Accommodation and food	0.4	0.2	2.1	10.7	19.6	0.3	0.8	2.7	7.9	21.1
Other	0.9	1.2	1.5	2.5	3.0	1.0	1.6	1.8	1.9	3.5
Public administration	4.1	9.0	6.5	3.8	1.9	2.2	13.0	9.4	2.5	1.0

Source: Authors' tabulations using microdata from U.S. Bureau of the Census (1992–2003).
Note: Columns sum to 100 percent.

Overall, these results suggest that the ability of less-skilled workers to get jobs in the highest-paying firms declined, because the best-paying jobs in manufacturing were replaced by well-paid jobs in professional and information services and the presence of the least-skilled workers declined in the manufacturing jobs that remained. Yet the growth of jobs in construction, health care, public administration, and elsewhere, and the growing shares of these jobs going to workers in the lowest skill groups suggest at least some possibilities for less-educated workers to still get good jobs.

One way to measure the availability of relatively good jobs for workers at different points in the distribution of skills is to focus on all those whose job quality is greater than what might be predicted on the basis of person quality and skills alone—in other words, those whose firm-effects quintiles are greater than their firm's person-effects quintiles. In table 2.6, we measure the distribution of all such workers across industries, separately by the person quintile of the firms in which they appear as well as overall.[21]

Table 2.6 shows that, for workers overall, *the extent to which manufacturing provides good jobs to workers has fallen by half*—from about 27 percent of all such cases in 1992 to 13.5 percent in 2003. While a number of industries, such as construction, wholesale trade, and professional services, have modestly expanded the share of such jobs that they provide (with a rise of about a percentage point in each case), the share accounted for by retail trade has risen the most—from 9 percent to nearly 17 percent. This industry—perhaps through its department stores and specialty shops—now provides good jobs to many workers in the fourth and fifth quintiles of skills who obtain jobs in higher quintiles of firm quality. Within other specific quintiles of workers, we find that health care, construction, and public administration provide increasing shares of better jobs to workers at firms in the second and third quintiles of skill.

On the other hand, it is likely that workers need greater skills to obtain such jobs than was true for the manufacturing jobs of the past. The jobs in construction and health care that pay above-average wages tend to be those in the middle-skill categories described in chapter 1—jobs that require some type of training or certification beyond high school. In health care, many of these are jobs as nurses, technicians, and therapy assistants that require certificates or degrees. In construction, these jobs include workers in the skilled crafts, such as plumbers, electricians, and the like. In manufacturing, the remaining jobs often require sophisticated numeric and computing skills, as in machinist jobs, or other specific skills (such as welding). And even in retail trade, an individual seems to need a range of communication and arithmetic skills to obtain one of the better-paying jobs.[22] The shift of better-paying jobs from manufacturing to other sectors

Table 2.6 Distribution of Employment by Industry Within Person-Effects Quintiles at Firms Where Firm Fixed-Effects Quintile Is Better Than Person Fixed-Effects Quintile

| | 1992 | | | | | 2003 | | | | |
| | Person-Effects Quintile (2 = Highest) | | | | | Person-Effects Quintile (2 = Highest) | | | | |
Industry	2	3	4	5	Total	2	3	4	5	Total
Agriculture	0.2%	0.5%	1.2%	2.8%	1.3%	0.2%	0.3%	0.9%	2.0%	0.9%
Mining	1.0	0.4	0.1	0.0	0.3	0.4	0.1	0.0	0.0	0.1
Utilities	1.3	0.2	0.0	0.0	0.3	1.0	0.1	0.0	0.0	0.2
Construction	6.5	3.8	1.7	0.9	2.9	7.6	3.7	3.1	2.0	3.8
Nondurable manufacturing	14.6	17.3	15.8	9.4	14.2	11.3	11.2	6.8	2.9	7.7
Durable manufacturing	24.1	16.8	10.0	2.8	12.4	10.8	7.7	5.1	1.5	5.8
Wholesale trade	6.2	5.4	2.5	1.3	3.6	6.3	5.5	5.5	1.9	4.7
Retail trade	4.7	5.4	9.0	15.6	9.1	5.2	7.0	19.2	30.3	16.6
Transportation	3.0	4.5	2.1	1.4	2.7	4.4	3.6	2.7	1.4	2.9
Services										
Information	7.1	2.9	1.1	0.8	2.6	4.3	2.5	1.0	0.8	1.9
Finance	6.1	6.1	4.0	0.9	4.1	10.3	5.7	2.1	0.5	4.0
Real estate	1.2	1.1	1.1	0.6	1.0	1.5	1.4	1.5	1.1	1.3
Professional services	4.2	2.0	1.4	1.2	2.0	7.7	2.9	2.1	1.7	3.2
Management	0.7	0.6	0.4	0.5	0.5	1.2	1.0	1.0	0.5	0.9
Administrative	3.2	3.4	3.2	10.9	5.3	4.3	4.1	5.9	15.8	7.9
Education	0.2	1.3	9.8	11.1	6.2	0.4	3.8	11.7	4.9	5.8
Health care	4.4	15.5	20.1	19.1	15.7	6.8	19.8	18.2	9.8	14.4
Entertainment	0.3	0.5	1.5	1.0	0.9	0.7	1.8	2.1	2.9	2.0
Accommodation and food	0.2	1.1	5.8	14.9	6.1	0.8	1.4	5.2	16.8	6.6
Other	2.1	1.7	2.4	2.4	2.2	1.9	1.9	1.9	2.7	2.1
Public administration	8.6	9.2	6.9	2.5	6.6	13.0	14.3	4.1	0.6	7.4

Source: Authors' tabulations using microdata from U.S. Bureau of the Census (1992–2003).
Note: Columns sum to 100 percent.

thus implies a higher set of skill needs to obtain better-paying jobs, even for those without college diplomas.

Before moving on to a more general consideration of how workers of different skill groups are matched to jobs of varying quality, we present a few more results by industry. For instance, are the pay premia by industry themselves changing over time, as industries restructure and shift employment toward higher- or lower-skill employees?

Table 2.7 compares the firm fixed effects paid in these industries in 1992 and 2003, as well as the person effects of workers hired in each year. The table shows that the pay premia by industry remain surprisingly constant over the twelve-year period. While information and professional services jobs appear to have been compensated somewhat better in the later years than the earlier ones, and those in mining and utilities paid a little worse, the changes in most other sectors were very modest. The pay premia in retail trade became just a bit less negative over time, confirming our earlier impression that the share of good jobs now appearing in this industry is rising. Meanwhile, the estimated firm effects in health care hewed to an average very close to zero, suggesting that this industry continued to provide a mix of high-paying and low-paying jobs.

As for worker skills, these results confirm what we saw in table 2.5—namely, that the skills of those being hired rose very clearly in construction and manufacturing, as well as in information services. This implies that, at least in two of the highest-paying industries that hire many less-skilled workers, it is now harder than in the past for the least-skilled workers to get jobs.

Overall, the results by industry tell a quite consistent story. Many high-wage jobs are still available and are being newly created in American labor markets. But they are less likely than before to be found in manufacturing and more likely to be found in a variety of service industries. Indeed, the magnitudes of the shifts in employment in good jobs across industries within roughly a decade are quite striking. And within manufacturing and elsewhere, the jobs that remain are becoming less accessible to workers whose personal skills are weak.

FIRM AND WORKER EFFECTS: WHO IS GETTING THE GOOD JOBS?

If the erosion of manufacturing employment and the relative growth of service industries have made good jobs less accessible to less-skilled workers, this should also be evident in data on which kinds of workers are getting which kinds of jobs, regardless of the industries in which they appear.

Table 2.8 presents data on this fundamental question. For workers in each of the five quintiles of person effects in 1992, and again in 2003, it

Table 2.7   Mean Firm Fixed Effects and Person Fixed Effects,
            by Industry

	Firm Fixed Effects		Person Fixed Effects	
Industry	1992	2003	1992	2003
Agriculture	−0.30	−0.29	−0.29	−0.25
Mining	0.15	0.12	0.13	0.15
Utilities	0.18	0.17	0.20	0.22
Construction	0.07	0.07	0.05	0.08
Nondurable manufacturing	0.03	0.05	−0.02	0.03
Durable manufacturing	0.10	0.11	0.07	0.11
Wholesale trade	0.07	0.09	0.05	0.06
Retail trade	−0.07	−0.06	−0.10	−0.11
Transportation	−0.01	−0.01	0.02	0.01
Services				
Information	0.10	0.13	0.09	0.13
Finance	0.08	0.12	0.09	0.10
Real estate	−0.01	−0.01	−0.04	−0.04
Professional services	0.13	0.15	0.13	0.13
Management	0.11	0.11	0.11	0.08
Administrative	−0.12	−0.12	−0.16	−0.13
Education	−0.10	−0.10	−0.05	−0.08
Health care	−0.01	0.00	−0.06	−0.05
Entertainment	−0.14	−0.13	−0.12	−0.14
Accommodation and food	−0.18	−0.19	−0.22	−0.22
Other	−0.07	−0.07	−0.11	−0.10
Public administration	0.04	0.05	0.02	0.02

Source: Authors' tabulations using microdata from U.S. Bureau of the Census (1992–2003).

shows the extent to which they were employed by firms in the various quintiles of the firm-effects distribution. In other words, table 2.8 shows us the extent to which "good workers" are matched to "good jobs" at the beginning and end of our period, and thus whether the tendency for these two categories to be matched is growing over time.

A number of striking findings appear in the table. As we noted earlier, over 60 percent of the very best workers (the top quintile of person effects) were employed at the very best-paying firms (the top quintile of firm effects), which is now evident for both 1992 and 2003. The same was true for the "worst" workers (at least as measured by their person effects), who ended up in the worst job quintile. Yet the other quintiles of workers show

Table 2.8 Distribution of Employment Across Firm-Effects Quintiles, 1992 Versus 2003

| | 1992 | | | | | 2003 | | | | |
| | Firm-Effects Quintile (1 = Highest) | | | | | Firm-Effects Quintile (1 = Highest) | | | | |
Person-Effects Quintile	1	2	3	4	5	1	2	3	4	5
Quintile 1	63.6%	26.3%	8.0%	1.9%	0.3%	67.7%	22.4%	7.6%	1.8%	0.6%
Quintile 2	25.8	34.1	23.2	13.0	3.9	24.9	38.6	24.4	9.9	2.2
Quintile 3	9.3	25.7	33.7	21.9	9.4	10.5	25.6	33.7	22.4	7.8
Quintile 4	2.4	12.6	25.5	37.9	21.6	3.7	6.8	24.2	40.0	25.4
Quintile 5	0.2	1.6	10.2	26.8	61.1	2.4	2.5	7.8	27.2	60.1

Source: Authors' tabulations using microdata from U.S. Bureau of the Census (1992–2003).
Note: Rows sum to 100 percent.

Figure 2.4   Employment over Time Within Person-Effects Quintile 1,
1992 to 2003

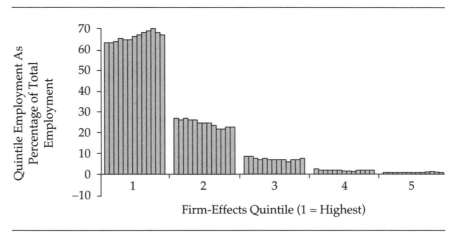

Source: Authors' tabulations using microdata from U.S. Bureau of the Census (1992–2003).

more tendency to be employed at either better or worse jobs than their person effect would predict: 30 to 40 percent in each worker quintile were employed in a comparable job quintile, and all the rest were employed at jobs in higher or lower pay quintiles.

In terms of changes over time, we find an increasing tendency of the very best workers to be concentrated in the very best firms (with the fraction rising from about 64 percent to 68 percent) and for the "nearly best" workers (those in the second quintile) to end up in the "nearly best" jobs (with that concentration rising from 34 to 39 percent). Among less-skilled workers, the largest changes are apparent for those in the fourth quintile of person effects—that is, those with relatively weak personal earnings capacity, though not the lowest. For this group, we see a distinct dropping off in the percentage of workers employed in the second and third quintiles of job quality (from 13 to 7 percent and 26 to 24 percent, respectively), while their concentration in the bottom two quintiles of firms rises.

A closer look at how workers of different skill levels are being increasingly linked to jobs of similar quality over time appears in figures 2.4 to 2.8. Separately for workers in each of the five quintiles of person effects (or skills), we present the annual shares of their employment in each of the five quintiles of firm effects. With the shares presented for each year in each figure, we can see the extent to which there has been a consis-

Figure 2.5   Employment over Time Within Person-Effects Quintile 2,
1992 to 2003

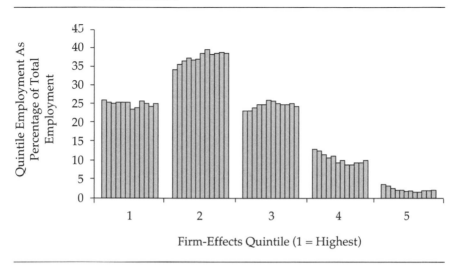

Source: Authors' tabulations using microdata from U.S. Bureau of the Census (1992–2003).

Figure 2.6   Employment over Time Within Person-Effects Quintile 3,
1992 to 2003

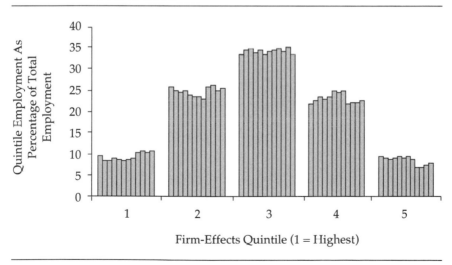

Source: Authors' tabulations using microdata from U.S. Bureau of the Census (1992–2003).

Figure 2.7   Employment over Time Within Person-Effects Quintile 4, 1992 to 2003

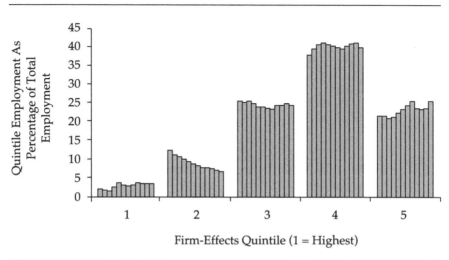

Source: Authors' tabulations using microdata from U.S. Bureau of the Census (1992–2003).

Figure 2.8   Employment over Time Within Person-Effects Quintile 5, 1992 to 2003

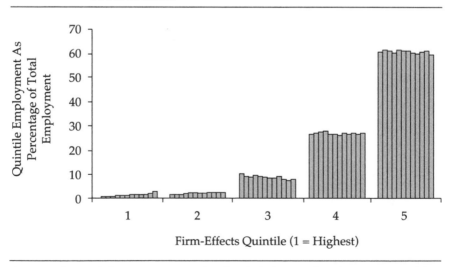

Source: Authors' tabulations using microdata from U.S. Bureau of the Census (1992–2003).

tent secular trend toward greater matching of high-skill workers to high-paying jobs and of low-skill workers to low-paying jobs.

The data tell the same story as table 2.8. The very best workers—those in the top quintiles of person effects—are consistently being more frequently matched to the very best jobs. The relatively high-quality workers of the second quintile are similarly being increasingly matched to quite high-paying jobs (the second quintile of firm effects) over the twelve-year period, and away from those in the bottom two quintiles. And workers in the fourth quintile—whose person effects are relatively weak but not among the very worst—clearly have more difficulty ending up in relatively good jobs (in the second or third quintiles) and more frequently end up at or near the bottom of the pay scale. With the most skilled workers increasingly obtaining the best jobs, and with fewer of these good jobs going to the less-skilled, it is little surprise that earnings inequality would be rising substantially with time.

But inequality depends not only on the distribution of more- and less-skilled workers between firms and jobs of different quality, but also on any changes occurring in relative rewards to these groups within firms. Given that workers end up in firms that pay relatively well or poorly, how have the fortunes of the most- and least-skilled workers evolved over time? Figure 2.9 presents the average ratio of earnings for workers in the ninetieth and tenth percentiles within firms in each of the firm-effects quintiles. The figure thus measures the trends in inequality between skill groups of workers but within firms of varying quality, as distinct from the question of whether different kinds of workers get hired at all at these firms.

The results show a rising ratio of pay among the highest- to lowest-paid workers in each quintile of job quality, as we might expect during an era of rising inequality. But these increases are most pronounced in the top two quintiles of firm and job quality. The rise of pay inequality within the best-paying firms at fixed parts of the pay ladders may at least partly reflect the rising concentration of highly skilled workers there, with the average quality of those at the ninetieth percentile rising relative to those at the tenth. But these results also reflect a greater tendency for the most-skilled workers to be relatively better compensated than the least skilled within firms and over time, even at fixed positions on the relative pay scale and for workers with given relative levels of ability.[23]

Either way, the overall results suggest that good jobs are becoming the province of good workers, as defined by their permanent earnings capacities. Such good jobs are increasingly out of reach for those with weak or poor skills, and their pay is relatively weakened even when they manage to be hired at well-paying firms.

Figure 2.9   Average Earnings Differential by Firm-Effects Quintile, 1992 Versus 2003

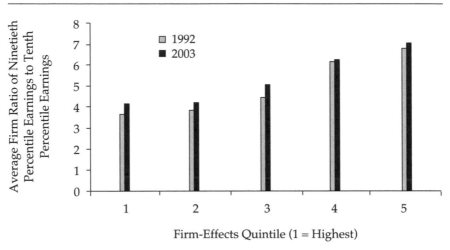

Source: Authors' tabulations using microdata from U.S. Bureau of the Census (1992–2003).

CONCLUSION

What kinds of jobs might be considered good jobs in the United States to-day, and who gets those jobs? Importantly, are good jobs disappearing in the United States? Our analysis of job quality and worker quality over a recent twelve-year period suggests that the answer to this last question is not a simple "yes" or "no."

To address these questions, we analyze an enormous body of longitudinal data on both workers and firms assembled by the U.S. Census Bureau. We develop measures of the quality of workers and jobs based on worker and firm fixed effects, which capture the earnings premia that workers receive and that firms pay over a period of years. We allow these effects to vary over time to allow for the possibility that firms might adjust their pay practices in response to changing economic circumstances and opportunities and that workers can also adjust the levels of skill they acquire. Indeed, the three time periods during which we estimate these effects—1992 to 1995, 1996 to 1999, and 2000 to 2003—reflect distinct periods of recovery, boom, and downturn in the U.S. economy that merit separate consideration. Though we do not have data reflecting the mild recovery in the labor market after 2003 and the Great Recession that came in 2008, we believe that our findings probably reflect long-term secular trends in the job market that remain relevant despite these major cyclical swings. Indeed, the ongoing decline in manufacturing employment since 2003 is very consistent with our findings before then, as is the rise in health care employment.

Like other analyses that have relied on similar measures, we find that the firm effects are strongly related to other characteristics like industry, firm size, and job turnover or churning. Worker effects are closely related to other characteristics such as race and gender, foreign-born status, and education. Indeed, our measures indicate that educational attainment is an important determinant of worker earnings capacity, but that such capacity also varies greatly for those at any given level of attainment. No doubt, this variation reflects the many dimensions of productivity and skill that years of education alone do not capture, as well as the systematic advantages and disadvantage that are still associated with race-ethnicity and gender in the United States. Overall, however, our results also confirm that our worker and firm effects measures are reasonably estimated and generally trustworthy.

What do our measures show regarding changes over time? At least in a relative sense, we can say that *good jobs are not disappearing in the United States*. We find that the jobs in the top quintile of quality grew most rapidly in the period 1992 to 2003 and that those in the second and third quintiles grew more slowly. The results are broadly consistent with the notion of the "hollowing of the middle" of the job market stressed by some recent analyses. But even though the differences in growth rates across these job quality categories seem substantial, the magnitudes of these changes are not large enough to dramatically change overall job availability at different levels of pay.

Perhaps more important, however, are *changes in the ability of less-educated workers to be employed in well-paid jobs*. Across industries, we find a dramatic shrinkage in the extent to which manufacturing—especially durable manufacturing—accounts for jobs in the top two quintiles. At the very top, these jobs are being replaced by those in professional services, information, and other sectors where good pay generally requires strong postsecondary credentials. And where jobs remain in manufacturing, they are increasingly being filled by workers from the top of the skills distribution.

Less-educated workers, who are largely concentrated in the lower to middle categories of skill as measured by person effects, increasingly find good jobs (as defined by fixed effects that are larger than their own person effects) in health care or retail trade rather than in the more traditional sources of these jobs in manufacturing, mining, and utilities. Construction continued to be a source of good jobs during this time period for these workers, but the subsequent bursting of the housing "bubble" raises some questions about that industry's ability to provide good jobs in the future. And even in these sectors, well-paid jobs require either postsecondary training and credentials (in health care and construction) or social-verbal and arithmetic skills (in retail trade) that go beyond what was needed for the good jobs of the past.

More broadly, we find a trend in which the quality of the jobs obtained by workers are more closely aligned with their personal skills—so that our measures of worker and job quality are lining up more closely than in the past. And within the best-paying firms the ratio of pay between the highest- and least-skilled employees is growing more than elsewhere, suggesting that, even within the well-paid jobs and firms, rewards are growing most rapidly for those with the best skills. These forces no doubt contribute to growing inequality over time, unless skill gaps begin to close.

What all this implies for policy is that the traditional bifurcation of discussions of labor market performance between advocates of "good workers" (those with education and skills) and "good jobs" (those that pay well even for unskilled workers) is gradually becoming obsolete. Of course, there remains a wide range of job qualities for workers of any skill level. Some industries still pay much better than others; large firms still offer better opportunities than small ones. And within industries and areas, firms still choose widely varying human resource practices that constitute a "higher road" in some cases and a "lower road" in others, with important consequences for the employment outcomes of the workers who end up in each type of firm. Policies that assist and encourage (or even require) more firms to travel the higher road still have an important place in these discussions, to which we return in chapter 6.

Still, the good jobs of today and tomorrow increasingly require good skills among the workers who get them. Therefore, the best strategies going forward should emphasize the creation of "better workers for better jobs," rather than a set of choices in which we need to choose between these options. How to best do so is fleshed out more fully in the remainder of this book.

And since job quality still matters importantly in our labor markets, some important questions remain about what happens to workers who have good jobs and then lose them. In a highly volatile job market such as the one we have, are workers losing these jobs more frequently, and are the consequences for those who lose good jobs more serious now than in the past? How hard is it to replace the lost jobs, and what happens when they are replaced by jobs of lower quality?

We turn to these questions in the next chapter and beyond.

APPENDIX: DATA, VARIABLES, AND FIXED-EFFECTS ESTIMATES

A full description of the LEHD data used in this book is available in Abowd et al. (2006). We follow their procedures in virtually everything we have done. Here we outline the issues that were most salient to the construction of our data.

The Data: Samples Used and Variables Calculated

Most of our estimates in this volume are based on samples of person-year observations, using a measure of annualized earnings that we have created for each person in each year they work (described later in this appendix). The use of annualized earnings is necessitated by the fact that many workers were employed by more than one firm in any given year; in such cases, the firm where that worker had the highest earnings in that year is defined as the "primary employer," and the observations with other employers for that year are deleted. But to make such observations consistent across cases where durations with the primary employer are longer or shorter, we convert all earnings to annualized measures, which are our best estimate of what workers would earn if they worked for the primary employer over an entire year.

We limit our analysis to observations where the worker was at least eighteen years of age at the start of the year and no older than sixty-four at the start of the year. Annualized earnings are converted to real 2003 dollars using the CPI-U and then converted to log annual earnings. One set of computations is performed for the entire twelve-year period (1992 to 2003), while other sets are done for each of our separate subperiods (1992 to 1995, 1996 to 1999, and 2000 to 2003). These computations are performed separately for each of the twelve states for which we have data covering the entire period: California, Colorado, Idaho, Illinois, Kansas, Maryland, Missouri, North Carolina, Oregon, Pennsylvania, Washington, and Wisconsin.

To generate annualized earnings for each person-year, we begin by categorizing every quarter in which a worker had positive earnings as either "full-quarter," "continuous," or "discontinuous" employment. It is full-quarter employment if a worker had positive earnings at the same firm in the previous quarter and the next quarter. Otherwise, it is continuous employment if the worker had positive earnings at the same firm in either the previous quarter or the next quarter. Employment that was neither full nor continuous is classified as discontinuous employment—the worker was employed in the current quarter, but was not employed in either the previous or subsequent quarter.

If a person has at least one quarter of full employment in a year, then annualized earnings for that person-year are defined as the average earnings for quarters of full employment times four. Otherwise, if he or she has at least one quarter of continuous employment in a year, then we compute the annualized earnings for that year as the average earnings for quarters of continuous employment times eight, relying on an assumption of expected employment duration of one-half for each quarter of continuous employment. If he or she has no full or continuous employment, then annualized earnings for that year are equal to the average earnings for quarters of discontinuous employment times twelve (using an assumption of expected employment duration of one-third for each quarter of discontinuous employment).[24]

We also create a series of variables for the time-varying characteristics of each individual in each year for inclusion in log earnings regressions, starting with experience. In the first year in which a worker appears in the data, experience is set equal to the year minus the year of the worker's birth minus the worker's imputed level of education minus six. Then, starting with that first year, for every quarter in which the worker had positive earnings, 0.25 is added to the level of experience in the next year. We then create a fourth-degree polynomial in the experience variable, which is included in the regressions (presented later in this appendix) that generated fixed-effects estimates.

We also create an additional set of dummy variables for each person-year. These include dummy variables for four full quarters of work and for other amounts of full-quarter work interacted with year dummies; a dummy variable if the only employment was discontinuous; and dummy variables for the number of full quarters worked. (The last two sets are not interacted with year.) All time-varying characteristics are also fully interacted with gender.

Firm-level employment and industry codes are added to the data set from our employer characteristics file (ECF). From this, we calculate the average monthly employment of each firm for the period, conditional on positive employment, including only those firms in the sample where average monthly employment was twenty-five months or more. Any person-year observations for firms that are not in this sample are deleted.

We then compute a set of measures for mean annual earnings for individuals (across years), for firms (across workers and years), and for all workers (across years), which we denote as $EARN_i$, $EARN_j$, and $EARN$, respectively. This is done separately for each of the twelve states and each of the four subperiods. Likewise, we compute mean time-varying characteristics for individuals, firms, and all workers (X_i, X_j, and X, respectively).

In calculating these means, we weight observations using the expected employment duration, as defined earlier. As with the calculation of annual earnings, quarters of continuous employment are not counted if there was at least one quarter of full employment, and discontinuous quarters are not counted if there was at least one quarter of full employment or continuous employment. For example, an observation with four full quarters of employment would have a weight of 4, an observation with three quarters of continuous employment would have a weight of 1.5 (or 3×0.5), and an observation with two quarters of discontinuous employment would have a weight of 0.667 (or 2×0.333).

The Calculation of Fixed Effects

Person and firm fixed-effects estimates are derived from earnings regressions on person-year observations in each state and time period that also include controls for time-varying worker characteristics. Alternatively, they are calculated in some cases from the means of earnings and time-varying characteristics. The exact methods we use (like those used by Abowd et al. 2006) were often necessitated by the limits on computational abilities for such enormous data sets.

In most states, we start with a sample of all person-years for those who worked at the two thousand largest firms, which amount to roughly half of the total number of observations in those states.[25] We ran regressions in which the dependent variable is the log annualized earnings for each person-year, and the time-varying characteristics and two thousand firm dummy variables are independent variables that "absorb" (or hold constant) the person fixed effects, again weighting by expected employment duration.[26] The firm fixed effect for each of these two thousand firms is then calculated as the coefficient on the firm dummy variable minus the mean of all firm dummy variables, thus generating a sample of firm effects with zero means:

$$\Psi_j = \beta_j - \beta,$$ (2.1)

where ψ is the firm effect for firm j, the β_js are coefficients on the firm dummies, and β is their mean.

The firm fixed effect for each of the other firms (those smaller in size than the largest two thousand firms) is calculated as follows:

$$\Psi_j = (EARN_j - EARN) - \Sigma \, \beta_x \, (X_j - X), \tag{2.2}$$

where β_x is the regression coefficient on each time-varying X variable. Thus, the firm effect is an estimate of the wage premium paid by each firm to its workers, holding all characteristics of the firm's workers—both observed and unobserved—constant.

The person fixed effect is calculated similarly. For each worker, the person effect is derived as follows:

$$\theta_i = (EARN_i - EARN) - \Sigma \, \beta_x (X_i - X), \tag{2.3}$$

now using individual worker means on $EARN$ and X rather than for firms. The resulting person effect is an estimate of the wage premium earned by each worker holding the employing firm and time-variant characteristics constant.

The resulting state-by-state data sets are pooled into aggregated data sets, one for each of the four time periods. To compute quintiles of firm and person effects that are fixed over time, all firms existing in 1992 are ordered by firm fixed effect, as calculated for the period of 1992 to 1995. These firms are divided into quintiles such that the total employment of each quintile in 1992 is as close as possible to one-fifth of the total employment of all firms existing in 1992. The range of firm fixed effects in each quintile is then used to place firms entering in later years into an appropriate quintile, based on each firm's fixed effect as calculated in the first four-year period in which it is observed.

Similarly, firms are divided into quintiles based on their mean person fixed effects. The quintiles are constructed based on 1992 employment such that employment within each quintile in 1992 is as close as possible to one-fifth of the total employment. As with the firm fixed-effects quintiles, the boundaries between the person fixed-effects quintiles created for 1992 are then used to place firms into fixed-effects quintiles from 1993 to 2003. However, because the workers who are employed at a particular firm vary in each year, the mean person fixed effect at a firm also varies. Therefore, each firm is assigned a person fixed-effects quintile for each year in which it existed from 1992 to 2003 based on its mean person fixed effect in that year. This is different from firm fixed-effects quintiles, where a firm is placed into a quintile based on its earliest firm fixed effect and has only one firm fixed-effects quintile associated with it.

Chapter 3 | Job Quality and Volatility: How Do They Affect Worker Earnings?

IN THE PREVIOUS CHAPTER, we showed that high-quality jobs are still relatively available in the United States, though apparently less so than before for workers with lower levels of education or skill. This relative change in the availability of good jobs for less-skilled workers could have important implications for recent and future trends in economic inequality.

This set of findings also raises some important questions regarding the relationship between job quality and volatility and what it might mean for worker *insecurity*. Of course, workers can change jobs for lots of reasons—some by choice, some not. Those who choose to change jobs might be doing so for good reasons and are often able to improve their economic circumstances when they do.

As we noted earlier, some prominent authors—like Peter Gosselin, Jacob Hacker, and Louis Uchitelle—have suggested that the risks of income or job loss are rising over the long term. But are workers at greater risk of losing jobs today than in earlier years owing to no fault of their own? How does job volatility—especially of the involuntary kind—vary across different categories of jobs, and particularly in high-quality jobs? And how are the odds of job change or job loss trending over time, both in the overall labor market and by level of job or worker quality?

Other questions involve not only the rate of job change or loss, but also the benefits or costs that job change or loss generates for workers. When involuntary job loss (or job displacement) occurs, what are the consequences for workers in terms of lost earnings and benefits, and how do those consequences differ from the effects of job change more generally? If high-quality jobs are becoming less available for some groups of workers, does this affect their ability to replace one good job with another? To what

57

extent are workers' earnings affected by this growing unavailability, as well as by the loss of job tenure they experience and any difficulties they have finding suitable employment again? And how are these impacts affected by the overall health of the nation's labor market?

We attempt to answer these questions in this chapter. We begin with a brief review of the empirical literature on job displacements. We then use our LEHD data to analyze the rates of job change overall and a measure of involuntary displacements that we have developed. We analyze differences in rates of job change and displacement across different categories of jobs (by firm effect, industry, size) and workers (by education, age, person effect) and look at how these rates have trended over time.

We then consider the impact of such job changes on worker earnings. Since earnings are heavily dependent on job quality, the effect of job change or loss on worker earnings should depend on the ability of job-changers or job-losers to replace them with comparable or better jobs. We analyze this ability and how it varies in different times and economic conditions, as well as what it means for the earnings changes of workers who suffer a job loss.

Finally, we summarize our findings and briefly review their implications for policy. We find that rates of job change and displacement increased only mildly over the 1990s. We also find that job change (and even displacement) can have either a positive or negative effect on a worker's earnings, depending to a large extent on the quality of the job that replaces the old one. Thus, a growing unavailability to less-skilled workers of good jobs over time might raise the costs associated with job change or displacement. Furthermore, the costs or benefits associated with job change and loss depend a great deal on the state of the overall labor market; much more positive earnings changes occur when the labor market is strong. But this implies quite serious negative effects of job displacement on many workers in the aftermath of the Great Recession.

JOB DISPLACEMENTS: WHAT DOES THE LITERATURE SHOW?

As we noted earlier, job changes can have either positive or negative effects on earnings, depending on the extent to which they are voluntary or involuntary (Bartel and Borjas 1981). Voluntary job changes, especially among young or low-income workers, are often associated with earnings increases. Indeed, these changes can account for large portions of the wage increases observed over time for these groups (Topel and Ward 1992; Andersson, Holzer, and Lane 2005).

But involuntary changes can generate a loss of job seniority (or "tenure," in the lingo of economists) and difficulties for the worker in finding another job, or especially one that pays as well, resulting in earnings losses over time. Some kinds of involuntary job loss—like being discharged for poor performance (at least in the eyes of the employer) or being individually laid off—do not necessarily generate large earnings losses, especially if they represent poor work performance that is generally associated with low wages for a given worker. But job *displacement*—which is defined as involuntary job loss associated with shutdowns or reorganizations of workplaces—results in earnings loss on average, especially for those who have accumulated some significant tenure in their jobs.

Initially, employment rates are lower for workers who have been displaced. Eventually, most find and accept new jobs, but often at lower levels of earnings than they previously enjoyed. The estimates to date suggest that, for workers with at least three years of job tenure, these losses average 15 to 25 percent, with the exact losses depending on local economic conditions (Jacobson, Lalonde, and Sullivan 1993; Couch and Placzek 2010). Losses are highest for older and less-educated workers, who lose the most job tenure and perhaps have the greatest difficulty finding acceptable new employment. If health insurance or other benefits provided by the employer are not available on the new job, these losses might be compounded and generate even greater insecurity—even if these workers were accepting lower wages to pay for the health benefits.[1]

Are the costs of job change and displacement worsening over time in the United States? This might be occurring for one or both of the following reasons: (1) the *incidence* of job change or displacement is rising, or (2) the *costs* associated with an incident of displacement are rising in terms of dollar earnings or lost benefits like employer-provided health insurance.

Those who say that worker and family incomes have become more volatile over time argue that this is at least partly true because the labor market is more volatile, with involuntary job loss rising.[2] Yet the extent to which this is true in the recent past in the United States has not been clear. For instance, some analyses of the overall income volatility of workers, using data like the Current Population Survey (CPS) or the Panel Survey of Income Dynamics (PSID), suggest that income volatility either has not increased at all or has done so only moderately (Dahl, DeLeire, and Schwabish 2008; Dynan, Elmendorf, and Sichel 2008; Shin and Solon 2008).

A somewhat different view emerges from recent work by Peter Gottschalk and Robert Moffitt (2009), who separate earnings inequality into *permanent* and *transitory* components and measure income volatility as the *variance* over time in the transitory component of earnings. They find clear evidence of rising transitory earnings variance among men. Yet the timing of these increases is quite uneven, with much of the recent increases occurring in the late 1970s and early 1980s and some also since the late 1990s. When they separate their samples by education or earnings levels, they find greater increases early on for less-educated men and more recently among the better-educated or those with higher earnings. Increases for women are less clear and differ somewhat in timing from those of men.

So, to the extent that earnings have become less stable over time, especially for men, to what extent can this be attributed to job market volatility and rising risks of worker displacement? There is some fairly clear evidence that jobs are becoming more unstable, in the sense that workers seem to be accumulating less tenure over time (Farber 2007; Hallock 2009). But it is much less clear that this is caused by higher risks of involuntary termination or displacements.

Henry Farber's (2005) analysis, using data from the Displaced Workers Survey (DWS), which supplements the Current Population Survey every two years in January, shows a strong countercyclical pattern in job displacement rates. Although his data suggest some elevated rates of job loss in the 1990s, especially given the strong state of the economy at that time, it is hard to discern a longer-term secular trend in that data. Furthermore, evidence of gross job creation and destruction, using "gross flows" measures of jobs based on administrative earnings data similar to what we use here (see, for example, Davis, Haltiwanger, and Schuh 1998; Davis 2008), does not show rising volatility. Indeed, job volatility seems to have declined somewhat over the past few decades (Davis et al. 2010), with fewer workers flowing into spells of unemployment as a result.[3] There is some evidence that rates of both new job creation and job destruction in the United States overall fell especially in the past decade (Mann 2006), implying even lower labor market volatility during that time. If true, this implies that any overall reductions in job tenure that we have observed might mostly be voluntary and based on an increasing tendency of workers to leave jobs. But whether this is true for all groups of workers, and for various kinds of jobs and levels of job quality, has been unclear in this work.

Has the long-term cost to workers associated with an incident of job displacement risen over time? Most analyses can focus only on pecuniary earnings and not on the possible loss of health insurance benefits. Farber (2005) has found some evidence of rising displacement costs among college-educated workers over time. Whether this is true for other groups has been less clear, and the extent to which any such trends might be related to changes in job quality and availability for different groups has not been addressed in this literature.

JOB CHANGES AND DISPLACEMENTS IN THE LEHD DATA

As we noted earlier, voluntary job changes (or "quits") are much more likely to generate earnings growth over time for individuals than involuntary changes, and among involuntary job changes it is important to distinguish changes related to worker performance (or "discharges") from those that are unrelated to worker performance and simply reflect changing economic contingencies faced by employers that limit worker opportunities (or "permanent dislocations"). Surveys of workers like the Current Population Survey (CPS) and the National Longitudinal Survey of Youth (NLSY) ask workers about why they lost or left their most recent job and can thus distinguish among these types of job changes, at least to some extent.[4]

Since here we are using administrative data on workers and their employers, we cannot directly distinguish voluntary from involuntary moves in general, or quits from discharges and layoffs in particular. But we can approximately identify permanent displacements as situations where workers change their employers at the same time that the firms for which they work initially are reducing their overall employment levels. Therefore, we define *job changes* as occurring when a worker's primary employer (the one with whom he or she has the greatest earnings in any given year) changes from one year to the next. In contrast, *job displacements* are the subset of such changes that occur for individuals when their employer also experiences a lasting decline in the size of its workforce of at least 30 percent.[5]

This definition does not perfectly distinguish between involuntary displacements and other kinds of job changes, but we feel that it is a reasonable first approximation to identifying job displacements within the limitations imposed on us by our data.[6] But to the extent that the distinction between general job changes and displacements is measured with some error here, differences in measured outcomes between the two are understated.

Also, following much of the literature on job displacement, we distinguish between workers who leave or lose their jobs fairly early in their time with a firm from those who leave after accumulating at least three years of job tenure, in which case the loss of rewards for seniority or firm-specific skills is relatively greater. Indeed, such separations should occur less frequently at this point, since both the firm and the worker have had more time to judge the quality of the "match" between them, and both have probably invested in the match if it has lasted longer.[7]

We begin our analysis of these different categories of job changes with figure 3.1, which presents the annual rates of job changes for workers averaged over the entire period of 1992 to 2003. We distinguish overall job changes from those that we designate as displacements, and we calculate these rates of job change for all workers and for those with at least three years of tenure on the job.

The results show, not unexpectedly, that many Americans change jobs

Figure 3.1   Rates of Job Change and Job Displacement, 1992
              to 2003

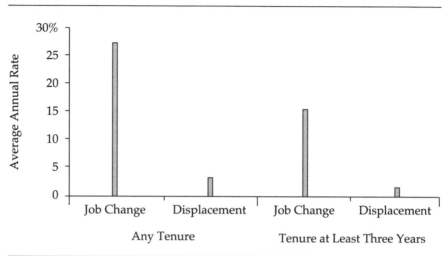

Source: Authors' tabulations using microdata from U.S. Bureau of the Census (1992–2003).

in any given year—indeed, about 28 percent of American workers do so. This rate of change is broadly consistent with the rates observed by Farber (1999) using survey data and by other researchers using LEHD and other sources of administrative data (Abowd and Kramarz 1999). In contrast, job displacements (at least by our definition) occur much less frequently and affect only about 2 percent of workers in an average year—a rate that is also consistent with the rates calculated by Farber. And for workers with at least three years of job tenure, job change in general and displacements in particular occur much less frequently, with annual rates of job change of approximately 16 percent and displacement rates in the 1 to 2 percent range.

Of course, these rates of job change and displacement probably vary across different kinds of firms and jobs as well as different categories of workers. In tables 3.1 and 3.2, we present data on how these job transition rates vary across categories of firms and workers. The data on firms include job change rates by industry, firm size category, and overall job quality—as measured by firm-effects quintile. The data on workers include changes by age, race, gender, education, and person-effects quintile.

The data in table 3.1 show that rates of job change do indeed vary quite a bit across industries. To some extent, rates of job change in general tend

Table 3.1   Rates of Job Change and Job Displacement, 1992 to 2003

Industry	Any Tenure		Tenure at Least Three Years	
	Job Change	Displacement	Job Change	Displacement
Agriculture	38.3%	12.5%	18.5%	4.3%
Mining	22.3	2.7	17.2	2.2
Utilities	12.6	0.6	12.2	0.7
Construction	33.3	4.8	17.0	1.9
Nondurable manufacturing	24.0	2.1	16.9	1.8
Durable manufacturing	21.2	1.7	16.0	1.6
Wholesale trade	26.1	2.0	17.5	1.6
Retail trade	33.5	1.7	18.6	1.2
Transportation	25.6	1.8	14.8	1.2
Services				
Information	27.1	2.2	18.7	1.7
Finance	26.0	1.3	18.5	0.9
Real estate	35.1	2.3	20.7	1.6
Professional services	31.7	2.5	20.4	1.6
Management	23.2	1.1	17.0	0.9
Administrative	51.3	4.0	24.4	2.3
Education	15.1	0.5	9.8	0.3
Health care	26.1	1.1	16.8	0.8
Entertainment	35.6	5.4	19.1	2.0
Accommodation and food	44.5	2.8	24.7	2.0
Other services	31.8	2.1	18.3	1.3
Public administration	16.0	0.2	12.3	0.1
Firm-effects quintile				
Quintile 1	24.6	1.9	17.0	1.4
Quintile 2	23.5	1.4	16.1	1.0
Quintile 3	25.4	1.5	15.4	1.0
Quintile 4	30.0	1.8	15.2	1.0
Quintile 5	38.1	3.7	18.2	1.8
Firm size				
25 to 49	32.0	3.2	17.8	2.1
50 to 99	32.2	3.1	18.0	1.9
100 to 999	29.3	2.3	16.9	1.4
1,000 to 9,999	24.8	1.1	15.3	0.8
10,000 or more	20.5	0.3	13.4	0.2

Source: Authors' tabulations using microdata from U.S. Bureau of the Census (1992–2003).
Note: Job change is defined as a change in a worker's primary employer from year t to year t + 1 (including non-employment in year t + 1). Displacement is defined as a job change where a displacement event (a decline of 30 percent or more in quarterly employment) occurred at the firm that is the primary employer in year t, and additionally the worker had positive earnings at the firm in the quarter of the displacement event, had positive earnings at the firm for at least one quarter prior to the event, and had zero earnings at the firm for at least two quarters after the event.

Table 3.2   Rates of Job Change and Job Displacement, 1992
to 2003

	Any Tenure		Tenure at Least Three Years	
	Job Change	Displace-ment	Job Change	Displace-ment
Person-effects quintile				
Quintile 1	23.2%	1.7%	16.9%	1.3%
Quintile 2	22.9	1.4	15.2	1.0
Quintile 3	24.9	1.5	14.9	0.9
Quintile 4	30.7	2.1	15.8	1.3
Quintile 5	40.5	3.6	20.6	2.0
Age				
Eighteen to thirty-four	32.6	2.2	17.4	1.2
Thirty-five to forty-four	20.6	1.7	13.0	1.1
Forty-five to sixty-four	22.9	1.7	18.8	1.2
Race				
White	26.3	1.8	15.8	1.1
Black	33.1	2.0	17.8	1.2
Hispanic	32.6	3.2	17.7	1.7
Asian–Pacific Islander	28.3	2.0	17.5	1.3
Native American	37.6	2.5	20.4	1.3
Gender				
Female	28.0	1.8	16.4	1.1
Male	27.7	2.2	16.1	1.3
Educational attainment				
Less than high school	33.2	3.0	18.1	1.9
High school	27.1	2.1	15.8	1.5
Some college	29.4	2.0	16.4	1.2
Associate's degree	25.2	1.8	15.4	1.2
Bachelor's degree	25.0	1.7	15.6	1.0
Master's degree	20.9	1.3	13.4	0.7
Professional degree	23.4	1.2	16.1	0.9
Doctoral degree	19.6	1.1	14.1	0.5

Source: Authors' tabulations using microdata from U.S. Bureau of the Census (1992–2003).
Note: Data on education come from the long form of the 2000 Decennial Census of Population, which includes approximately one-sixth of the workers in our data. Education results are calculated solely for these workers and solely for the year 2000.

to correlate with those of displacement, though not perfectly. Some industries (agriculture, construction, administrative services, and entertainment) have high rates of job change in both categories, while others (manufacturing—especially durable—finance, management, health care, and, especially, utilities, education, and the public sector) have low rates in both. In contrast, retail trade is an example of an industry that has relatively high rates of job change but not of displacement.

The notion that utilities and the public sector provide greater job security to their workers and fewer inducements to leave is not terribly surprising, given the relative lack of competition they face in product and labor markets.[8] In other sectors, displacements probably reflect variability in product demand (perhaps unforeseen at the time of hiring) or in the production process. High rates of voluntary and involuntary job changes more generally might well reflect low wages and working conditions, lack of investments by one or both sides in firm-specific skills, a lack of job "ladders" and promotion possibilities in these jobs or firms, and generally low attachments to the employment relationship, as both Henry Farber (1999) and Donald Parsons (1987) have noted.[9]

Of course, a relative lack of permanence in a job may not be uniformly or monotonically related to the compensation level it offers or the skills of the workers who fill it, especially since worker incentives to stay in any job are greater when their compensation is high relative to their other market opportunities, while for firms the incentives might be the opposite (especially when such compensation is not fully offset by higher productivity).[10]

In fact, our data on job change rates by firm-effects quintile confirm this. Rates of job change in general are just a bit higher in the highest-quality jobs than in the middle categories, but tend to rise substantially in the lowest-quality jobs, and displacement rates show a more pronounced J-shape with regard to firm effects. But both kinds of job change decline much more uniformly with firm size, perhaps reflecting the strong relationship between firm size, compensation levels, and the quality of human resources policies that has been noted elsewhere (Brown, Hamilton, and Medoff 1990).

A number of interesting relationships between our measures of job change and personal characteristics of workers appear in table 3.2, and these relationships are mostly consistent with earlier work on this topic (Farber 2005; Parsons 1987). For instance, job changes rise substantially at firms in the bottom two quintiles of person effects, while displacement rates are somewhat higher at the top quintile of this skills measure, as well as at the bottom. Thus, being highly skilled does not guarantee a worker's security on the job, at least not by this measure. Job change rates are U-shaped with respect to age, with both younger and older workers showing more employment variation and less attachment to their employers than prime-age workers, while displacement is higher for the young when they have less job tenure. By race, we find high rates of both job change and displacement among Hispanic workers, which are probably especially high among (undocumented) immigrants. In contrast, rates of job change are somewhat high among blacks and Native Americans, though displacements are not.[11] Women have slightly higher rates of job change than men—probably a reflection of their need to juggle work with family responsibilities—while men tend to be more frequently displaced. And both kinds of job change tend to fall fairly uniformly with the worker's level of education.

TRENDS IN JOB CHANGES AND DISPLACEMENT OVER TIME

For our purposes, an important question is whether or not these rates of job change and, especially, displacement have varied over time, either for all workers or for specific categories. In particular, has the incidence of job displacement risen over time, generating greater insecurity among some or all workers?

Figure 3.2 presents rates of overall job change and displacement for each year—for all workers over the period 1992 to 2003 and for those with at least three years of job tenure over the period 1995 to 2003—with each bar in the diagram representing the job change or displacement rate for a particular year in the period.[12]

Overall, the data show that *there was some trend toward higher rates of job change and job displacement over the 1990s*, especially among those workers with lower levels of job tenure. That displacement rates would increase during the downturn of 2001 is not at all surprising, given that involuntary layoffs and permanent displacements always follow a clear countercyclical pattern. But the pattern here also appears over much of the 1990s, during which time the labor market was growing increasingly tight. Furthermore, in a tightening job market, we might well expect voluntary job changes to accelerate as workers gain more confidence that they can leave a job and replace it with another one of comparable or better quality and appeal. Indeed, overall job changes peak in the very tight labor market environment of 1999, but the apparent tendency for an increase in job displacements (albeit a mild one) during this time period is also notable.

This last finding is consistent with Farber's suggestion of high job displacement in the 1990s, adjusting for the cyclical state of the economy at that time, and also with the Gottschalk-Moffitt evidence of greater transi-

Figure 3.2   Rates of Job Change and Job Displacement over Time, 1992 to 2003

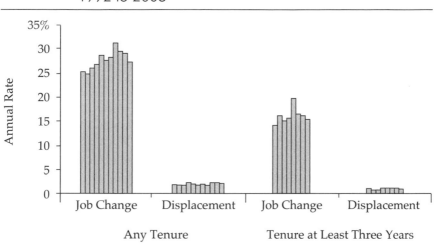

Source: Authors' tabulations using microdata from U.S. Bureau of the Census (1992–2003).
Note: Bars represent the rate of job change or displacement for each year from 1992 to 2002.

tory earnings variation during this period. Of course, whether this relatively high rate of displacement activity persisted beyond the recession of 2001 is less clear, given the drop in observed rates of job destruction (as well as creation) in the United States that we noted earlier.

But are these changes in job mobility and displacement more pronounced for some categories of jobs and workers than others? We consider this issue in figures 3.3 and 3.4, where we present the trends over time in rates of job displacement for each of the five quintiles of firm effects and person effects, respectively. Despite some outliers within any given year for any particular quintile, we find that *there was an overall tendency for displacement rates to rise over the 1990s for most groups of workers and for most groups of firms.*[13] The increases in most cases are modest, with displacement rates for most groups rising by less than a percentage point. If anything, they seem to be largest among the highest-skill workers and the best jobs, though the overall tendency toward rising displacement can be found throughout the other quintiles of the worker and jobs distribution as well. Likewise, our analysis of displacement trends by industry and personal characteristics (not shown here) did not indicate clear differences in these trends by economic sector or demographic group.

Figure 3.3   Rates of Job Displacement over Time by Firm-Effects
              Quintile, 1992 to 2003

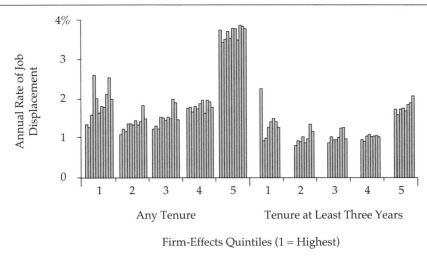

Source: Authors' tabulations using microdata from U.S. Bureau of the Census (1992–2003).
Note: Bars represent the rate of job displacement for each year from 1992 to 2002.

Figure 3.4   Rates of Job Displacement over Time by Person-Effects
              Quintile, 1992 to 2003

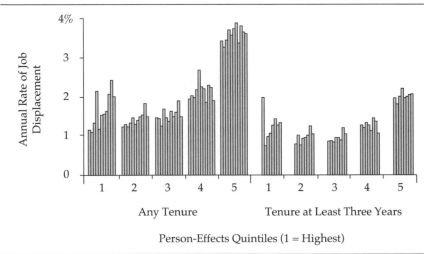

Source: Author's tabulations using microdata from U.S. Bureau of the Census (1992–2003).
Note: Bars represent the rate of job displacement for each year from 1992 to 2002.

THE GAINS AND COSTS OF JOB CHANGE AND DISPLACEMENT

The previous section suggests that the incidence of job change and job displacement might have risen for most groups of workers and jobs in the 1990s. But the magnitudes of these changes were modest and might not have lasted into the decade of the 2000s.

Either way, what are the implications of job changes and displacements for the quality of the new jobs in which workers are ultimately employed, and what happens to their wages? The answers might differ markedly between the two categories of job change, since we would expect voluntary job changes to be much more likely to generate positive changes in job quality and earnings over time than involuntary changes, especially displacements. Workers with more tenure at the time of a change are also more likely to lose earnings associated with that tenure, all else being equal.

Tables 3.3 and 3.4 present data on the changes in job quality and in earnings, respectively, that occur for workers who become displaced, both overall and among those with at least three years of job tenure. These tables present the effects of displacements over the long run, covering the entire twelve-year period of 1992 to 2003; they focus on workers who lost jobs in 1992 and who were employed elsewhere in 2003 but remained in the state labor market. (Tables 3A.1 and 3A.2 provide similar data for the broader pool of job-changers over this time period.)

Since no data are available before 1992, we can measure the group with only three years of tenure as of 1995. Thus, we present job transitions and earnings changes for the latter group over the period 1995 to 2003, and we also include results for the same time period for the broader sample, so that we can compare results across the same time period for the higher-tenure and the more general samples.

For any workers who were displaced in 1992 (or 1995), table 3.3 shows the distribution of firm effects on the jobs they ultimately held in 2003 across firm-effects quintiles, separately for each firm-effects quintile in which their initial jobs were located. The table thus presents a set of "transition matrices" on job quality between old and new jobs, allowing for the adjustments to these changes that are made by workers over many years and that may mitigate their overall effects.

Table 3.3 indicates that, *after a displacement, workers frequently end up in jobs of either higher or lower quality* than what they had initially. For instance, among workers at all levels of tenure who started in jobs in the highest quintile of firm effects and changed jobs in 1992 or 1995, 40 to 50 percent

Table 3.3 Distribution of Displaced Workers Across New Firm-Effects Quintiles, 1992 to 2003 and 1995 to 2003

	Any Tenure, 1992 to 2003						Tenure at Least Three Years, 1992 to 2003					
	1	2	3	4	5	Total	1	2	3	4	5	Total
Original firm-effects quintile changed to a firm in . . .												
Quintile 1	47.2%	23.4%	20.5%	17.2%	13.5%	22.5%	N/A	N/A	N/A	N/A	N/A	N/A
Quintile 2	22.2	38.0	22.1	17.9	16.1	21.7	N/A	N/A	N/A	N/A	N/A	N/A
Quintile 3	13.7	17.6	29.3	20.7	19.0	19.8	N/A	N/A	N/A	N/A	N/A	N/A
Quintile 4	10.1	13.8	16.3	27.0	22.5	19.1	N/A	N/A	N/A	N/A	N/A	N/A
Quintile 5	6.9	7.2	11.9	17.1	28.8	17.0	N/A	N/A	N/A	N/A	N/A	N/A

	Any Tenure, 1995 to 2003						Tenure at Least Three Years, 1995 to 2003					
	1	2	3	4	5	Total	1	2	3	4	5	Total
Original firm-effects quintile changed to a firm in . . .												
Quintile 1	58.7	27.7	17.6	16.1	13.4	29.0	69.8%	23.8%	18.2%	16.1%	10.6%	38.2%
Quintile 2	18.1	30.9	24.7	16.8	14.8	20.1	13.7	34.4	19.2	15.4	13.3	18.2
Quintile 3	10.3	20.2	28.2	22.0	18.2	18.7	7.6	19.7	34.8	23.5	19.1	17.7
Quintile 4	7.5	14.1	17.6	25.3	22.3	16.8	5.5	16.5	17.2	26.3	23.6	14.6
Quintile 5	5.4	7.0	11.9	19.8	31.2	15.4	3.5	5.7	10.6	18.7	33.4	11.4

Source: Authors' tabulations using microdata from U.S. Bureau of the Census (1992–2003).
Note: Columns sum to 100 percent. The sample is restricted to workers employed at the beginning and end of each period. Displacements occurred in 1992 or 1995, while final job is observed in 2003. The table presents the distribution of workers across firm-effects quintiles in 2003 for each quintile in which workers started in 1992 or 1995.

Table 3.4 Earnings Growth of Workers by Displacement, Firm-Effects Quintile, and Tenure, 1992 to 2003 and 1995 to 2003

	Any Tenure, 1992 to 2003 Firm-Effects Quintile in 1992 (1 = Highest)						Tenure at Least Three Years, 1992 to 2003 Firm-Effects Quintile in 1992 (1 = Highest)					
	1	2	3	4	5	Total	1	2	3	4	5	Total
Workers who remained in the same firm	36.2%	28.7%	23.1%	29.3%	29.4%	29.7%	N/A	N/A	N/A	N/A	N/A	N/A
Workers who were displaced to a firm . . .												
In a better firm-effects quintile	N/A	53.5	49.8	71.3	106.6	77.3	N/A	N/A	N/A	N/A	N/A	N/A
In the same firm-effects quintile	48.1	38.7	31.5	40.9	33.7	40.6	N/A	N/A	N/A	N/A	N/A	N/A
In a worse firm-effects quintile	14.7	12.8	11.1	21.5	N/A	14.4	N/A	N/A	N/A	N/A	N/A	N/A
Total	32.6	33.9	34.5	54.9	85.2	46.8	N/A	N/A	N/A	N/A	N/A	N/A

	Any Tenure, 1995 to 2003 Firm-Effects Quintile in 1995 (1 = Highest)						Tenure at Least Three Years, 1995 to 2003 Firm-Effects Quintile in 1995 (1 = Highest)					
	1	2	3	4	5	Total	1	2	3	4	5	Total
Workers who remained in the same firm	30.0	23.7	21.2	24.1	25.3	25.2	24.5%	19.7%	16.7%	19.3%	20.1%	20.3%
Workers who were displaced to a firm . . .												
In a better firm-effects quintile	N/A	33.1	46.5	64.2	85.4	60.3	N/A	10.7	27.6	23.9	34.1	24.2
In the same firm-effects quintile	33.0	20.9	25.4	38.6	35.3	31.3	27.1	8.9	13.2	16.5	13.9	23.1
In a worse firm-effects quintile	-0.6	13.1	15.2	24.3	N/A	6.5	-17.1	1.7	2.9	9.6	N/A	-8.7
Total	21.5	22.1	32.4	50.4	70.4	32.4	15.7	6.9	16.4	19.6	27.6	15.5

Source: Authors' tabulations using microdata from U.S. Bureau of the Census (1992–2003).

Note: Columns sum to 100 percent. The sample is restricted to workers employed at the beginning and end of each period. Displacements occurred in 1992 or 1995, while final job is observed in 2003. The table presents the distribution of workers across firm-effects quintiles in 2003 for each quintile in which workers started in 1992 or 1995.

ultimately had jobs in the lower quintiles of firm effects. Not surprisingly, the lower the quintile in which their initial jobs were found, the greater the likelihood that job quality improved with a job change. For instance, those in the second quintile of jobs initially remained in the top two quintiles about 60 percent of the time and thus ended up with jobs of lower quality in roughly 40 percent of all cases. Twenty to 30 percent of job-changers who initially were in the third or fourth quintiles found themselves with lower-quality jobs (as measured by quintiles). In contrast, those initially in the bottom quintile ended up in better jobs about 70 percent of the time.

Thus, those with worse jobs initially are more likely to benefit from a job change, all else being equal, while those with better jobs more frequently experience a decline in quality. In general, similar patterns appear for the displaced as for the broader category of job-changers, though the latter are often a bit more likely to stay within the same quintiles in which they started—showing neither improvements nor deterioration in the jobs they fill many years later (comparing tables 3.3 and 3A.1). Job improvements are likely to be more pronounced among those who move voluntarily, but the general category of movers also includes those who have been discharged or laid off in a nondisplacement situation and who may on average be of lower quality as workers than some of the displaced.[14] And comparing all those who changed jobs or were displaced in 1995 with those who had at least three years of tenure, we find that displaced workers and job-changers with more tenure were also less likely to experience a change of job quality.

What are the consequences of these changes in job quality for changes in earnings over time? Table 3.4 presents percentage earnings changes between 1992 and 2003 for displaced workers who remained in the labor market for the entire twelve-year period and between 1995 and 2003 for those with at least three years of job tenure. Estimates are presented separately for those who remained in the same firm over the entire period and for those who were displaced (by our definition). Within each group of displaced workers, we provide separate estimates for those whose new jobs were of roughly the same quality as their earlier ones (as measured by the firm-effects quintile), of better quality, or of worse quality. We also provide these estimates separately for each quintile of the firm-effects distribution in which a worker started, thus controlling for initial job quality. Similar results appear in table 3A.2 for all job-changers.

Table 3.4 shows us that almost all workers who were in the labor market over this entire period enjoyed some real earnings growth. But the magnitudes of such growth differ markedly according to whether individuals stayed with the same firm or changed jobs, and especially by what happened to the quality of their jobs if they changed them. Specifically, workers who changed jobs generally enjoyed more earnings growth than those who stayed with the same employer over the entire period, but *the effects of job displacements were much more positive for those whose job quality improved and more negative for those whose job quality deteriorated* relative to those whose job quality remained roughly the same.

For workers of all levels of tenure, those who stayed with the same firm enjoyed earnings growth of roughly 30 percent over the entire period 1992 to 2003, with those in both the highest and lowest quintiles of job quality enjoying higher growth than those in the middle. Table 3A.2 shows that, among the entire set of job-changers, virtually all groups enjoyed earnings growth, but those who managed to improve the quality of their jobs experienced substantial growth (of over 100 percent) on average, with those in the bottom quintile initially enjoying the strongest growth in earnings. In contrast, job-changers who maintained roughly similar job quality enjoyed strong growth as well (about 56 percent overall), with growth highest for those in the highest job quality quintile. And those whose job quality deteriorated had much lower earnings growth (only about 26 percent over the twelve-year period). The same pattern holds for job changes in 1995, though the magnitudes of earnings growth are lower for the shorter period, as we would expect.

Table 3.4 clearly indicates, however, that there was a cost in earnings for those displaced in 1992 or 1995, even over the long run. For the subset of workers at all levels of tenure who were apparently displaced from their jobs in 1995, earnings growth in every category was somewhat lower than among job-changers overall. Indeed, earnings growth was quite modest (about 6 percent) for those displaced who ended up in a worse job quintile, and it was nonexistent for those who began in the highest quintile and ended in a worse one.

Also, for those who began with at least three years of job tenure, earnings growth over the period 1995 to 2003 was considerably lower among both job-changers and those displaced than among those with all levels of tenure. This implies that the loss of returns to job tenure for this group entailed serious costs that reduced the gains from job mobility to a large extent. Thus, displaced workers with at least three years of tenure at the time of displacement on average had only 15 percent earnings growth over the entire period 1995 to 2003, and earnings for the displaced who ended up in worse jobs than they had before were 9 percent lower, even after eight years. Those who began in the top quintile of jobs but were displaced into jobs of lower quality after at least three years of tenure suffered the biggest losses (17 percent).

Overall, what are we to make of these data? In our earlier work (Andersson, Holzer, and Lane 2005), we showed that job changes can lead to major improvements in earnings for workers—especially early in their careers, before they have become attached to any particular firm or line of work, and when they can gain some new skills (either before taking a new job or on a new job) and ultimately work for a better firm. The findings here are consistent with that analysis and show the potential of low earners to improve their earnings with the right kind of job change. Indeed, the right workforce development policies can help them gain new skills and employment in better jobs than they had before (Holzer 2004).

At the same time, job changes can have quite negative consequences for other workers, especially those who had been attached to a well-paying firm and were benefiting from their seniority there. Most such workers are not choosing to find new jobs and have not been discharged for cause; they are likely to have become involuntarily unemployed as part of a larger dislocation. And they frequently have difficulty regaining employment in firms or jobs as good as the ones they previously had. These workers, too, might be assisted in gaining new skills or finding better jobs from appropriate policy interventions (as we discuss later in the chapter), though the costs of investing in new careers might be relatively higher for older and less-educated workers, and the horizons over which they can reap returns on such investments much shorter.

Of course, those who remain in the same state labor market over an entire twelve-year period are a somewhat unique subset of all workers (for instance, they are less likely to be in the younger or older age categories), as are those who stay with the same firm over the entire period. Looking at job-stayers versus job-changers within shorter time periods generates samples of workers who are somewhat differently "selected" than over such a long period, with fewer leaving the labor market. And perhaps more importantly, looking at job-changers and displaced workers over shorter time periods enables us to infer the effects of very different labor market characteristics on the outcomes we observe for them, since the periods of 1992 to 1995, 1996 to 1999, and 2000 to 2003 represent periods of job market recovery, boom, and downturn, respectively.

Therefore, in tables 3.5 and 3.6, we reproduce our analyses from tables 3.3 and 3.4, but now we present separate results for displaced workers in the periods of 1992 to 1995, 1996 to 1999, and 2000 to 2003. As before, all job displacements occur in the first year of each period. In both cases, we focus on all those employed at both the beginning and end of each period in that state. Once again, the first table (table 3.5) presents data on the extent to which displaced workers obtained jobs of better, similar, or worse quality, according to the job quality quintile in which they began, while the second one (table 3.6) presents data on percentage earnings changes for those staying in the same jobs or being displaced within each period.

Separate data are again presented for job-changers more generally in tables 3A.3 and 3A.4, and for the years 1996 to 1999 and 2000 to 2003, separate results appear for those with at least three years of tenure versus those at all levels of tenure initially.

The results displayed in table 3.5 generally confirm those of table 3.3. In general, workers who were displaced experienced either improvements or deterioration in job quality in large numbers. Job quality was somewhat less likely to change for those with at least three years of tenure. In general, workers displaced from jobs in the boom period of 1996 to 1999 were a bit more likely to experience improvements in job quality, while those displaced during the recession experienced less improvement.

Similarly, the results of table 3.6 (and table 3A.4 for all job-changers) generally confirm those of table 3.4, but with some additional findings generated by the comparisons across time periods. In general, earnings growth was higher among job-changers than job-stayers, but lower among those displaced than among the more general group of job-changers. Earnings growth was generally lower for those with three or more years of tenure among the displaced. Once again, earnings changes were far greater for those who managed to improve the quality of their jobs and worse for those whose job quality deteriorated relative to those who maintained roughly equal job quality.

Although this general pattern of relative outcomes appears in all three subperiods, the effects of different labor market conditions on the levels of these outcomes are now quite striking. Specifically, earnings growth was strong in the boom period of 1996 to 1999 and quite weak in the recessionary period of 2000 to 2003, with the recovery period of 1992 to 1995 falling somewhere in between.

In 1996 to 1999, virtually all groups enjoyed real earnings growth, including those who had been displaced and who ended up in worse jobs. Earnings growth for displaced workers at all levels of tenure who improved their jobs was very strong—about 35 percent in just three years and even higher for those who started in low-quality jobs. For those who regained jobs of similar quality, earnings growth averaged about 20 percent and was higher for those in high-quality jobs. And even those whose job quality deteriorated had real earnings growth of about 8 percent. These numbers are all lower for those who lost significant job tenure or for the displaced, though not substantially so. Only those who were displaced after losing three or more years of tenure on their earlier jobs, and who also ended up in worse jobs than they had originally, experienced modest real earnings losses after three years.

In contrast, earnings increases for all groups were lower in the 1992 to 1995 (recovery) period, and especially in the 2000 to 2003 (recessionary)

Table 3.5 Distribution of Displaced Workers Across New Firm-Effects Quintiles, Three Subperiods

	Any Tenure, 1992 to 1995						Tenure at Least Three Years, 1992 to 2003					
	1	2	3	4	5	Total	1	2	3	4	5	Total
Original firm-effects quintile changed to a firm in . . .												
Quintile 1	54.5%	22.2%	19.0%	11.9%	8.5%	20.6%	N/A	N/A	N/A	N/A	N/A	N/A
Quintile 2	20.5	43.5	21.9	16.1	13.2	20.9	N/A	N/A	N/A	N/A	N/A	N/A
Quintile 3	11.8	20.3	34.6	23.3	15.6	20.1	N/A	N/A	N/A	N/A	N/A	N/A
Quintile 4	8.1	9.0	16.3	31.7	22.6	18.9	N/A	N/A	N/A	N/A	N/A	N/A
Quintile 5	5.1	5.1	8.2	17.0	40.1	19.4	N/A	N/A	N/A	N/A	N/A	N/A

	Any Tenure, 1996 to 1999						Tenure at Least Three Years, 1996 to 1999					
	1	2	3	4	5	Total	1	2	3	4	5	Total
Original firm-effects quintile changed to a firm in . . .												
Quintile 1	47.9	25.2	13.7	12.1	9.8	21.4	53.3%	27.2%	11.6%	10.0%	7.7%	22.8%
Quintile 2	23.1	37.9	23.5	14.7	11.7	21.2	24.2	39.4	22.8	13.2	9.7	23.3
Quintile 3	13.7	18.5	34.4	21.5	16.5	20.5	13.1	19.5	41.9	21.5	16.9	23.4

	Any Tenure, 2000 to 2003						Tenure at Least Three Years, 2000 to 2003					
	1	2	3	4	5	Total	1	2	3	4	5	Total
Quintile 4	8.9	10.7	16.4	30.2	21.1	17.6	6.5	8.7	13.7	34.9	21.4	15.7
Quintile 5	6.4	7.6	12.1	21.4	40.9	19.3	2.9	5.3	10.0	20.4	44.3	14.8

Original firm-effects quintile changed to a firm in . . .	1	2	3	4	5	Total	1	2	3	4	5	Total
Quintile 1	58.5	28.5	14.4	12.9	9.1	25.8	64.1	28.1	9.6	10.2	6.0	28.2
Quintile 2	19.3	31.1	21.6	15.2	12.2	19.1	16.7	31.7	21.6	13.2	9.8	19.2
Quintile 3	10.3	19.6	33.6	22.6	15.4	19.7	10.0	20.9	40.8	24.4	13.0	21.8
Quintile 4	7.1	12.8	19.7	28.3	22.6	17.7	5.5	12.5	20.1	31.4	24.9	16.9
Quintile 5	4.9	7.9	10.7	21.0	40.6	17.7	3.7	6.7	7.9	20.7	46.3	13.9

Source: Authors' tabulations using microdata from U.S. Bureau of the Census (1992–2003).

Note: Columns sum to 100 percent. The sample is restricted to workers employed at the beginning and end of each period. Displacements occurred in the first year of each subperiod, while the final job is observed in the last year. The table presents the distribution of workers across firm-effects quintiles in the last year for each quintile in which the workers started in the first year.

Table 3.6 Earnings Growth of Workers by Job Change, Firm-Effects Quintile, and Tenure, Three Subperiods

	Any Tenure Firm-Effects Quintile in 1992 (1 = Highest)						Tenure at Least Three Years Firm-Effects Quintile in 1992 (1 = Highest)					
	1	2	3	4	5	Total	1	2	3	4	5	Total
1992 to 1995												
Workers who remained in the same firm	9.2%	5.2%	4.8%	6.2%	5.6%	6.6%	N/A	N/A	N/A	N/A	N/A	N/A
Workers who were displaced to a firm . . .												
In a better firm-effects quintile	0.0	12.5	12.4	20.3	35.5	22.9	N/A	N/A	N/A	N/A	N/A	N/A
In the same firm-effects quintile	9.0	4.3	0.7	6.3	11.3	6.8	N/A	N/A	N/A	N/A	N/A	N/A
In a worse firm-effects quintile	-8.3	-8.6	-8.7	-4.0	N/A	-8.0	N/A	N/A	N/A	N/A	N/A	N/A
Total	2.2	2.5	3.4	12.3	26.2	8.6	N/A	N/A	N/A	N/A	N/A	N/A

	Any Tenure Firm-Effects Quintile in 1996 (1 = Highest)						Tenure at Least Three Years Firm-Effects Quintile in 1996 (1 = Highest)					
	1	2	3	4	5	Total	1	2	3	4	5	Total
1996 to 1999												
Workers who remained in the same firm	24.8	13.3	12.1	14.3	13.6	17.0	20.7%	10.9%	9.2%	11.5%	10.0%	13.6%
Workers who were displaced to a firm . . .												
In a better firm-effects quintile	N/A	23.1	21.9	34.7	58.3	35.7	N/A	13.8	12.6	10.7	18.9	13.9

	Any Tenure Firm-Effects Quintile in 2000 (1 = Highest)						Tenure at Least 3 Years Firm-Effects Quintile in 2000 (1 = Highest)					
	1	2	3	4	5	Total	1	2	3	4	5	Total
In the same firm-effects quintile	24.5	16.2	12.0	18.7	18.3	19.6	14.0	12.3	5.8	6.3	4.3	10.4
In a worse firm-effects quintile	7.8	7.2	5.4	10.9	N/A	7.5	−0.6	−2.2	2.3	1.2	N/A	−0.4
Total	17.0	15.6	14.3	25.3	42.3	20.9	7.9	8.7	7.4	7.5	12.8	8.4
2000 to 2003												
Workers who remained in the same firm	1.1	6.6	6.0	6.5	6.0	4.4	−2.9	4.3	3.6	4.1	3.3	1.5
Workers who were displaced to a firm . . .												
In a better firm-effects quintile	N/A	12.4	6.4	18.8	36.4	18.7	N/A	8.3	−2.2	4.2	11.1	4.7
In the same firm-effects quintile	−1.5	3.8	6.2	3.8	7.6	1.1	−4.7	4.1	3.1	−3.9	1.2	−2.2
In a worse firm-effects quintile	−12.0	−7.2	−5.4	−1.9	N/A	−9.0	−18.8	−10.1	−9.2	−7.7	N/A	−14.1
Total	−4.8	3.0	3.4	10.9	25.4	3.1	−8.6	0.5	−1.7	−0.4	5.8	−3.6

Source: Authors' tabulations using microdata from U.S. Bureau of the Census (1992–2003).

period. Real earnings declines are now more apparent, primarily among those whose job quality deteriorated. In the recession, even among displaced workers who managed to maintain job quality, some earnings losses were apparent, especially among those who experienced declining job quality and/or lost significant job tenure when they changed jobs. Thus, real earnings losses averaged about 9 percent among displaced workers at all levels of tenure whose job quality deteriorated in the recession. Among those with at least three years of tenure at the time of displacement, earnings losses averaged 14 percent for the displaced, and earnings losses for this latter group were almost 20 percent among those who began in the highest-quality jobs and lost job quality thereafter.

Consistent with recent results from the work of Kenneth Couch and Dana Placzek (2010), the effects of job displacement and changes more broadly are very sensitive to business cycle and overall labor market conditions. During boom periods, employers face tighter labor markets and need to pay more to attract workers of sufficient quality (Holzer, Raphael, and Stoll 2006). This enables job-changers, and even those who have been displaced, to more easily find good jobs and/or higher wages to replace what they had previously. In contrast, during recessionary periods, or periods with slack labor markets more generally, employers have much less difficulty finding workers with the necessary skills to perform the work needed, and therefore they do not have to pay new workers much to attract and retain them. This clearly works to the disadvantage of those seeking new employment, either voluntarily or involuntarily.[15] And it implies very serious challenges for many displaced workers during the likely slow recovery that will follow the Great Recession of 2005 and beyond.

These findings raise important questions about the average effects of job changing and displacement in the entire twelve-year period, as well as the subperiods, and how the findings might be affected by controlling for underlying worker characteristics as well as changes in job quality and tenure. We therefore present the results of some estimated regression models for the log of real earnings growth in table 3A.5 in the appendix to this chapter. (Readers without any interest in these more technical results can proceed to the conclusion.)

We present regressions for changes in the log of annual real earnings over the period of 1992 to 2003 and for each of the three subperiods (1992 to 1995, 1996 to 1999, and 2000 to 2003) for workers who were employed in both the beginning and end years of each period. For the latter two subperiods, separate estimates are presented for those with at least three years of tenure. The models are run on samples that include job-stayers as well as job-changers, and dummy variables are always included for non-displaced and displaced changers (with job-stayers as the reference category). Controls are included for the worker's age in 1992 and his or her person effect, thus controlling for important personal skills and characteristics that might well affect the success of that person's job search.

Three models are then estimated for each sample: a basic one containing only the variables listed here; one that adds the change in the firm effect across jobs (or across periods for the same job); and one that controls for changes in job tenure. The estimated models thus explore the extent to which changes in job quality and tenure can account for the effects of displacement and nondisplacement job changes on real wages over time, and they address possible doubts about the causality of the quality of the new job with respect to a change in the worker's earnings.[16]

The results include several findings that are broadly consistent with the summary results discussed earlier. Relative to those who stay in the same job, those who change jobs generally enjoy higher real wage gains over time than job-stayers; on average, both groups, but especially the changers, do better in stronger labor markets and worse in weaker ones. Those who are apparently displaced have lower earnings increases, on average, than those job-changers who are not displaced, and those who lose job tenure at the time of a move lose substantially more in real earnings, even relative to job-stayers.

Changes in job quality have strong positive effects on earnings growth, and controlling for such changes tends to partly account for any positive effects of job-changing on earnings. Changes in job tenure also have strong positive effects; controlling for the loss of tenure associated with job changes tends to strengthen the positive effects of the latter. Indeed, controlling for both changes in job quality and tenure turns all effects of job change and displacement into positive ones, relative to staying in the same job. In general, older workers gain much less from changing jobs than younger ones (with each year of age reducing earnings growth by 0.01 to 0.03 log points), and highly skilled workers (as measured by the person effect) generally have more positive earnings growth in all but recessionary periods.

Overall, then, the message of these results is clear: job-changing in general and displacement in particular can result in either positive or negative effects on earnings—depending on the extent to which the quality of an individual's job improves or deteriorates (and whether he or she sacrifices job tenure). For young workers or those stuck in low-quality jobs, a voluntary job change before they have accumulated significant tenure can lead to improved earnings—as we have demonstrated in our earlier work (Andersson, Holzer, and Lane 2005)—especially if they receive some assistance in finding good jobs and appropriately enhance their skills to get there. For older workers or those already in fairly high-wage jobs, the risks of losing earnings grow, especially in a weaker job market, where these workers' odds of ultimately having a worse job, with potentially greater losses of job tenure, grow more serious.

Over longer periods of time, most workers enjoy earnings growth, and thus any negative effects of job changes on earnings can be attenuated. But even over a longer time period the odds of significant gains in earnings diminish if high-quality jobs are in short supply at a particular skill level or if labor market slack persists for lengthy periods of time.

CONCLUSION

In our opening chapter, we noted that American workers are growing more insecure about their jobs. To gain some sense of why they are becoming more insecure and how changes in job quality affect job insecurity, we posed a number of questions in this chapter: Are job displacement rates (and job changes more generally) rising in the U.S. labor market? If so, what kinds of jobs are affected, and which workers? More broadly, what are the effects of job changes and displacements on job quality and earnings changes over time? And to what extent are these changes affected by the state of the overall labor market? We have sought to examine both the incidence and the benefits and costs associated with job changes and displacement and the relationship of all these factors to job quality.

Overall, we find some evidence of rising job mobility and displacement over the 1990s, even before the recession of 2001. The increases appear to have been widespread across skill and job quality categories, though they were mostly modest in magnitude. Whether these changes persisted into the 2000s, or even beyond 2003, is not at all apparent.

More importantly, we find that job changes and even displacements can lead to jobs of either higher or lower quality for workers. When job quality improves, earnings are likely to improve as well; when job quality deteriorates, earnings are likely to decline (or to grow only modestly). Consistent with our earlier work, we find that younger workers or those in low-quality jobs might benefit most from a job change, especially if they can acquire new skills or gain employment in a higher-wage firm. In contrast, older and less-skilled workers who have been attached to a relatively good job are likely to have more difficulty replacing it. The loss of job tenure in these cases almost always reduces earnings; thus, such earnings losses are best kept low when workers (especially younger ones) change jobs early in the tenure cycle.

We also find that the impacts of job changes on job quality and especially earnings are heavily dependent on overall labor market conditions: the strong labor market of the late 1990s generated mostly earnings increases for job-changers, while the recession period after 2000 generated more earnings losses, especially among those who were losing good jobs and replacing them with ones of lower quality. Indeed, it appears as though extensive periods of labor market slack—like the one experienced even beyond the recession earlier in this decade, and especially like the one we have experienced since the severe downturn of 2008—make it harder for workers to successfully change jobs and find earnings levels as good as (or better than) what they had before.

The analysis presented here certainly has some major limitations. For one thing, our ability to clearly identify job displacements is no doubt hampered by measurement error, which tends to reduce the differences that we estimate in the effects of displacements and the effects of job changing; to the extent that the nondisplaced in our sample include those discharged for cause or laid off (job performance often tends to be weaker among both groups), our comparisons between the displaced and other job-changers are further blurred. Beyond that, our inability to observe losses of job benefits such as health insurance weakens this analysis, as does our lack of data beyond the year 2003. The extent to which our analyses hold up in the relatively weaker expansion of the early 2000s and then the severe downturn that followed it remains unclear. And some questions might remain about the extent to which our measure of job quality the firm effect—successfully separates the quality of jobs from the quality of the workers who fill them.

Nevertheless, our results have important implications for how we view job market volatility and worker insecurity in the United States. In the previous chapter, we noted that good jobs are not disappearing in this country over the long term, but they are probably becoming less available for workers who lack educational or occupational credentials and important basic skills. To the extent that these workers lose good jobs involuntarily—especially older workers with substantial job tenure in manufacturing and other industries—their ability to replace them with jobs of comparable quality is now lower, and their odds of suffering lost earnings over time will rise. An inability to find new jobs that offer employer-provided health insurance no doubt reinforces these potential losses (though the newly enacted health reform legislation might mitigate these losses by making it easier to replace lost health insurance).

So, even though many workers gain better jobs and enjoy upward earnings movement in a turbulent job market, others are hurt by it. And for those who remain employed but who feel (often correctly) that they are at risk of losing employment, the insecurity that they feel may well have a foundation in reality. This insecurity cannot be reduced without policies that improve the odds that the displaced will find good jobs to replace their old ones or that provide them with more assistance when they cannot do so. We discuss these policies in chapter 6.

The fact that the impacts of job displacements and job mobility in general are so sensitive to economic conditions might well have implications for local labor markets as well as the aggregate business cycle. In local areas that have generated substantial employment growth, especially in sectors with lots of good jobs, the negative impacts of job losses on displaced workers might be mitigated by the availability of good replacement jobs. In contrast, in local areas where overall job growth has lagged and new good jobs have not replaced those that have been lost—especially for older and less-educated workers who formerly benefited from manufacturing or other high-wage employment—the consequences of involuntary job loss are likely to be more serious.

We turn in the next chapter to an analysis of the effects of employment growth and job loss at the metropolitan level and their relationship to job quality.

APPENDIX

(Follows on next page.)

Appendix 3A.1 Distribution of Workers Who Changed Firms Across New Firm-Effects Quintiles, 1992 to 2003 and 1995 to 2003

Original firm-effects quintile changed to a firm in . . .	Any Tenure, 1992 to 2003						Tenure at Least Three Years, 1992 to 2003					
	1	2	3	4	5	Total	1	2	3	4	5	Total
Quintile 1	48.8%	25.5%	18.6%	17.7%	14.9%	24.0%	N/A	N/A	N/A	N/A	N/A	N/A
Quintile 2	20.3	33.1	22.4	18.9	17.3	21.9	N/A	N/A	N/A	N/A	N/A	N/A
Quintile 3	13.4	19.1	28.7	21.2	19.4	20.5	N/A	N/A	N/A	N/A	N/A	N/A
Quintile 4	10.3	13.7	18.4	26.1	23.0	19.0	N/A	N/A	N/A	N/A	N/A	N/A
Quintile 5	7.3	8.7	11.9	16.2	25.3	14.7	N/A	N/A	N/A	N/A	N/A	N/A

Original firm-effects quintile changed to a firm in . . .	Any Tenure, 1995 to 2003						Tenure at Least Three Years, 1995 to 2003					
	1	2	3	4	5	Total	1	2	3	4	5	Total
Quintile 1	51.6	26.8	18.4	17.9	14.5	25.5	59.6%	26.5%	16.1%	15.0%	11.3%	28.8%
Quintile 2	19.9	31.9	22.2	17.8	16.3	21.4	17.4	36.9	22.3	16.2	14.2	22.4
Quintile 3	12.8	19.6	29.7	20.8	19.0	20.4	11.1	18.4	36.5	22.3	18.3	21.1
Quintile 4	9.3	13.1	17.6	26.0	22.1	17.9	7.1	11.3	15.7	30.9	22.3	15.9
Quintile 5	6.5	8.6	12.0	17.4	28.0	14.7	4.8	6.8	9.4	15.6	33.8	11.9

Source: Authors' tabulations using microdata from U.S. Bureau of the Census (1992–2003).
Note: Columns sum to 100 percent. The sample is restricted to workers employed at the beginning and end of each period. Job changes occurred in 1992 or 1995, while the final job is observed in 2003. The table presents the distribution of workers across firm-effects quintiles in 2003 for each quintile in which workers started in 1992 or 1995.

Appendix 3A.2 Earnings Growth by Job Change, Firm-Effects Quintile, and Tenure, 1992 to 2003 and 1995 to 2003

	Any Tenure, 1992 to 2003 Firm-Effects Quintile in 1992 (1 = Highest)						Tenure at Least Three Years, 1992 to 2003 Firm-Effects Quintile in 1992 (1 = Highest)					
	1	2	3	4	5	Total	1	2	3	4	5	Total
Workers who remained in the same firm	36.2%	28.7%	23.1%	29.3%	29.4%	29.7%	N/A	N/A	N/A	N/A	N/A	N/A
Workers who changed to a firm...												
In a better firm-effects quintile	N/A	76.9	87.2	116.6	143.5	109.9	N/A	N/A	N/A	N/A	N/A	N/A
In the same firm-effects quintile	61.2	46.9	49.6	62.3	53.8	56.0	N/A	N/A	N/A	N/A	N/A	N/A
In a worse firm-effects quintile	23.1	23.7	30.2	40.6	N/A	26.0	N/A	N/A	N/A	N/A	N/A	N/A
Total	44.2	47.1	60.6	90.3	119.4	65.4	N/A	N/A	N/A	N/A	N/A	N/A

	Any Tenure, 1995 to 2003 Firm-Effects Quintile in 1995 (1 = Highest)						Tenure at Least Three Years, 1995 to 2003 Firm-Effects Quintile in 1995 (1 = Highest)					
	1	2	3	4	5	Total	1	2	3	4	5	Total
Workers who remained in the same firm	30.0	23.7	21.2	24.1	25.3	25.2	24.5%	19.7%	16.7%	19.3%	20.1%	20.3%
Workers who changed to a firm...												
In a better firm-effects quintile	N/A	63.0	74.5	99.4	123.6	90.9	N/A	39.9	43.8	48.4	54.8	45.9
In the same firm-effects quintile	49.7	40.1	41.8	54.3	49.5	47.2	34.8	24.3	24.0	26.3	24.0	30.0
In a worse firm-effects quintile	17.7	21.0	29.2	34.9	N/A	22.0	-0.9	4.6	7.7	13.3	N/A	2.9
Total	36.9	40.4	52.7	76.8	102.0	53.5	22.5	22.8	28.5	36.5	44.4	27.0

Source: Authors' tabulations using microdata from U.S. Bureau of the Census (1992–2003).
Note: Job changes occurred in 1992 or 1995. Tenure is measured as of the beginning of the period. "Better/same/worse" quintile represents a comparison of the quintile of the worker's primary employer in the end year to the quintile of the worker's primary employer in the start year.

Appendix 3A.3   Distribution of Workers Who Changed Firms Across New Firm-Effects Quintiles, Three Subperiods

	Any Tenure, 1992 to 1995						Tenure at Least Three Years, 1992 to 1995					
	1	2	3	4	5	Total	1	2	3	4	5	Total
All workers who changed firms												
Original firm-effects quintile changed to a firm in . . .												
Quintile 1	56.3%	25.1%	14.7%	12.9%	9.8%	22.5%	N/A	N/A	N/A	N/A	N/A	N/A
Quintile 2	18.9	38.7	22.9	16.7	14.1	21.6	N/A	N/A	N/A	N/A	N/A	N/A
Quintile 3	10.7	17.8	35.5	21.2	17.1	20.4	N/A	N/A	N/A	N/A	N/A	N/A
Quintile 4	8.6	11.1	16.3	33.0	24.6	19.5	N/A	N/A	N/A	N/A	N/A	N/A
Quintile 5	5.5	7.4	10.7	16.1	34.4	15.9	N/A	N/A	N/A	N/A	N/A	N/A

	Any Tenure, 1996 to 1999						Tenure at Least Three Years, 1996 to 1999					
	1	2	3	4	5	Total	1	2	3	4	5	Total
All workers who changed firms												
Original firm-effects quintile changed to a firm in . . .												
Quintile 1	54.0	30.8	16.2	14.7	11.5	25.2	62.4%	37.6%	14.3%	11.7%	11.3%	30.2%
Quintile 2	19.8	32.5	22.4	15.8	13.7	20.8	17.9	33.7	24.9	14.2	11.4	22.4

(Table continues on p. 88.)

Appendix 3A.3 (Continued)

	Any Tenure, 1992 to 1995						Tenure at Least Three Years, 1992 to 1995					
	1	2	3	4	5	Total	1	2	3	4	5	Total
Quintile 3	12.0	17.5	32.3	19.6	17.5	19.8	9.5	14.6	36.8	19.0	16.0	19.1
Quintile 4	8.3	11.9	17.2	32.2	23.1	18.8	6.2	9.8	15.5	40.6	24.3	17.3
Quintile 5	5.8	7.3	11.8	17.7	34.1	15.4	3.9	4.4	8.6	14.4	39.1	11.1

	Any Tenure, 2000 to 2003						Tenure at Least Three Years, 2000 to 2003					
	1	2	3	4	5	Total	1	2	3	4	5	Total

All workers who changed firms

Original firm-effects quintile

changed to a firm in . . .

	1	2	3	4	5	Total	1	2	3	4	5	Total
Quintile 1	52.6	24.6	15.6	14.0	10.4	24.0	58.5	24.0	13.5	11.5	8.1	26.4
Quintile 2	20.0	34.1	20.2	15.4	13.0	20.2	18.9	38.8	20.4	13.9	11.3	21.8
Quintile 3	12.0	19.2	31.8	20.5	17.2	19.9	10.4	19.1	37.7	22.2	15.7	21.1
Quintile 4	9.0	13.1	19.5	30.1	23.0	18.9	7.3	11.2	18.6	34.6	22.2	17.3
Quintile 5	6.4	9.0	12.8	20.1	36.4	16.9	4.8	6.8	9.8	17.8	42.7	13.4

Source: Authors' tabulations using microdata from U.S. Bureau of the Census (1992–2003).
Note: Columns sum to 100 percent. The sample is restricted to workers employed at the beginning and end of each period. Job changes occurred in the first year of each subperiod, while the final job is observed in the last year. The table presents the distribution of workers across firm effects quintiles in the last year for each quintile in which the workers started in the first year.

Appendix 3A.4 Earnings Growth by Job Change, Firm-Effects Quintile, and Tenure, Three Subperiods

1992 to 1995

	Any Tenure Firm-Effects Quintile in 1992 (1 = Highest)						Tenure at Least Three Years Firm-Effects Quintile in 1992 (1 = Highest)					
	1	2	3	4	5	Total	1	2	3	4	5	Total
Workers who remained in the same firm	9.2%	5.2%	4.8%	6.2%	5.6%	6.6%	N/A	N/A	N/A	N/A	N/A	N/A
Workers who changed to a firm . . .												
In a better firm-effects quintile	N/A	20.0	27.3	42.1	55.6	37.6	N/A	N/A	N/A	N/A	N/A	N/A
In the same firm-effects quintile	13.6	10.6	9.7	14.6	14.2	12.6	N/A	N/A	N/A	N/A	N/A	N/A
In a worse firm-effects quintile	-8.7	-4.6	-0.5	3.3	0.0	-5.1	N/A	N/A	N/A	N/A	N/A	N/A
Total	5.3	8.7	14.6	27.3	41.3	15.9	N/A	N/A	N/A	N/A	N/A	N/A

1996 to 1999

	Any Tenure Firm-Effects Quintile in 1996 (1 = Highest)						Tenure at Least Three Years Firm-Effects Quintile in 1996 (1 = Highest)					
	1	2	3	4	5	Total	1	2	3	4	5	Total
Workers who remained in the same firm . . .	24.8	13.3	12.1	14.3	13.6	17.0	20.7%	10.9%	9.2%	11.5%	10.0%	13.6%
Workers who changed to a firm . . .												
In a better firm-effects quintile	N/A	27.1	37.8	54.9	72.7	46.5	N/A	14.8	20.4	23.2	33.0	20.2

(Table continues on p. 90.)

Appendix 3A.4 (Continued)

	Any Tenure Firm-Effects Quintile in 1992 (1 = Highest)						Tenure at Least Three Years Firm-Effects Quintile in 1992 (1 = Highest)					
	1	2	3	4	5	Total	1	2	3	4	5	Total
In the same firm-effects quintile	34.8	19.4	21.1	26.1	25.8	28.3	24.0	11.1	9.5	12.1	8.5	17.0
In a worse firm-effects quintile	8.0	8.3	12.2	16.4	N/A	9.6	-4.2	-2.8	-1.2	0.9	N/A	-2.9
Total	24.8	18.9	26.0	39.5	56.8	29.1	14.9	9.3	11.8	16.0	23.4	13.3

	Any Tenure Firm-Effects Quintile in 2000 (1 = Highest)						Tenure at Least Three Years Firm-Effects Quintile in 2000 (1 = Highest)					
	1	2	3	4	5	Total	1	2	3	4	5	Total
2000 to 2003												
Workers who remained in the same firm	1.1	6.6	6.0	6.5	6.0	4.4	-2.9	4.3	3.6	4.1	3.3	1.5
Workers who changed to a firm . . .												
In a better firm-effects quintile	N/A	15.0	22.5	32.1	48.0	29.7	N/A	6.0	10.4	13.0	24.8	12.2
In the same firm-effects quintile	-4.0	9.5	11.3	12.9	11.9	2.5	-13.0	3.7	3.1	0.7	4.5	-6.2
In a worse firm-effects quintile	-8.4	-3.2	0.1	3.6	N/A	-4.7	-17.4	-9.5	-7.7	-4.5	N/A	-12.9
Total	-5.6	6.9	12.8	21.5	35.2	7.7	-14.4	0.3	3.2	6.1	16.4	-3.8

Source: Authors' tabulations using microdata from U.S. Bureau of the Census (1992–2003).
Note: Job change occurs at beginning of the period. Tenure is measured as of the beginning of the period. "Better/same/worse" quintile represents a comparison of the quintile of the worker's primary employer in the end year to the quintile of the worker's primary employer in the start year.

Appendix 3A.5   Regressions on Log Change in Earnings

	Model 1		Model 2		Model 3	
	Coeffi-cient	t-Value	Coeffi-cient	t-Value	Coeffi-cient	t-Value
1992 to 2003, all workers						
Intercept	1.100	1449	1.003	1382	0.961	1327
Displaced	0.143	98	0.071	51	0.104	76
Changed jobs, not displaced	0.232	511	0.196	455	0.231	532
Age in 1992	−0.024	−1206	−0.022	−1141	−0.024	−1225
Person effect	0.156	251	0.152	256	0.121	205
Change in firm effect			1.117	1207	1.117	1217
Change in tenure					0.019	490
R-squared	0.137		0.221		0.234	
1995 to 2003, all workers						
Intercept	0.906	1569	0.846	1382	0.809	1463
Displaced	0.087	77	0.030	51	0.074	69
Changed jobs, not displaced	0.190	502	0.162	455	0.198	542
Age in 1992	−0.020	−1277	−0.019	−1141	−0.020	−1308
Person effect	−0.031	−59	−0.026	256	−0.042	−85
Change in firm effect			1.026	1207	1.021	1241
Change in tenure					0.020	564
R-squared	0.121		0.197		0.212	
1995 to 2003, tenure at least three years						
Intercept	0.612	754	0.578	737	0.554	715
Displaced	−0.015	−9	−0.079	−50	−0.009	−6
Changed jobs, not displaced	0.061	104	0.047	83	0.106	186
Age in 1992	−0.014	−650	−0.013	−630	−0.014	−702
Person effect	0.046	73	0.046	75	0.031	52
Change in firm effect			0.937	767	0.933	774
Change in tenure					0.018	491
R-squared	0.055		0.118		0.143	
1992 to 1995, all workers						
Intercept	0.332	848	0.295	785	0.247	622
Displaced	0.054	62	−0.008	−10	0.027	32
Changed jobs, not displaced	0.127	464	0.095	361	0.129	464
Age in 1992	−0.007	−750	−0.006	−692	−0.007	−748
Person effect	0.114	342	0.111	348	0.099	311
Change in firm effect			1.082	1318	1.098	1340
Change in tenure					0.031	363
R-squared	0.054		0.132		0.137	
1996 to 1999, all workers						
Intercept	0.458	1286	0.440	1273	0.416	1183
Displaced	0.089	111	0.070	89	0.104	132

(Table continues on p. 92.)

Appendix 3A.5   (Continued)

	Model 1		Model 2		Model 3	
	Coefficient	t-Value	Coefficient	t-Value	Coefficient	t-Value
Changed jobs, not displaced	0.135	542	0.116	477	0.147	571
Age in 1992	−0.009	−996	−0.009	−976	−0.009	−998
Person effect	0.022	65	0.023	72	0.021	64
Change in firm effect			0.818	1170	0.820	1175
Change in tenure					0.017	354
R-squared	0.069		0.124		0.129	
1996 to 1999, tenure at least three years						
Intercept	0.295	639	0.285	630	0.271	600
Displaced	−0.011	−10	−0.017	−15	0.037	32
Changed jobs, not displaced	0.017	49	0.006	17	0.056	149
Age in 1992	−0.006	−510	−0.006	−500	−0.006	−528
Person effect	0.049	129	0.049	133	0.045	123
Change in firm effect			0.783	697	0.793	708
Change in tenure					0.014	289
R-squared	0.028		0.069		0.076	
2000 to 2003, all workers						
Intercept	0.281	870	0.263	840	0.223	697
Displaced	0.011	14	−0.011	−14	0.040	54
Changed jobs, not displaced	0.076	297	0.063	252	0.107	409
Age in 1992	−0.007	−787	−0.007	−749	−0.007	−750
Person effect	−0.092	−270	−0.081	−245	−0.080	−243
Change in firm effect			0.791	1156	0.782	1149
Change in tenure					0.021	529
R-squared	0.039		0.095		0.106	
2000 to 2003, tenure at least three years						
Intercept	0.203	436	0.193	423	0.167	206
Displaced	−0.051	−44	−0.053	−47	0.044	156
Changed jobs, not displaced	−0.010	−25	−0.010	−27	0.077	209
Age in 1992	−0.005	−422	−0.005	−406	−0.005	−398
Person effect	−0.077	−186	−0.072	−178	−0.072	−173
Change in firm effect			0.805	673	0.784	662
Change in tenure					0.018	342
R-squared	0.018		0.059		0.076	

Source: Authors' tabulations using microdata from U.S. Bureau of the Census (1992–2003).
Note: Control variables used in all three models are the worker's age in years as of the beginning of 1992 and the worker's person fixed effect calculated over the period 1992 to 2003. Models 2 and 3 include an additional variable for the change in the firm fixed effect from the worker's employer in the start year to the employer in the end year. Model 3 includes an additional variable for change in the worker's tenure from the start year to the end year.

Chapter 4 | Job Quality and Volatility in Metropolitan Areas: A Tale of Two (Kinds of) Cities

THE PREVIOUS TWO chapters have demonstrated the importance of job quality in U.S. labor markets and indicated that the access of less-skilled workers to high-quality jobs might be diminishing over time. Job volatility can also have either positive or negative impacts on workers, depending on the extent to which workers can replace the high-quality jobs that they lose or leave with others of equal or better quality. The previous chapter clearly showed that the overall state of the labor market has very important implications for the ability of displaced workers to obtain good jobs to replace those that they have lost.

All of this implies that, when analyzing the issues of job quality and volatility, it is important to consider them in the context of *local labor markets*. Local labor markets in the United States—which are usually measured at the metropolitan level—differ from one another quite dramatically in terms of both industrial structure (on the demand side) and demographics (on the supply side). And their growth trajectories and compositional changes over time have also varied a lot.

In this chapter, we analyze the issues of job quality and volatility across and within metropolitan areas. After reviewing the research literature on metropolitan labor markets, we consider data on two groups of metro areas within our sample of twelve states: one consisting of all large metropolitan areas (MSAs) within these states, and the other consisting of a sample of somewhat smaller metropolitan areas that had relatively high levels of manufacturing employment in the early 1990s and thus experienced considerable economic restructuring in the past two decades and

93

major labor market changes. Though the latter group is clearly not a random sample of smaller metro areas, we argue that their characteristics and experiences are not terribly different from those of other MSAs of similar size across many dimensions.

In this chapter, we compare the labor market experiences of these two groups of cities and metropolitan areas, with a strong focus on job quality and volatility. We begin with some data on average employment and earnings growth over the periods 1992 to 2000 and 1992 to 2003 in the two categories of MSAs. We consider in particular the extent to which jobs of different levels of quality and in different industries have grown in each set of areas, as well as the employment and earnings growth of workers in different skill categories in these areas.

Next we analyze the correlates of earnings growth across MSAs—both for all workers and for those at different skill levels. Although we cannot say too much about exactly which relationships represent true causal effects, we can at least identify the characteristics of metro areas that are associated with higher or lower earnings growth overall and for specific skill groups. For instance, what kinds of job growth have been associated with the greatest earnings growth for workers, in both the largest metro areas and the smaller ones? Is it overall job growth that contributes most to earnings growth, or does growth in particular kinds of jobs generate earnings increases for particular groups of workers? Is there evidence of "trickle-down" from the growth of high-wage and high-skill jobs to the earnings of less-educated workers? And do the correlates differ between large and smaller MSAs, perhaps indicating differences across the two kinds of areas in the processes by which workers benefit?

Finally, we look at the issues of job volatility within metro areas and the extent to which workers are hurt by job displacement, especially those with at least three years of job tenure. As in chapter 3, we first consider rates of job displacement, as well as the extent to which mobility and displacement result in workers having better or worse jobs and higher or lower earnings. To what extent do these costs vary between the larger and smaller metro areas and in the industries in which jobs are lost and gained by individual workers in these areas?

Overall, we show that the large and medium-sized metro areas have shared some labor market trends over the past few decades, but in other ways their experiences have diverged. The largest metro areas have experienced the greatest employment growth overall; this higher growth is particularly pronounced at both the top and bottom of the labor market, especially during the boom years of the late 1990s. In contrast, the smaller metro areas analyzed here—again, admittedly not a random sample of all such areas of this size but chosen because of their experience with industrial restructuring—showed less polarization between the top and the bottom groups of firms and workers, but were more sensitive to the business cycle, experienced less of a boom in the late 1990s, and have had greater difficulty replacing lost manufacturing jobs. The workers who lost such jobs, especially if they were older and less-educated, also had the greatest difficulty adapting to labor market restructuring in these smaller metro areas.

Thus, the two kinds of metro areas presented here illustrate a broader set of principles. Challenges clearly exist for low-wage and displaced workers in all areas of the United States. But larger areas seem to attract both jobs and workers of higher quality, which seems to be associated with better labor market performance even for those who fill lower-quality jobs or whose skills are of lower quality. And those who suffer from job volatility in these larger and growing regions are more successful at replacing their lost earnings than those who experience volatility in smaller areas that have undergone a great deal of economic restructuring. Displaced workers in both kinds of areas, but especially the smaller ones, will face challenges in the aftermath of the Great Recession over the next several years.

In chapters 5 and 6, we consider the implications of these findings for the economic development and job training policies of state and local governments trying to respond to economic changes and those hurt by them.

MSAS AND EMPLOYMENT: WHAT THE LITERATURE SAYS

It has long been established that metropolitan areas vary enormously in terms of overall economic performance and employment levels and that these factors strongly affect the employment outcomes of major subgroups in the population. If anything, less-educated workers and minorities are more affected by the strength of local MSA economies and employment than are other groups (see, for example, Bartik 2001; Freeman and Rodgers 2000; Hoynes 2000).

Furthermore, the industrial composition of MSAs matters as well, in terms of the earnings and employment of local residents. For instance, manufacturing employment levels and their changes over time seem to have strong effects on the employment and earnings of less-educated and male workers, especially among minorities, even adjusting for the overall strength of local economies (Bound and Holzer 1993; Kasarda 1995).

In more recent years, the cities with the most professional jobs in high-wage service industries and the most-educated workforces have had the highest earnings and the fastest rates of earnings and employment growth over time. Some of these findings have been popularized by authors such as Joel Kotkin (2000) in his work on the "new geography" and the digital revolution and Richard Florida (2004, 2008), who writes on the "creative class" in growing cities.

Economic analysts of the "new urban geography," like Paul Krugman (1991) and Edward Glaeser (for example, Glaeser and Gottlieb 2009), have also focused on these developments. This literature emphasizes the "agglomeration economies" that favor cities and metropolitan areas over rural locations, as well as cities with larger (or denser) populations over smaller ones, in generating productive workers and jobs. Economic theory and at least some empirical evidence suggest that lower transportation and information costs tend to improve productivity in these areas, with the latter being especially important in knowledge-based service industries that rely heavily on social interactions and the spreading of ideas. Labor markets with more workers and jobs per geographic area should also enable more efficient "sorting" of workers into jobs, further encouraging greater productivity. These factors might encourage the location in such areas of jobs requiring more skills and workers with higher levels of education, and that movement of jobs would further tend to raise earnings levels and their growth rates over time in these areas. There are enormous differences in such characteristics across cities, however, even within size categories, and a variety of other factors—such as industrial history, proximity to the coasts, and even some key natural amenities such as warm weather—may lure these workers as well.

Furthermore, economic opportunities are not evenly spread across geographical locations *within* metropolitan areas. Economists have long debated the impact of "spatial mismatch" on the employment levels of minorities. In this hypothesis, the combination of the residential segregation of lower-income workers—especially minorities within inner-city areas—with the growing decentralization of employment to the suburbs creates disadvantages for these job-seekers.

The preponderance of empirical evidence in recent years has tended to support the mismatch hypothesis, at least to some extent (see Holzer 1991; Ihlanfeldt and Sjoquist 1998; Kain 1992). And spatial mismatch can occur even within heterogeneous parts of the suburbs, with lower-income workers and minorities increasingly located in older and lower-income suburban neighborhoods while job growth in general, and higher-wage jobs in particular, become more commonly located in the higher-income areas (Stoll, Holzer, and Ihlanfeldt 2000; Andersson, Holzer, and Lane 2005; Holzer and Stoll 2007).

Finally, there are a number of ways in which metropolitan areas can adjust to economic shocks that weaken employment opportunities there (Bartik 2001; Blanchard and Katz 1992; Bound and Holzer 2000). For instance, employment might rebound over time as local economies recover from the effects of business cycles or as new industries develop to replace those that have diminished or disappeared. Wages might have to adjust to shifts in local labor demand, with slower wage growth needed to help employment recover. And finally, workers might have to relocate to other, more thriving areas, though the older and less-educated do so much more slowly than others.

A number of questions remain about these findings, however, especially regarding labor market differences across metropolitan areas over time. In particular, how do the issues of job quality and volatility matter at the local level, and how do these forces play out in different metro areas? Are there systematic differences in the ability of different metro areas to attract and retain both workers and jobs of different quality, either across industries or within them, as Glaeser's work suggests? Are large MSAs more likely to attract and retain these workers and jobs than smaller ones? Is there some complementarity between the ability of local areas to attract both high-wage and lower-wage workers (for example, professionals and immigrants) and the jobs each group fills? Do the benefits of higher education and better jobs in fact have positive "externalities" (or spillovers) that benefit less-skilled workers as well, whether they are themselves employed in high- or low-quality jobs? And is it in fact the jobs that attract the workers to these areas, or vice versa?

Similarly, the effects of job displacement might play out quite differently in different metropolitan locations. Some areas might have higher rates of dislocation than others, or their new jobs might grow more slowly and be of lower average quality. For instance, a high concentration of manufacturing jobs in an area might imply greater hardship for those areas during periods in which manufacturing employment has declined, as has recently occurred. In areas that have suffered disproportionately from such job loss, how do dislocated workers fare? Does their ability to replace the good jobs they have lost—and remedy the subsequent earnings effects of displacement—depend on where they live?

Answering all of these questions systematically is clearly beyond the scope of this chapter and this book. But we can at least present some basic facts on job quality and volatility across and within different kinds of metropolitan areas and discuss what they mean for the workers who live in those places. We provide such evidence in this chapter—after we define the categories of metropolitan areas we use to explore these issues.

TWO KINDS OF METROPOLITAN AREAS

As we explore the issues of job quality and volatility in a metropolitan context, we need some way to categorize different metropolitan areas that captures the systematic differences between them that are relevant for these issues.

In this chapter, we categorize the MSAs in our sample of twelve states into two groups. The first is a sample of all large metropolitan areas—those with populations of at least 1 million residents as of the year 2000—located in these states. The second is a sample of smaller metro areas in these states that had higher-than-average levels of manufacturing employment as of the early 1990s and subsequently lost significant numbers of jobs in that sector.[1]

To make the analysis tractable, we had to limit ourselves to just two sets of metropolitan areas, and there were substantive reasons to focus on the second group in this research.[2] Of course, the set of larger MSAs is a complete one, while the set of smaller ones has been chosen nonrandomly on the basis of employment composition and the changes over time in which we have a particular interest. This limits the extent to which we can make broad inferences from this work about larger versus smaller metro areas. On the other hand, given our strong interest in how economic restructuring affects job quality and its effects on worker outcomes in specific kinds of local geographic settings, a comparison of these two kinds of areas seems appropriate and useful for this work. Moreover, an analysis of summary data on the smaller MSAs in our twelve states that we do not include here suggests that the MSAs on which we focused are not terribly unrepresentative of the entire smaller group.[3]

We have thirty-five MSAs in all, with about half in the group of larger MSAs and the rest in the group of smaller ones.[4] Since our sample of states reflects a diverse set of regions and economic and demographic characteristics, the same is true of these metro areas. At least a few of the larger metro areas (such as Chicago, Milwaukee, and Pittsburgh) were once areas of strong manufacturing employment, though most were not, and even these few areas underwent significant restructuring before 1992—the beginning of our study period.

The metro-specific outcomes (in both our data and the data published by the Census Bureau) indicate a great diversity of trends over time across these areas, within each subsample. Employment growth has been relatively weak in some metro areas, both large and smaller ones (such as Pittsburgh and Reading, Pennsylvania), and relatively strong in others (like San Diego, California, and Boulder, Colorado). Earnings growth also shows high variance across metro areas and also across states, with stronger growth in all metro areas of some states (like California) and weaker growth in others (like Pennsylvania). And some areas were apparently much more sensitive than others to the mild recession of the early 2000s, as measured by the differences in measured employment growth between

Figure 4.1   Earnings, Large Versus Small MSAs

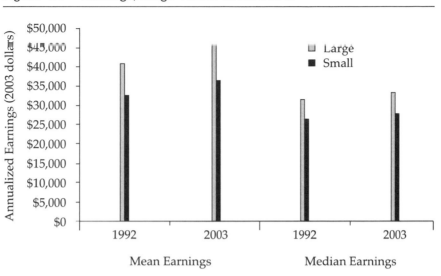

Source: Authors' tabulations using microdata from U.S. Bureau of the Census (1992–2003).

the period 1992 to 2000 and the period 1992 to 2003. We return to this issue later in the chapter.

EMPLOYMENT TRENDS IN LARGER AND SMALLER METRO AREAS

The average labor market characteristics of the two samples of metro areas (as of 1992) and their labor market trends over time are summarized in figures 4.1 and 4.2.[5] Average earnings appear in figure 4.1, presented as both means and medians for each period to enable us to distinguish results that mostly reflect the upper- or lower-most tails of the earnings distribution in each MSA from those mostly reflecting the middle of each. In figure 4.2, we present the data on changes for the periods 1992 to 2000 and 1992 to 2003; only the latter period includes the mildly recessionary period of 2000 to 2003.

A number of important differences can be seen between the labor markets of our larger and smaller MSAs. The summary data on earnings in figure 4.1 show that *average earnings were substantially higher in the larger MSAs.* This is true whether earnings are measured as means or as medians, though the larger differences in means indicate that the gaps are particularly large

Figure 4.2   Employment and Earnings Change, Large Versus Small
MSAs

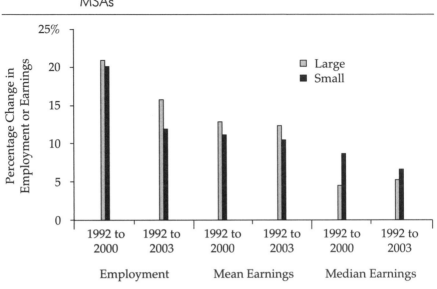

Source: Authors' tabulations using microdata from U.S. Bureau of the Census (1992–2003).

among the uppermost earners in these areas. Of course, the higher average earnings in larger MSAs could reflect many different factors: cost-of-living differences, higher average levels of education and skills, and greater concentrations of higher-paying jobs, both across and within industries. Indeed, our data show that all of these factors apply, except for cost-of-living differences; this finding is consistent with the predictions of the urban agglomerations literature that more productive workers and jobs locate in larger areas. And other data (see, for example, Hirsch and McPherson 2003) show higher costs of living in the larger MSAs as well.

Several differences in employment and earnings growth over time between the larger and smaller MSAs appear in figure 4.2. In particular:

- Employment growth was higher in the larger MSAs over the entire period.

- The recession years of 2000 to 2003 reduced employment in the smaller MSAs by greater amounts, suggesting that they remain more cyclically sensitive than the larger areas.

- Mean earnings growth was higher in the larger MSAs, but median

Figure 4.3   Employment Change by Firm-Effects Quintile, Large
              Versus Small MSAs

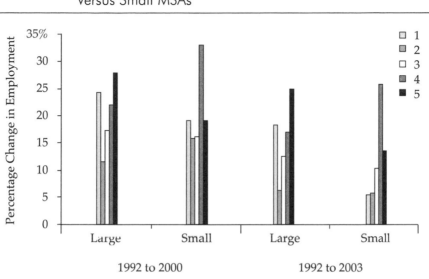

Source: Authors' tabulations using microdata from U.S. Bureau of the Census (1992–2003).

growth was higher in the smaller ones, indicating that the top and bottom earners experienced relatively more earnings growth in the larger
areas while middle earners did somewhat better in the smaller regions.

Of course, the underlying populations and their characteristics are
changing over time in both kinds of areas, with more rapid population
growth in the larger areas. The greater numbers of younger and immigrant workers in the larger MSAs reduces the average earnings and
growth found in those areas. And to the extent that out-migration and labor market withdrawal are higher in the smaller areas—the former occurs
more frequently among more-educated younger workers and the latter
among older workers who have lost good jobs—the median growth of
earnings appears higher among those who remain.

But exactly whose employment and earnings are rising in these areas?
In figures 4.3 through 4.8, we present summary data on employment and
earnings growth across the quintiles of the firm- and person-effects distributions in our samples of larger and smaller MSAs. These distributions
measure the quality of jobs and workers, respectively; thus, these figures
indicate the extent of employment and earnings growth in high-paying

Figure 4.4   Employment Change by Person-Effects Quintile, Large
Versus Small MSAs

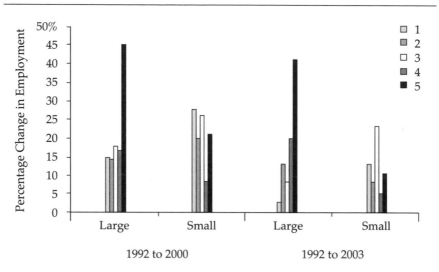

Source: Authors' tabulations using microdata from U.S. Bureau of the Census (1992–2003).

Figure 4.5   Mean Earnings Change by Firm-Effects Quintile, Large
Versus Small MSAs

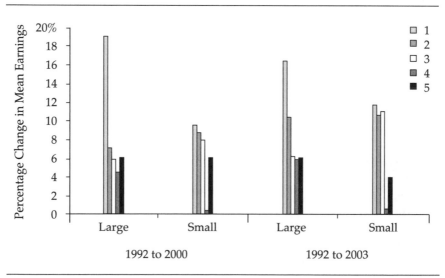

Source: Authors' tabulations using microdata from U.S. Bureau of the Census (1992–2003).

Figure 4.6   Mean Earnings Change by Person-Effects Quintile, Large Versus Small MSAs

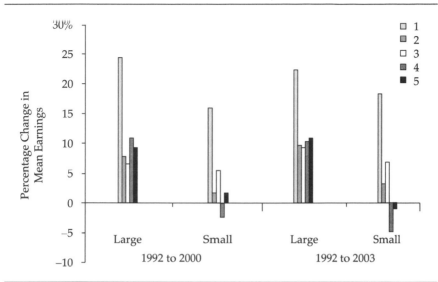

Source: Authors' tabulations using microdata from U.S. Bureau of the Census (1992–2003).

Figure 4.7   Median Earnings Change by Firm-Effects Quintile, Large Versus Small MSAs

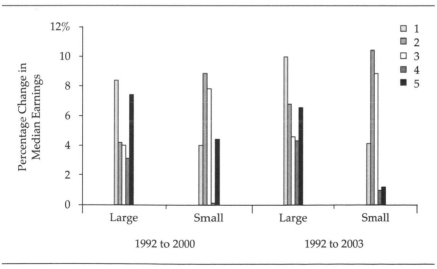

Source: Authors' tabulations using microdata from U.S. Bureau of the Census (1992–2003).

Figure 4.8   Median Earnings Change by Person-Effects Quintile, Large Versus Small MSAs

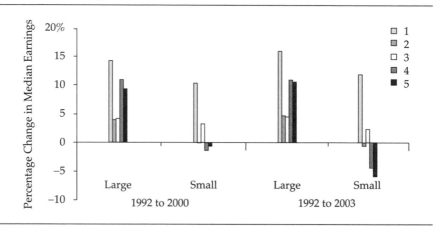

Source: Authors' tabulations using microdata from U.S. Bureau of the Census (1992–2003).

versus low-paying jobs as well as by the skills of the workers who fill them in these areas. Figures 4.3 to 4.8 present the growth rates of employment, mean earnings, and median earnings, respectively, across quintiles of firm- and person-effects distributions for larger and smaller areas.

A number of striking findings appear in these figures. For instance, employment growth was greatest in both the best- and worst-paying jobs in large metropolitan areas in the 1990s (but in the fourth quintile for smaller metro areas); employment growth was highest by far in the lowest-skill group of workers in the large metro areas but was more evenly distributed in the smaller areas; and earnings growth was dramatic in the highest quintiles of jobs and workers in the largest metro areas and was also quite high for the most highly skilled workers in the smaller areas as well.

Together these figures show a story of growing inequality and polarization in all labor markets in the 1990s, but especially the largest ones. High-paying jobs were growing rapidly in the largest labor markets, generating strong earnings growth for the most highly paid employees. The even stronger growth of employment in the lowest-paid jobs was more than matched by a growth of workers in the lowest-skilled categories, at least partly reflecting both immigration and an influx of low-income single mothers into the labor force during the period of welfare reform; indeed, it appears as though the increase in the supply of workers to these jobs was sufficient to keep their earnings from growing as rapidly as those at the top, where supply growth was more limited.[6] Inequality also grew in the smaller metro areas, but not as dramatically across job categories or workers.

The growing polarization of the U.S. labor market in the 1990s, with more employment and earnings growth in high-wage and low-wage jobs than in the middle of the wage (or skill) spectrum, has been noted by Frank Levy and Richard Murnane (2004) and by David Autor, Lawrence Katz, and Melissa Kearney (2006). But why would such polarization have been greater in the largest MSAs? The growth of jobs for highly educated workers there might have been encouraged by the greater efficiencies in these labor markets for information-sharing, as Glaeser and others have noted, or by a greater tendency of educated workers to live in areas that provide the urban amenities they value. In contrast, the growing shares of immigrants and low-income women in these labor markets might well reflect other trends and policies (like economic developments in immigrant source countries and domestic welfare reform, respectively) that directly drove labor supplies in these areas. But it is also possible that the two trends are more directly linked to one another—for instance, that high-earning young professionals directly created demand for low-wage service employment through their need for child care, landscaping services, restaurants, dry cleaners, and the like, and that immigrants and low-income women responded to this demand in their labor force and migration decisions.

Some more light is shed on these developments in table 4A.1. We present data on employment and earnings growth across firm- and person-effects categories, similar to what appears in figures 4.3 to 4.8, but the data now appear separately for the three subperiods of 1992 to 1996, 1996 to 2000, and 2000 to 2003—which correspond to the period of recovery from recession, the late 1990s boom, and the recession of the early 2000s, respectively. A number of findings appear there. The smaller MSAs were more sensitive to business cycles, with higher overall growth rates in employment and earnings during the 1992 to 1996 recovery period but also greater deterioration in these measures as the economy reentered a recession after 2000. In contrast, the larger MSAs enjoyed greater employment and mean earnings growth during the boom period of the late 1990s. Consistent with the earlier figures, we find dramatic growth in both employment and earnings in the largest MSAs in the top and bottom quintiles of jobs and workers during the boom period; some evidence of polarization in this period also appears in the smaller MSAs, but much less dramatically, with substantial growth in employment and earnings in the third quintile as well during the boom.

Given this set of findings, an immediate question arises about the extent to which these employment changes at the metro level have shifted across industries over time. Table 4.1 presents data on employment shares

Table 4.1   Employment Shares by MSA Group and Industry

	Small MSAs			Large MSAs		
	1992	2000	2003	1992	2000	2003
Construction	3.01%	3.77%	3.71%	3.38%	4.36%	4.35%
Nondurable manufacturing	16.85	13.14	11.91	8.21	6.77	5.88
Durable manufacturing	18.94	17.62	14.38	12.42	10.74	8.34
Wholesale trade	3.89	3.24	3.91	5.36	4.56	4.65
Retail trade	13.36	14.37	14.89	13.68	13.81	14.37
Transportation	3.43	3.80	3.65	4.65	4.50	4.43
Information	2.63	2.98	2.80	4.13	5.07	4.68
Finance	4.45	4.49	4.70	7.16	6.41	6.53
Professional services	2.09	2.47	2.49	5.60	6.60	6.14
Administrative	4.53	6.89	6.55	6.11	8.92	8.39
Health care	12.46	13.08	15.35	11.99	11.50	13.25
Entertainment	1.05	1.27	1.38	1.76	2.12	2.46
Accommodation and food	7.88	7.95	8.78	8.44	8.43	8.99
Other services	1.57	1.72	1.84	2.29	2.29	2.37
Other industries	3.85	3.20	3.68	4.81	3.93	5.18

Source: Authors' tabulations using microdata from U.S. Bureau of the Census (1992–2003).
Note: "Other industries" includes agriculture, mining, utilities, real estate and leasing, management of companies, and the remainder of education.

in smaller and larger MSAs for the years 1992, 2000, and 2003 for major industries; data on shares and their changes (rather than growth rates) more clearly illustrate where employment is concentrated at any point in time and how this concentration evolves over time.[7]

The table illustrates a number of differences in patterns of industrial structure and growth between the larger and smaller MSAs during these periods. As of 1992, there was considerably more concentration of employment in durable and nondurable manufacturing in the smaller MSAs (about 36 percent of the total) than in the larger ones (about 21 percent); this concentration, of course, reflects the MSAs that we deliberately chose in each sample. In contrast, employment in the larger metro areas is more concentrated in high-paying service industries such as information, finance, and professional services, with about 17 percent of all jobs in larger MSAs located in these sectors in 1992 (as opposed to 9 percent in the smaller areas). This, of course, is fully consistent with Glaeser's observations.

Over the next several years, manufacturing employment shrank quite rapidly in both kinds of areas, but especially in the smaller MSAs, where shares of employment dropped by ten percentages points (from 36 to 26 percent), compared with a seven-point drop in the larger areas (from 21 to 14 percent). Employment shares in the high-paying services also grew in both larger and smaller areas, but a bit more strongly in the former. In contrast, employment shares in the smaller MSAs rose relatively more in retail trade and, especially, health care. Indeed, because employment in health care is relatively noncyclical, its share grew quite strongly, especially in smaller MSAs, in the downturn of 2000 to 2003.

To what extent are the trends in industry employment patterns shown in table 4.1 responsible for (or at least correlated with) the differences across firm- and person-effects quintiles shown in table 4A.1? Our online appendix table 4OA.1 presents industry shares of employment in smaller and larger MSAs in each year, separately by firm-effects quintiles; similar data appear for person-effects quintiles in online appendix table 4OA.2.[8]

The data in table 4OA.1 confirm that manufacturing employment accounts for fewer of the good jobs in both kinds of areas over time, while the high-paying services account for more, especially in the larger metro areas. Health care accounts for more jobs among middle- and upper-quintile workers, as shown in tables 4OA.1 and 4OA.2, especially in the smaller MSAs over time.

While highly skilled workers largely maintained their employment shares in manufacturing, *there was a virtual collapse in manufacturing employment for less-skilled workers in the smaller MSAs*. For instance, table 4OA.2 shows that the share of employment of workers in the fourth quintile of skills employed in manufacturing dropped from nearly 7 percent to about 2.5 percent in the smaller MSAs between 1992 and 2003, with a considerably smaller drop observed in the larger areas (from 2.8 to 2.0 percent).

Clearly, then, the largest metropolitan economies of the United States had become less dependent on manufacturing employment by the 1990s and experienced a boom in professional service and other employment that seemed to benefit both the most-educated and least-educated workers. These areas experienced the greatest labor market growth overall, but also the most polarization. In contrast, smaller metro areas (at least those studied here) continued to suffer lower employment growth from the loss of manufacturing jobs, especially during recessions, while relying more heavily on diverse sectors such as retail trade and health care to replace those jobs.

THE CORRELATES OF EARNINGS GROWTH IN METRO AREAS

The average employment and earnings growth rates for larger and smaller MSAs presented here raise some fairly obvious questions about what gen-

Table 4.2   Correlations Between Earnings and Employment Growth Across MSAs, 1992 to 2000: Correlations with Overall Employment Growth, Earnings Growth, and Job Creation/Destruction

	All MSAs	Small MSAs	Large MSAs
Mean earnings growth and . . .			
Employment growth	0.502	0.588	0.457
Median earnings growth	0.876	0.904	0.886
Job creation	0.212	0.451	0.052
Job destruction	−0.027	−0.292	0.174
Median earnings growth and . . .			
Employment growth	0.412	0.494	0.272
Mean earnings growth	0.876	0.904	0.886
Job creation	0.300	0.524	0.011
Job destruction	−0.177	−0.414	0.130

Source: Authors' tabulations using microdata from U.S. Bureau of the Census (1992–2003).

erates successful labor market outcomes in metro areas. Our analysis of the data indicates that some areas are much more successful than others at generating employment or earnings growth, within either broad category. But what are the attributes of MSA employment growth most frequently correlated with success in earnings growth, and who enjoys that success when it happens? Does greater employment growth for more-educated workers in high-paying jobs also provide positive "externalities," or spillovers, for other workers, as Glaeser and others suggest?

With a fairly small sample of MSAs and measures of employment and earnings growth across industries and other categories of jobs and workers, it would be quite difficult to formally test hypotheses about what causes employment and earnings growth. But we can measure the correlates of labor market success in these areas and the extent to which job growth in specific categories is related to the earnings growth of workers in specific categories or more broadly. We can also infer the extent to which such earnings growth overall is widely shared across groups, and whether the success of the most highly skilled groups is positively correlated with that of their less-skilled counterparts.

Accordingly, tables 4.2 to 4.4 present correlations between earnings growth and several measures of employment growth across MSAs. The correlations are calculated for all MSAs and then separately for the larger

Table 4.3   Correlations Between Earnings and Employment Growth Across MSAs, 1992 to 2000: Correlations with Employment Growth by Firm-Effects Quintile

	All MSAs	Small MSAs	Large MSAs
Mean earnings growth and . . .			
Firm-effects quintile 1 employment growth	0.528	0.533	0.424
Firm-effects quintile 2 employment growth	0.129	0.030	0.203
Firm-effects quintile 3 employment growth	0.132	−0.175	0.496
Firm-effects quintile 4 employment growth	−0.164	0.131	−0.286
Firm-effects quintile 5 employment growth	0.219	0.432	0.144
Median earnings growth and . . .			
Firm-effects quintile 1 employment growth	0.461	0.446	0.247
Firm-effects quintile 2 employment growth	0.138	0.133	0.096
Firm-effects quintile 3 employment growth	−0.080	−0.319	0.323
Firm-effects quintile 4 employment growth	−0.188	0.028	−0.375
Firm-effects quintile 5 employment growth	0.379	0.596	0.081

Source: Authors' tabulations using microdata from U.S. Bureau of the Census (1992–2003).

and smaller ones, respectively, to see whether the same patterns hold across these groups. Correlations are shown for the period of 1992 to 2000, while similar results for the period of 1992 to 2003 appear in tables 4A.2 to 4A.4 of the appendix, in case the observed patterns of employment and earnings growth during the recessionary years of the early 2000s differ substantially from those of the growth years in the 1990s.

The correlations between earnings and employment growth are also calculated for various measures of employment growth. We begin with overall net employment growth and overall rates of job creation and job destruction (table 4.2). We then present separate estimates of correlations between overall earnings growth and employment growth in firm-effects quintiles (table 4.3) and in different industries (table 4.4). Finally, while tables 4.2 to 4.4 present the correlations across MSAs between mean and median earnings growth for all workers and the various measures of employment growth, online appendix table 4OA.3 presents these correlations separately for workers in the five person-effects quintiles, which tell us the extent to which different skill categories of workers share in the growth generated in various categories of jobs.

A number of findings appear in tables 4.2 to 4.4. In table 4.2, we see that overall earnings growth and employment growth were positively corre-

Table 4.4   Correlations Between Earnings and Employment Growth Across MSAs, 1992 to 2000: Correlations with Employment Growth by Industry

	All MSAs	Small MSAs	Large MSAs
Mean earnings growth and . . .			
Agriculture employment growth	−0.269	−0.330	−0.206
Mining employment growth	0.304	0.250	0.155
Utilities employment growth	−0.197	0.099	−0.335
Construction employment growth	0.560	0.804	0.429
Manufacturing employment growth	0.154	0.186	−0.045
Wholesale employment growth	0.251	0.672	0.275
Retail employment growth	−0.143	0.161	−0.076
Transportation employment growth	−0.152	0.006	−0.265
Information employment growth	0.027	0.204	0.485
Finance employment growth	−0.125	0.055	−0.296
Real estate employment growth	−0.079	0.102	0.171
Professional employment growth	0.699	0.584	0.767
Management employment growth	0.200	0.681	−0.116
Administrative employment growth	−0.192	−0.097	0.017
Education employment growth	0.185	0.377	0.304
Health care employment growth	−0.179	−0.178	−0.122
Entertainment employment growth	−0.268	0.161	−0.589
Food and hotels employment growth	−0.129	−0.057	−0.150
Other services employment growth	0.100	0.248	0.154
Median earnings growth and . . .			
Agriculture employment growth	−0.278	−0.387	−0.122
Mining employment growth	0.208	0.232	0.001
Utilities employment growth	−0.006	0.275	−0.145
Construction employment growth	0.662	0.809	0.467
Manufacturing employment growth	0.159	0.122	−0.005
Wholesale employment growth	0.457	0.782	0.232
Retail employment growth	−0.050	0.241	−0.127
Transportation employment growth	−0.161	−0.067	−0.240
Information employment growth	0.066	0.203	0.449
Finance employment growth	−0.194	−0.118	−0.222
Real estate employment growth	0.023	0.177	0.290
Professional employment growth	0.683	0.610	0.699
Management employment growth	0.371	0.689	−0.227
Administrative employment growth	−0.103	0.168	−0.295
Education employment growth	0.110	0.157	0.233
Health care employment growth	−0.243	−0.209	−0.215
Entertainment employment growth	−0.276	0.021	−0.657
Food and hotels employment growth	−0.078	−0.026	−0.058
Other services employment growth	0.156	0.385	0.104

Source: Authors' tabulations using microdata from U.S. Bureau of the Census (1992–2003).

lated, especially during the boom years of the 1990s and in the smaller MSAs. When employment and earnings growth are positively correlated, economists often infer that employment results across areas are primarily driven by *shifts in labor demand*—since, in our simplest analytical models of labor markets, positive shifts in labor demand increase both employment and earnings outcomes while negative shifts tend to decrease them.[9] Thus, areas that experience increasing demand for labor—probably associated with rising demand for the kinds of goods and services they produce—show increases in both employment and earnings rates, while those that experience decreases (or relatively smaller increases) in such demand show relatively smaller improvements in both employment and earnings.

Another broad finding in this table is that earnings growth tends to be more correlated with overall *job creation* than with job destruction, especially in the smaller areas. If new job creation is strong enough, it can overcome the negative effects of job destruction on overall earnings and the likely effects of displacement that job destruction implies. But this raises major questions about exactly who benefits from newly created jobs and who is hurt by displacement from destroyed jobs; we explore these questions further later in the chapter.

To what extent does employment growth in different job categories translate into earnings growth overall at the MSA level? The results in table 4.3 imply that:

- Job growth in the top quintile of job quality generally is most highly correlated with overall earnings growth across metro areas.

- Job growth in the bottom quintile is quite highly correlated with earnings growth as well.

- Correlations for both of these quintiles are generally higher than for other quintiles closer to the middle of the job quality distribution.

The results generally can be found in both large and small MSAs, and for both mean and median earnings growth over time; only in the smaller MSAs and for median earnings growth does growth in the bottom quintile matter more than in the top quintile between 1992 and 2000, though even here both of these correlations are much higher than those for the middle quintiles. These results also mostly hold up when we consider the correlations (in the appendix) over the period of 1992 to 2003—which also includes the recession period of the early 2000s—though the magnitudes weaken considerably in the larger MSAs.

When we consider employment growth across industries in table 4.4, some similar results appear. For instance, employment growth in construction was highly correlated with earnings growth, as was growth in wholesale trade employment (at least in smaller metro areas); employment growth in manufacturing was just modestly correlated with earnings growth of any kind in both sets of places; and *employment growth in professional services and management services (in the small areas) was strongly correlated with overall earnings growth as well*—even for median earnings.

Quite importantly, these results appear to hold in online appendix table 4OA.3 for all parts of the personal skill distribution. Thus, workers in the middle and lower quintiles of person effects still benefit in areas where employment growth is strong in the highest quintile of firm effects and in professional services. The correlations of earnings growth with employment growth at the top end of the jobs and skills spectrums tend to weaken somewhat as we move down the quintiles of the skill distribution, but they generally remain fairly strong nonetheless.[10]

Of course, these correlations do not necessarily imply causation. In some cases—like construction and wholesale trade—employment growth might be completely endogenous to prosperity and the high incomes generated at the top by other forces. Growth in finance and construction might reflect temporary "bubbles" (in technology stocks and then in housing) to some extent. But the results do suggest that, whatever economic and labor market forces generated strong growth in the top quintile of jobs and in professional services sectors of many large metro areas, they ultimately provide or overlap with benefits to other groups.

Perhaps employment growth in high-wage and high-skill jobs generates a broader prosperity that spills over to less-educated workers, as Glaeser suggests. It remains unclear whether it is the supply of such workers already in the area (drawn by urban amenities) that draws the jobs, or the labor market benefits of density that first draws the jobs and then the workers. And if the benefits of the more-educated do spill over to the less-educated, exactly why is unclear as well. Maybe there is some complementarity between the demands for workers with high and low skills in an area, as we noted earlier—with a growing high-income professional or managerial class requiring the services of lower-skill groups in their personal lives, if not directly in the workplace. Indeed, the literature on immigration suggests some complementarity between labor market demands for more-educated native workers and less-educated immigrants.[11] Of course, it is also possible that any such "trickle-down" stories are not true and that these correlations are purely spurious or coincidental.

At a minimum, the estimated correlations show that lower-skill workers often do well in the same places where higher-skill workers in high-wage jobs are growing and prospering and that they do less well in areas where the gains for high-skill groups are weaker. In the final chapter, we consider the types of policies that could improve the access of less-skilled workers to the growing number of good jobs in these areas and ways to make sure that prosperity of any kind is more widely shared.

DISPLACEMENT AND ITS EFFECTS IN LARGER AND SMALLER METROPOLITAN AREAS

If job creation and net employment growth, especially in high-wage job categories and in the professional services, are associated with overall earnings growth in local labor markets, what happens to those who are displaced from their jobs in such markets? The data in the previous chapter suggested that workers with some amount of tenure accumulated in their previous jobs get hurt by displacement, especially if they lose good jobs. These losses depend importantly, however, on the quality of the new jobs they obtain and on the strength of the overall labor market.

How do the effects of job loss and displacement vary across these metropolitan areas? Are displacement rates higher in the smaller areas that have experienced much restructuring? Do workers there have more difficulty finding good new jobs to replace their previous ones in such areas, and are earnings losses greater? And given the net loss of employment in manufacturing for less-skilled workers, to what extent do all of these results depend on whether the earlier jobs were in manufacturing?

In this section, we present results on displacement rates and their effects, separately for our samples of smaller versus larger metro areas and for those who lose manufacturing jobs versus nonmanufacturing jobs in each. Using the same (admittedly imperfect) definition of displacement as in chapter 3, we present data on rates of job displacement, changes in the quality of jobs for those displaced, and changes in earnings associated with such displacements—separately for our four subsamples. We focus primarily on those with at least three years of job tenure, since these are the workers upon whom job displacement imposes the largest costs.

Figure 4.9 presents data on job displacement rates averaged over the entire period of 1992 to 2003—for manufacturing and nonmanufacturing employees, in large and smaller MSAs, and for the overall sample of workers as well as for those with at least three years of job tenure.[12] As before, displacement rates are considerably higher in all cases for workers with less than three years of tenure than it is for those with more tenure. For the broader sample of employees, displacement rates outside of manufacturing are considerably higher than those in manufacturing in both sets of MSAs, which was also apparent in the data of chapter 3.

For those with at least three years of tenure, displacement rates in these metro areas averaged 1 to 1.5 percent a year. Displacement rates in manu-

Figure 4.9   Rates of Job Displacement, 1992 to 2003, Large Versus
               Small MSAs

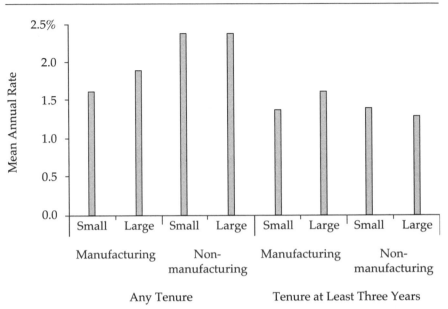

Source: Authors' tabulations using microdata from U.S. Bureau of the Census (1992–2003).
Note: Job change is defined as a change in a worker's primary employer from year *t* to year
t + 1 (including non-employment in year *t* + 1). Displacement is defined as a job change
where a displacement event (a decline of 30 percent or more in quarterly employment) occurred at the firm that is the primary employer in year *t*, and additionally the worker had
positive earnings at the firm in the quarter of the displacement event, had positive earnings
at the firm for at least one quarter prior to the event, and had zero earnings at the firm for at
least two quarters after the event. For workers with tenure of at least three years, the period
is 1995 to 2003.

facturing for these workers were a bit higher than in other industries in
the largest metro areas, but they were more comparable in the smaller areas, despite the greater net loss of employment in manufacturing employment over this period. And displacement rates outside of manufacturing
were just a bit higher in the smaller than in the larger MSAs.

To what extent do displaced workers subsequently have higher, similar,
or lower job quality after they become reemployed in these areas, and
where do those jobs appear? For displaced workers who remained in their
metro areas and were still employed there, table 4.5 presents the industries in which the old and new jobs appeared, while table 4.6 presents data

Table 4.5   Industry Distribution of 2003 Employment for Workers
Displaced in 1996

| | Original Industry | | | |
| | Small MSAs | | Large MSAs | |
New Industry	Manufac-turing	Other	Manufac-turing	Other
Construction	1.9	3.3	1.4	6.9
Nondurable manufacturing	46.4	4.5	12.8	3.4
Durable manufacturing	30.1	5.9	67.3	4.4
Wholesale trade	2.7	4.5	3.0	8.0
Retail trade	4.7	15.6	2.5	16.1
Transportation	1.1	3.4	1.3	3.7
Information	0.9	8.3	0.9	5.4
Finance	0.6	10.0	0.7	7.4
Professional services	1.3	3.5	2.6	6.5
Administrative	3.4	7.5	3.1	7.8
Health care	4.3	21.4	1.4	14.7
Entertainment	0.1	2.7	0.3	1.8
Accommodation and food	0.8	3.5	0.5	7.3
Other services	0.5	0.9	0.5	1.6
Other industries	1.1	4.9	1.7	5.0

Source: Authors' tabulations using microdata from U.S. Bureau of the Census (1992–2003).
Note: Columns sum to 100 percent. "Other" industries includes agriculture, mining, utilities, real estate and leasing, management of companies, and the remainder of education. Workers are those with at least three years of tenure as of 1996.

on the percentages of displaced workers who ultimately had higher, similar, or lower job quality (as measured by quintile of firm effects), both overall and according to the quality of the jobs in which they started. Again, both sets of data are presented for displaced workers with at least three years of tenure at the time of displacement and separately for those in small versus large MSAs and in manufacturing versus nonmanufacturing jobs originally.[13]

The results shown in table 4.5 reveal a surprising fact: many displaced workers who began in manufacturing obtained a new job there. Indeed, this was true for roughly three-quarters of our original manufacturing workers in smaller MSAs and roughly 80 percent in the larger ones. Those who did not end up in manufacturing ultimately found work in health care or retail trade, among other industries, in the smaller MSAs. Displaced manufacturing workers in the larger metro areas ended up in a

Table 4.6   Fraction of Displaced Workers Who Moved into Jobs of Similar or Changing Quality

	Original Industry							
	Manufacturing				Non-Manufacturing			
	1996 to 2000		1996 to 2003		1996 to 2000		1996 to 2003	
	Small MSA	Large MSA	Small MSA	Large MSA	Small MSA	Large MSA	Small MSA	Large MSA
Better	23.3%	14.3%	22.9%	15.2%	30.4%	30.0%	33.4%	33.1%
Same	34.6	71.8	38.8	70.9	39.2	41.2	35.2	38.9
Worse	42.1	13.9	38.3	13.9	30.3	28.8	31.4	28.0

Source: Authors' tabulations using microdata from U.S. Bureau of the Census (1992–2003).
Note: Workers are those with at least three years of tenure as of 1996. "Better/same/worse" quintile represents a comparison of the quintile of the worker's primary employer in the end year to the quintile of the worker's primary employer in the start year.

wide range of industries, though retail trade and health care again appeared frequently as new job destinations there as well.

The results reported in table 4.6 also show a wide range of outcomes for displaced workers, in terms of new job versus old job quality. Overall, many workers ended up with jobs of better or similar quality than those they started in, but significant fractions (14 to 40 percent) wound up in worse jobs, even after seven years. Displaced workers who originally had manufacturing jobs were much less likely than others to obtain better new jobs, in all locations and time periods. In small metro areas, they were much more likely to end up in worse jobs after displacement than those who lost nonmanufacturing jobs; in larger metro areas, those displaced from manufacturing were more likely to end up in jobs of similar quality than those who began elsewhere. More generally, *displaced workers in smaller MSAs were more likely to end up in worse new jobs than the ones they had before, while those in larger MSAs were more likely to end up in jobs of similar quality to what they had before,* though these differences are much more pronounced among workers who were originally in manufacturing than among those in nonmanufacturing jobs.

Finally, what do these changes in jobs among displaced workers imply for the earnings changes they experienced after reemployment? Figure 4.10 presents data on earnings changes for displaced workers with at least three years of tenure according to whether or not job quality improved, stayed the same, or declined between jobs. Separate data are presented not

Figure 4.10   Change in Mean Earnings of Displaced Workers by MSA
Group, Starting Industry, Period, and Change in Firm-
Effects Quintile

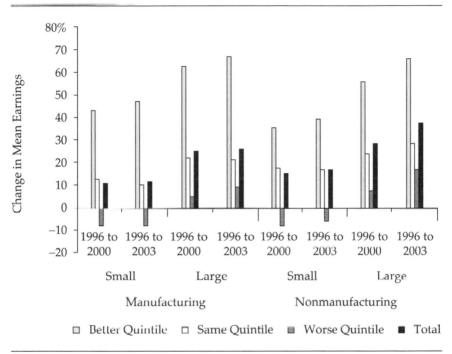

Source: Authors' tabulations using microdata from U.S. Bureau of the Census (1992–2003).
Note: Workers are those with at least three years of tenure as of 1996.

only for large and small MSAs and for jobs originally in manufacturing
versus elsewhere but also for the periods of 1996 to 2000 and 1996 to 2003.

The exact results vary a lot across particular groups and locations and
depend strongly on the quality of the new jobs obtained relative to workers' original jobs. But overall, *earnings gains were much more positive for displaced workers who managed to obtain jobs of similar or especially higher quality
than those they had originally.* More specifically, we find that, for those with
job quality worse than before, earnings changes were negative after four
to seven years in the smaller MSAs and generally positive but quite low in
the larger ones; for those with job quality that held roughly steady, earnings gains were modest—mostly in the range of 10 to 20 percent after four
years and 15 to 30 percent after seven. For those whose job quality improved, the gains were quite large—in the range of 35 to 65 percent—and

on average those in large MSAs experienced larger earnings gains (or smaller losses) than those in smaller metro areas; results for those originally in manufacturing versus nonmanufacturing are mixed.

Thus, the results show that displaced workers were most likely to suffer earnings losses (or smaller gains) when they ended up in worse jobs than before in small metro areas. It appears that manufacturing workers can often find new jobs, in that sector or elsewhere, that still reward them for the general or sectoral skills they have developed. But since displaced manufacturing workers in small metro areas are the ones most likely to experience deteriorating job quality (as we saw in table 4.6), they are also most likely to suffer the earnings losses that are apparent for this group in figure 4.10.

It is important to remember that these results probably understate the negative effects of displacement—both because of our imperfect ability to identify those displaced (so we probably capture at least some voluntary changers in our definition) and because those with earnings losses might well have left the local labor market, either by moving elsewhere or by leaving employment entirely.[14] Nevertheless, these data indicate both the importance of new job quality versus old job quality on the effects of displacement, as well as the benefits of living in large metro areas for workers who become displaced. The stronger labor markets there and the larger range of available jobs in growing sectors no doubt enable displaced workers to find new employment that is more consistent with their levels of skill.

To shed a bit more light on the earnings changes of displaced workers, we present results from regressions for earnings changes between old and new jobs in table 4A.5. (Again, readers can skip to the conclusion if they are so inclined.) Like those in chapter 3, these regressions compare earnings changes for displaced and nondisplaced job-changers to earnings changes for those who have stayed on the same jobs in the same time period, but only for those who began with at least three years of tenure. This time we also add net employment growth at the MSA level as an additional independent variable (model 2), and we include equations in which the effects of an individual's job change (displaced or otherwise) are interacted with net employment growth in the MSA (model 3). Results appear for the periods of 1996 to 2000 and 1996 to 2003 and separately for small and large MSAs and for workers who were in manufacturing versus non-manufacturing jobs at the beginning of the period.

The results reported in table 4A.5 largely confirm what we have seen in the earlier tables. The effects of displacement were mostly near zero or negative (except for manufacturing workers in large metro areas); the effects of job changing more generally, however, were decidedly mixed, since workers were losing valuable job tenure when they changed jobs, even if they got better jobs. The costs of displacement were most negative for those who started in manufacturing in smaller MSAs.

The second and third models clearly show that net employment growth at the MSA level generally has a positive effect on earnings growth for all workers and that the effects of displacement are mostly more positive (or less negative) in growing metro areas. Results for the periods that exclude or include the recessionary downturn (through 2003) generally reflect these findings as well. On the other hand, the higher net employment growth in the larger MSAs does not account for much of the better earnings performance of displaced workers in these areas.

Overall, then, our results show once again that job changing in general and involuntary displacements in particular can have either positive or negative effects, depending in part on the quality of the new job attained relative to the one lost. Both the size and the extent of employment growth in the MSA, as well as the industries in which workers originated and end up, contribute to how well displaced workers adapt to the difficult restructuring process that many workers faced in the 1990s and still face today. While difficulties no doubt exist for displaced workers in all areas, those in the smaller MSAs—and especially those displaced from manufacturing jobs—have faced the greatest challenges in maintaining or improving their real earnings over time. Finally, the benefits of higher overall growth associated with increasing labor market opportunities for all workers, especially the highly educated, might benefit displaced workers looking for new work, as well as the less-educated.

CONCLUSION

In this chapter, we have analyzed U.S. labor markets at the metropolitan level, looking at the kinds of jobs that have grown in different metropolitan areas, the changes correlated with labor market success for different groups of workers in these places, and what happens to displaced workers there. We argue that recent changes in job quality and volatility and in their consequences differ between the two kinds of metropolitan areas that we analyze here: the largest MSAs versus medium-sized ones that underwent significant restructuring and lost many manufacturing jobs in the 1990s.

What we find is that both employment and earnings grew more rapidly in the largest MSAs in the 1990s—especially during the boom years of the late 1990s. But employment growth rates were large in the highest and especially the lowest job quality categories there, while earnings grew the most for workers with the highest skills. Still, earnings growth for most groups of workers was highly correlated with such growth at the top of the skill distribution.

In contrast, the medium-sized MSAs considered here—ones with relatively more manufacturing jobs as of 1990 and thus, admittedly, not a random sample—were more cyclical and experienced less dramatic polarization during the boom years, but also lower job growth. Employment growth in professional services and other highly paid job categories was lower in these areas, which were more dependent on growth in retail trade and health care to replace the lost jobs in manufacturing. And the consequences of job displacement were more negative (in terms of earnings changes) in the smaller MSAs—especially for those workers who suffered a loss in job quality, which was especially true for those who had held manufacturing jobs. These workers will also likely face the greatest challenges in the aftermath of the Great Recession over the next several years.

Of course, it is important to acknowledge some caveats to this analysis. As noted earlier, our ability to identify accurately those workers who were involuntarily displaced is limited, and that limitation might lead us to understate negative outcomes. Our samples of the largest MSAs are complete only within the twelve states we analyze here, and our sample of smaller MSAs is deliberately chosen to reflect the experience of heavily restructuring areas. One can easily think of large MSAs that have also done relatively badly, at least in terms of employment and earnings growth, during this time period (for instance, Detroit), and even worse more recently, as well as smaller ones whose experiences have been a bit more positive than those studied here.

Indeed, our inability to extend this analysis beyond 2003 is a major limitation to this work. It would have been very useful to know the extent to which the much more modest labor market boom of 2003 to 2007 generated similar patterns in terms of job quality, job volatility, and their consequences in smaller and larger areas. Also, we would like to know the extent to which the Great Recession of 2008 and beyond has disproportionately hurt areas that were dependent on construction and financial services as well as manufacturing for their good jobs and employment growth, in both the short and longer runs. Specifically, did the broader sharing of these gains with middle-skill workers depend on booms in the financial market and then in housing that ultimately proved to be ephemeral?

Other uncertainties limit our ability to clearly interpret the results for the 1990s. Exactly why did employment grow so much more rapidly for highly skilled professional workers in the largest MSAs, and why did growth in the highest and lowest categories of job quality correlate with one another? In both cases, did the job growth drive the growing supplies of workers in these areas, or vice versa?

No doubt, displaced workers and the less-educated experience major challenges in our largest metropolitan areas, where fewer good jobs are available to those with lower skills and those labor markets remain volatile. But whatever the challenges for these workers in the larger metro areas analyzed here, those in the smaller MSAs (and in some larger MSAs of the industrial Midwest) face more serious ones. How can these formerly industrial areas attract or generate good jobs of high quality for less-educated workers as well as the more-educated? Aside from simply improving worker skills and education, are there economic development strategies that have been relatively successful in these places, and have they achieved some level of scale?

Whether the smaller areas have any hope of replicating even some of the successes enjoyed in larger metro areas is unclear, since they lack the amenities that draw highly educated young workers or the density that creates network efficiencies in the best-paying jobs. In the end, it is possible that the best hopes for the less-educated in these areas may be to simply move to other regions where job growth is more robust (or will be when the United States eventually recovers from the Great Recession).

Before we analyze potential policy responses to these labor market issues, we need a bit more evidence on how jobs at different levels of quality grow or do not grow, especially at the firm level. This will give us more insight into what kinds of economic development policies might be cost-effective in creating good jobs, and at what scale, in conjunction with skill development and other policies. We turn to these issues in the next chapter.

APPENDIX

(Follows on next page.)

Table 4A.1   Percentage Change in Employment or Earnings by MSA and by Period

	Small MSAs			Large MSAs		
	1992 to 1996	1996 to 2000	2000 to 2003	1992 to 1996	1996 to 2000	2000 to 2003
Change in employment						
Total	10.8%	8.6%	−7.0%	9.4%	10.5%	−4.2%
Firm-effects quintile						
1	11.0	7.4	−9.7	9.5	16.8	−7.3
2	10.2	5.4	−8.8	6.9	5.8	−5.9
3	10.9	4.5	−5.2	8.0	9.0	−4.7
4	17.4	12.1	−5.6	13.0	7.7	−4.5
5	5.9	11.7	−5.4	9.5	16.4	−3.8
Person-effects quintile						
1	16.2	9.9	−11.2	7.8	6.1	−10.1
2	15.4	3.7	−9.7	6.7	7.1	−1.1
3	11.8	12.7	−2.0	10.0	7.0	−8.0
4	7.8	0.5	−3.1	5.5	10.4	3.0
5	4.1	16.5	−9.1	18.0	23.0	−2.3
Change in mean earnings						
Total	3.4	7.4	−0.4	0.4	12.2	−0.4
Firm-effects quintile						
1	1.6	7.9	2.0	2.2	16.5	−2.1
2	0.5	8.2	1.7	−0.8	8.0	3.1
3	−2.2	10.5	2.8	−1.6	7.6	0.4
4	−4.9	5.7	0.2	−3.7	8.6	1.3
5	−1.5	7.9	−2.0	−4.6	11.2	0.0
Person-effects quintile						
1	4.6	10.8	2.0	5.0	18.5	−1.8
2	−1.5	3.2	1.6	−0.6	8.5	1.8
3	−2.9	8.7	1.4	−1.8	8.5	2.5
4	−7.8	5.9	−2.5	−3.3	14.8	−0.4
5	−4.7	6.9	−2.5	−4.1	13.9	1.6
Change in median earnings						
Total	0.8	7.9	−1.8	−2.9	7.6	0.7
Firm-effects quintile						
1	−1.3	5.4	0.1	−1.3	9.9	1.4
2	−0.2	9.1	1.5	−1.7	6.0	2.5
3	−4.1	12.4	1.0	−3.2	7.4	0.7
4	−6.9	7.5	0.8	−6.1	9.9	1.2
5	−4.3	9.1	−3.1	−5.9	14.1	−0.8
Person-effects quintile						
1	1.2	9.0	1.4	1.9	12.1	1.6
2	−4.4	4.5	−0.5	−2.1	6.1	0.5
3	−4.9	8.7	−0.9	−3.1	7.3	0.4
4	−6.9	5.9	−3.3	−3.0	14.4	−0.2
5	−5.9	5.7	−5.8	−5.1	15.3	1.2

Source: Authors' tabulations using microdata from U.S. Bureau of the Census (1992–2003).

Table 4A.2   Correlations Between Earnings and Employment Growth
Across MSAs, 1992 to 2003: Correlations with Overall
Employment Growth, Earnings Growth, and Job Creation
and Destruction

	All MSAs	Small MSAs	Large MSAs
Mean earnings growth and . . .			
Employment growth	0.249	0.492	−0.147
Median earnings growth	0.907	0.935	0.834
Job creation	0.208	0.370	−0.058
Job destruction	−0.148	−0.234	0.017
Median earnings growth and . . .			
Employment growth	0.195	0.348	−0.274
Mean earnings growth	0.907	0.935	0.834
Job creation	0.211	0.380	−0.161
Job destruction	−0.171	−0.295	0.093

Source: Authors' tabulations using microdata from U.S. Bureau of the Census (1992–2003).

Table 4A.3   Correlations Between Earnings and Employment Growth
Across MSAs, 1992 to 2003: Correlations with
Employment Growth by Firm-Effects Quintile

	All MSAs	Small MSAs	Large MSAs
Mean earnings growth and . . .			
Firm-effects quintile 1 employment growth	0.510	0.545	0.045
Firm-effects quintile 2 employment growth	0.011	0.059	−0.347
Firm-effects quintile 3 employment growth	0.014	0.038	0.052
Firm-effects quintile 4 employment growth	−0.322	−0.078	−0.567
Firm-effects quintile 5 employment growth	0.321	0.603	0.120
Median earnings growth and . . .			
Firm-effects quintile 1 employment growth	0.412	0.339	−0.081
Firm-effects quintile 2 employment growth	0.060	0.194	−0.477
Firm-effects quintile 3 employment growth	−0.044	−0.059	0.012
Firm-effects quintile 4 employment growth	−0.374	−0.226	−0.551
Firm-effects quintile 5 employment growth	0.451	0.703	0.158

Source: Authors' tabulations using microdata from U.S. Bureau of the Census (1992–2003).

Table 4A.4   Correlations Between Earnings and Employment Growth Across MSAs, 1992 to 2003: Correlations with Employment Growth by Industry

	All MSAs	Small MSAs	Large MSAs
Mean earnings growth and . . .			
Agriculture employment growth	−0.384	−0.370	−0.328
Mining employment growth	0.042	−0.036	0.205
Utilities employment growth	−0.124	0.191	−0.246
Construction employment growth	0.393	0.594	0.133
Manufacturing employment growth	0.130	0.211	−0.226
Wholesale employment growth	0.039	0.606	−0.153
Retail employment growth	−0.183	0.225	−0.316
Transportation employment growth	−0.145	0.046	−0.274
Information employment growth	−0.043	0.254	0.227
Finance employment growth	−0.177	0.101	−0.446
Real estate employment growth	−0.121	0.227	−0.196
Professional employment growth	0.348	0.407	0.362
Management employment growth	0.089	0.665	−0.219
Administrative employment growth	−0.201	0.138	−0.342
Education employment growth	0.093	0.158	0.243
Health care employment growth	−0.325	−0.240	−0.287
Entertainment employment growth	−0.153	−0.248	−0.321
Food and hotels employment growth	−0.257	−0.112	−0.518
Other services employment growth	0.152	0.316	0.117
Median earnings growth and . . .			
Agriculture employment growth	−0.421	−0.435	−0.314
Mining employment growth	−0.047	−0.099	0.037
Utilities employment growth	−0.015	0.269	−0.070
Construction employment growth	0.452	0.559	0.241
Manufacturing employment growth	0.174	0.071	0.013
Wholesale employment growth	0.186	0.673	−0.181
Retail employment growth	−0.118	0.226	−0.328
Transportation employment growth	−0.142	0.012	−0.303
Information employment growth	0.012	0.278	0.108
Finance employment growth	−0.203	−0.001	−0.511
Real estate employment growth	−0.019	0.221	0.048
Professional employment growth	0.351	0.408	0.262
Management employment growth	0.177	0.639	−0.371
Administrative employment growth	−0.119	0.273	−0.493
Education employment growth	−0.002	−0.007	0.124
Health care employment growth	−0.391	−0.240	−0.479
Entertainment employment growth	−0.199	−0.286	−0.371
Food and hotels employment growth	−0.203	−0.086	−0.402
Other services employment growth	0.149	0.317	0.026

Source: Authors' tabulations using microdata from U.S. Bureau of the Census (1992–2003).

Table 4A.5   Regressions on Log Change in Earnings for Workers with Tenure at Least Three Years

	Model 1		Model 2		Model 3	
	Coefficient	t-Value	Coefficient	t-Value	Coefficient	t-Value
1996 to 2000, small MSAs, non-manufacturing workers						
Intercept	0.355	84.3	0.327	68.0	0.331	67.7
Displaced	0.020	2.13	0.019	2.08	−0.102	−4.89
Changed jobs, not displaced	0.051	16.7	0.051	16.9	0.035	4.78
Age in 1992 (years)	−0.007	−64.1	−0.007	−63.9	−0.007	−63.9
Person fixed effect	0.046	13.7	0.046	13.5	0.046	13.5
MSA employment change (per 100 percent change)			0.124	11.8	0.105	9.22
Displaced*employment change					0.552	6.48
Job change*employment change					0.079	2.54
R-squared	0.021		0.021		0.021	
1996 to 2000, small MSAs, manufacturing workers						
Intercept	0.311	74.4	0.247	53.3	0.245	52.1
Displaced	−0.257	−24.6	−0.274	−26.2	−0.335	−13.8
Changed jobs, not displaced	−0.005	−1.66	−0.005	−1.70	0.026	3.35
Age in 1992 (years)	−0.007	−68.7	−0.007	−68.8	−0.007	−68.7
Person fixed effect	0.092	24.2	0.079	20.8	0.079	20.8
MSA employment change (per 100 percent change)			0.311	30.9	0.322	30.3
Displaced*employment change					0.231	2.73
Job change*employment change					−0.155	−4.41
R-squared	0.029		0.033		0.033	
1996 to 2000, large MSAs, non-manufacturing workers						
Intercept	0.434	329.4	0.410	286.1	0.416	286.8
Displaced	−0.058	−19.2	−0.058	−19.1	−0.072	−11.9
Changed jobs, not displaced	0.000	0.29	0.001	0.78	−0.045	−23.4
Age in 1992 (years)	−0.009	−260.3	−0.009	−260.6	−0.009	−260.5
Person fixed effect	0.089	84.2	0.089	84.5	0.089	84.5
MSA employment change (per 100 percent change)			0.110	41.9	0.081	28.7
Displaced*employment change					0.063	2.61
Job change*employment change					0.212	27.2
R-squared	0.028		0.028		0.028	
1996 to 2000, large MSAs, manufacturing workers						
Intercept	0.339	176.4	0.312	151.4	0.311	148.9
Displaced	0.239	80.1	0.236	79.3	0.232	36.8

(Table continues on p. 126.)

Table 4A.5   (Continued)

	Model 1		Model 2		Model 3	
	Coeffi-cient	t-Value	Coeffi-cient	t-Value	Coeffi-cient	t-Value
Changed jobs, not displaced	−0.033	−23.1	−0.034	−23.6	−0.016	−5.51
Age in 1992 (years)	−0.007	−150.5	−0.007	−150.7	−0.007	−150.7
Person fixed effect	0.200	120.5	0.195	117.3	0.195	117.3
MSA employment change (per 100 percent change)			0.127	34.9	0.135	34.6
Displaced*employment change					0.018	0.77
Job change*employment change					−0.081	−6.84
R-squared	0.041		0.042		0.042	
1996 to 2003, small MSAs, non-manufacturing workers						
Intercept	0.517	93.8	0.487	84.9	0.486	84.3
Displaced	−0.020	−1.77	−0.022	−1.86	−0.011	−0.57
Changed jobs, not displaced	0.065	18.1	0.066	18.4	0.075	13.2
Age in 1992 (years)	−0.011	−73.7	−0.011	−73.5	−0.011	−73.5
Person fixed effect	−0.013	−2.88	−0.010	−2.30	−0.010	−2.28
MSA employment change (per 100 percent change)			0.213	18.7	0.222	18.2
Displaced*employment change					−0.075	−0.66
Job change*employment change					−0.068	−1.97
R-squared	0.028		0.030		0.030	
1996 to 2003, small MSAs, manu-facturing workers						
Intercept	0.372	65.2	0.350	60.4	0.350	60.1
Displaced	−0.262	−19.5	−0.268	−19.9	−0.404	−18.5
Changed jobs, not displaced	−0.010	−2.50	−0.010	−2.38	0.003	0.50
Age in 1992 (years)	−0.010	−69.3	−0.010	−69.7	−0.010	−69.6
Person fixed effect	0.169	33.2	0.159	31.1	0.159	31.1
MSA employment change (per 100 percent change)			0.217	20.0	0.219	19.3
Displaced*employment change					1.006	7.88
Job change*employment change					−0.115	−3.01
R-squared	0.037		0.039		0.040	
1996 to 2003, large MSAs, non-manufacturing workers						
Intercept	0.616	372.9	0.603	350.7	0.605	349.7
Displaced	−0.058	−15.9	−0.059	−16.1	−0.072	−13.3
Changed jobs, not displaced	0.049	47.5	0.050	48.8	0.043	28.2
Age in 1992 (years)	−0.014	−307.3	−0.014	−306.8	−0.014	−306.6
Person fixed effect	0.014	10.7	0.015	11.8	0.016	11.9
MSA employment change (per 100 percent change)			0.070	26.0	0.062	21.2

Table 4A.5   (Continued)

	Model 1		Model 2		Model 3	
	Coefficient	t-Value	Coefficient	t-Value	Coefficient	t-Value
Displaced*employment change					0.077	3.36
Job change*employment change					0.046	6.04
R-squared	0.039		0.039		0.039	
1996 to 2003, large MSAs, manufacturing workers						
Intercept	0.441	165.5	0.447	162.0	0.446	160.8
Displaced	0.223	57.0	0.222	56.8	0.345	50.6
Changed jobs, not displaced	−0.028	−15.0	−0.028	−15.1	−0.023	−7.83
Age in 1992 (years)	−0.011	−156.4	−0.011	−156.5	−0.011	−156.7
Person fixed effect	0.217	96.7	0.217	96.6	0.216	96.4
MSA employment change (per 100 percent change)			−0.040	−9.01	−0.026	−5.46
Displaced*employment change					−0.886	−22.0
Job change*employment change					−0.032	−2.19
R-squared	0.042		0.042		0.042	

Source: Authors' tabulations using microdata from U.S. Bureau of the Census (1992–2003).
Note: Control variables used in all three models are the worker's age in years as of the beginning of 1992 and the worker's person fixed effect calculated over the period of 1992 to 2003. Models 2 and 3 include a control variable for the percentage change in employment at the worker's MSA. Model 3 includes interaction variables for MSA employment change with dummies representing whether a worker was displaced or changed jobs without being displaced, from the start year to the employer in the end year. Model 3 includes an additional variable for change in the worker's tenure from the start year to the end year.

Chapter 5 | Good Jobs and Firm Dynamics

"A GIANT SUCKING SOUND" was the way Ross Perot described the effect of globalization on middle-income American jobs during the 1982 presidential election. The alleged vanishing of well-paid jobs has been a theme of newspaper and magazine articles ever since. These concerns make sense. Although the forces of technological change, globalization, and deregulation may lead to greater productivtity, this is hardly reassuring to workers who face the loss of current jobs and suffer uncertainty about the earnings in their future jobs.

The previous chapters have identified the importance of good jobs—and the economic costs borne by workers who lose good jobs and cannot replace them, especially in smaller metro areas with much restructuring and less growth. But it is also important to understand how good jobs can be regenerated. What has happened to the number and type of jobs within each industry through boom and bust? What is the role of new and exiting employers in determining the number of jobs? Have the employers offering good jobs been replaced by employers offering worse jobs than before? And what do these changes mean for job stability—the retention of workers in existing jobs? In sum, what is the role of employer dynamics and job volatility?

There is strong evidence that many employers make a business decision to pay a wage premium: in earnings per worker, output per worker, and worker mix across businesses within narrowly defined industries, there are substantial and persistent differences that remain even after controlling for the observable characteristics of workers and firms. There is also good evidence that employer dynamics play an important role in determining the mix of good jobs—new businesses exhibit even greater heterogeneity in earnings and productivity than do mature businesses—and that they adjust their worker mix in a manner consistent with learning over time and with market selection based on that learning. As firms age, businesses that have made "errors" with their worker mix (and on other dimensions) either exit or adjust their worker skill mix in the direction of the profiles of mature businesses (Haltiwanger, Lane, and Spletzer 2007). And as noted in chapter 2, there are distinct patterns of pay by industry and firm size categories.

The magnitude of the relationship between job volatility and the turbulence associated with employer dynamics is hard to overstate: in any given quarter, about one in four job matches either begins or ends, one in thirteen jobs is created or destroyed, and one in twenty establishments closes or is born (Brown, Haltiwanger, and Lane 2006). Forty percent of new businesses die within three years of their birth, and more than half of all jobs destroyed in any three-year period are due to the death of establishments (Spletzer 2000). Anderson and Meyer (1994) and Simon Burgess, Julia Lane, and Kevin McKinney (2009) estimate that the quarterly worker reallocation rate exceeds 40 percent.[1] John Abowd and Lars Vilhuber (2010), in updated research, found that the average worker reallocation rate is 46.4 percent; the average job reallocation rate is 12.6 percent; and the excess reallocation rate (churning), or the difference between the two, is 33.8 percent. In other words, there is neither a "fixed" number of good jobs in the United States nor any guarantee that a worker, once in a good job, will retain it.[2]

Not only is that turbulence a fact of life, but it has important positive effects on economic growth. By some estimates, firm entry and exit were responsible for more than one-quarter of the increase in aggregate productivity between 1977 and 1987 and more than half of U.S. postwar productivity growth (Foster, Haltiwanger, and Krizan 2001, 2006; Gabler and Licandro 2006). The importance of allowing workers to reallocate across firms is clear from some recent research that suggests that the industry index of labor productivity in the average U.S. manufacturing industry is 50 percent higher than it would be if employment shares were randomly allocated within industries; the same differential, however, is only twenty to thirty log points in western Europe, and close to zero in the very inflexible economies of central and eastern Europe at the beginning of their transition to a market economy (Bartelsman, Haltiwanger, and Scarpetta 2009). Similar work using matched employer-employee data shows that changes in the allocation of workers to firms and changes in the size and number of high-wage firms directly affect the earnings distribution (Burgess, Lane, and McKinney 2009).

So, to the extent that worker productivity and wages are linked, labor market turbulence—both firm entry and exit, as well as labor reallocation across firms—is directly related to the availability of good jobs. In addition, there is evidence that entry and exit are associated with an increased sorting of low-wage workers into low-wage firms and high-wage workers into high-wage firms over time, as good workers help good firms survive while others disappear. This is consistent with the idea that the driving force of economic change is the entry and exit of firms, which can be linked to the selection of new technologies and associated workforces by new firms (Lane 2009).

Of course, the impact of turbulence is not borne equally by all workers. Reallocation is higher in low-wage industries like retail trade and lower in high-wage industries like manufacturing. Turnover is much higher for younger than for older workers, for less-educated workers than the more-educated, and for women than for men. Work by Golan et al. (2007), who tracked the transitions of workers within and across jobs and industries, revealed that about 21 percent of workers switch jobs every year—with about half of these job-switchers (11 percent) staying in the same major industry division and half (10 percent) switching out.

Also, groups of workers who have experienced high degrees of turbulence in prior years are much more likely to experience turbulence in the next period. Golan and his colleagues (2007) show that only a relatively small subset of all workers is shuffled across jobs—both within and across industries—in the economy. Although the levels of reallocation vary across demographic group, the basic pattern of job persistence for most workers does not; this is because worker reallocation is disproportionately accounted for by workers who have already been reshuffled at least once. Notably, worker reallocation *within* industries is disproportionately accounted for by workers who have already been reshuffled *within* industries at least once, and worker reallocation *across* industries is disproportionately accounted for by workers who have already been reshuffled *across* industries. Finally, workers who are employed in industries that provide low returns to industry tenure are much more likely to reallocate both within and across industries.

Of key importance for this chapter is the evidence that the net impact of firm entry and exit is to increase earnings at the bottom end of the distribution more than at the top. Since firm wage premia primarily reflect a lack of market competition, unionization, and/or efficiency wage payments (see chapter 1), wage-setting institutions are clearly important for workers at the bottom end of the skills distribution and represent a way for them to improve their overall earnings (Lane 2009). The fact that firms that successfully generate high wages survive over time, while those that do not disappear, contributes to the ability of some workers to find and retain good jobs.

This chapter begins to answer some of the questions about what has happened to the number and type of jobs within each industry through boom and bust and in each area. It examines employer dynamics to determine whether good jobs have been replaced by worse jobs as high-paying employers shrink and low-paying employers grow, or whether the reverse is true. We do this by establishing a set of facts about employer dynamics in our data. We then examine what has happened to both jobs and good jobs in different industries and urban areas of interest as well as to the jobs that workers held in 1992. We particularly focus on the dynamics for exiting and entering employers in comparison to those employers that survived to 2003.

As noted earlier, our reliance on employer identification numbers (EINs) to measure firm identities limits our ability to distinguish between establishments and firms in some situations and might cause us to overstate firm births and deaths in some cases. Our results on the magnitudes of firm dynamics are not qualitatively different from what has been found with other data sets (such as the BDS data discussed in chapter 3) in which firm identities can be measured more accurately. Nevertheless, when we discuss "employer dynamics" here, our findings should be interpreted to refer broadly to the entry and exit of establishments within firms as well as the entry and exit of firms per se.[3]

THE BASIC FACTS

We opened the chapter by asking what has happened to the number and type of jobs within each industry. Figure 5.1 shows that there are quite stark differences. Even though there was a 15 percent growth rate in jobs overall, and a 12 percent growth rate in good jobs, between 1992 and 2003, these were not uniformly distributed across industries.[4] As we noted in chapter 2, employment in manufacturing (and mining) declined; employment in professional, management, and support services soared—particularly in good jobs.

We also asked about the role of new and exiting employers in determining the number of jobs. Our analysis of the data shows that there was tremendous change: one in four jobs held in 2003 was with an employer that did not exist in 1992; one in five of the jobs lost by 2003 was due to employers exiting. Good employers (employers in the top quintile of em-

Figure 5.1   Employment Change Between 1992 and 2003

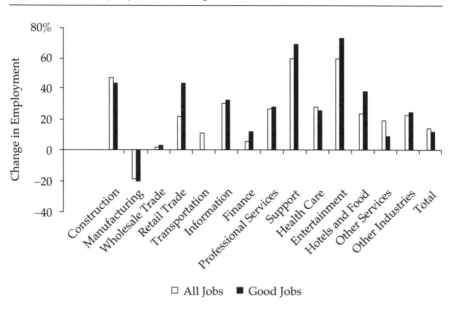

□ All Jobs   ■ Good Jobs

Source: Authors' tabulations using microdata from U.S. Bureau of the Census (1992–2003).

ployer fixed effects) were much more likely to enter and expand jobs. Employers offering poor-quality jobs (in the bottom quintile of the fixed-effects distribution) were much more likely to contract and exit. However, expanding employers did so by adding younger workers—the proportion of their workforce under age thirty-five went from 40 percent in 1992 to 60 percent in 2003. Contracting employers shed these workers roughly proportionately.

These differences vary substantially by industry. Industries with the biggest job losses (more than 25 percent) due to exit were hotels and food, retail trade, real estate, construction, agriculture, and mining; those industries that gained the most (more than 30 percent) from entry were information services, professional and support services, and education. The most stable industries (those with employers whose employment changed by less than 20 percent, either positively or negatively) between 1992 and 2003 were utilities, transportation, management, and health care. There were also substantial differences by region: small MSAs gained much more employment from employer entry than did large MSAs.

Another way of examining the impact of employer entry and exit on jobs is to decompose the net increase in jobs of 15 percent between 1992 and 2003 into three parts: the net job change at continuing employers, the job creation from entering employers, and the job destruction from exiting employers.

Many points are clear as a result of this exercise. One of the first is that the enormous amount of job creation and destruction associated with employers entering and exiting the labor market dwarfs the contribution of continuing employers. The *net* increase in employment was over 2.5 million jobs, but 8.5 million jobs were lost to employers exiting, 10 million jobs were gained by employers entering, and something under 1 million jobs were added on net by employers that survived the entire period.[5]

The potential for change is clear from examining the columns in table 5.1 that document the contribution of employer entry and exit to overall net job change.[6] Every single industry lost jobs through employers exiting between 1992 and 2003. The largest industries, notably manufacturing and health care, contributed the most to job loss through employer exit, but even the education and utilities industries saw a loss of employers. Of course, as table 5.1 also shows, even declining industries (like manufacturing) still added jobs through employer entry. In addition, the major growth industries—like support services, retail trade, and health care—expanded employment primarily through the entry of new employers (although in the case of the retail industry there was a notably large contribution to growth from continuing employers).

The second set of points is that the sources of growth of good jobs are quite different from the sources of all jobs. For example, although manufacturing continued to provide a disproportionately large amount of good jobs, and retail trade a disproportionately small amount of good jobs, there was much faster growth in good jobs in retail trade than in retail trade overall—as chapter 2 suggested. Interestingly, two industries that are important sources of good jobs for low-wage workers—health care and retail trade—not only contribute substantially to net job change but also do so disproportionately from existing employers.

We also asked what employer dynamics meant for the retention of workers in existing jobs—another way of measuring job stability. Of course, one of the challenges of examining the impact of employer entry and exit on workers is that the workforce changes over time. Indeed, of the roughly 17 million workers employed in 1992, only about half were still employed in the same states in 2003—out of a 2003 workforce of more than 20 million.[7] Another way of saying this is that only about 40 percent of the 2003 workforce consisted of workers in the same states who had been in the 1992 workforce. This change was due to the natural aging of the workforce—young workers enter and older workers retire—and geographic mobility. Job stability in an industry can be examined by looking at industry workforce retention rates and comparing across industries. As

Table 5.1 Employment Dynamics, Worker Retention, and Firm Entry and Exit

Industry	Retention Rate	Contribution of Employers to Net Job Change			Number of Employers		
		Exit	Entry	Continuing	Exiting	Entering	Continuing
All jobs							
Agriculture	22.12%	−1.62%	1.52%	0.04%	647	602	597
Mining	31.69	−0.72	0.47	−0.16	228	183	125
Utilities	59.23	−1.08	1.67	−2.80	135	237	289
Construction	47.59	−9.73	15.85	4.25	4,099	6,715	5,101
Manufacturing	42.14	−69.85	51.32	−10.16	13,898	12,652	13,252
Wholesale	42.04	−19.55	18.54	1.55	7,744	7,797	5,555
Retail	36.24	−42.83	49.93	12.38	11,084	12,357	8,535
Transportation	52.09	−12.17	15.14	0.32	3,265	3,675	2,475
Information	63.85	−11.70	19.35	0.17	2,387	3,511	1,344
Finance	51.68	−22.93	23.65	2.22	5,036	5,229	3,570
Real estate	40.60	−5.09	7.22	0.92	2,177	3,007	1,527
Professional	45.38	−19.14	26.31	2.06	5,506	8,555	4,395
Management	85.03	−3.68	9.33	0.06	740	1,793	639
Support	41.46	−23.16	43.61	2.38	5,389	9,136	3,451
Education	41.01	−0.99	1.85	0.12	471	744	296
Health care	55.95	−32.77	43.70	11.87	5,326	8,601	5,908
Entertainment	42.38	−4.48	9.76	1.32	1,281	2,099	1,741
Hotels and food	25.59	−28.35	40.61	0.53	8,906	13,639	6,483
Other services	33.75	−6.80	8.02	1.72	2,835	3,562	2,789

Good jobs

Agriculture	22.65	−0.77	0.45	−0.01	108	84	54
Mining	33.72	−1.42	0.88	−0.34	172	141	90
Utilities	60.77	−2.34	3.59	−6.40	113	210	250
Construction	51.77	−15.01	23.74	7.70	2,643	4,380	3,905
Manufacturing	46.54	−114.09	83.73	−20.88	7,173	6,953	7,164
Wholesale	46.27	−31.81	30.51	2.79	5,329	5,356	4,034
Retail	50.35	−22.09	33.68	12.46	4,111	4,474	3,627
Transportation	56.88	−13.52	14.77	−1.12	1,564	1,767	1,300
Information	66.06	−19.99	34.00	0.06	1,751	2,775	832
Finance	55.84	−44.83	47.53	7.11	4,123	4,419	2,865
Real estate	45.75	−6.17	8.13	1.67	1,113	1,460	691
Professional	48.07	−34.17	47.60	4.32	4,229	6,843	3,797
Management	91.91	−6.83	17.83	0.26	560	1,332	488
Support	62.87	−15.13	29.42	2.13	2,065	3,144	1,136
Education	50.38	−0.77	1.76	0.14	164	274	115
Health care	62.06	−48.37	62.00	18.16	2,422	3,836	2,388
Entertainment	47.56	−2.40	5.42	0.64	314	439	243
Hotels and food	30.61	−8.31	12.09	1.10	909	1,837	644
Other services	37.38	−6.32	6.72	0.69	1,142	1,289	1,076

Source: Authors' tabulations using microdata from U.S. Bureau of the Census (1992–2003).

table 5.1 demonstrates, workforce retention tends to be lowest in the lowest-paid industries: only one in four of the workers who were employed in 2003 in the accommodations and food services industry was in the workforce in 1992, compared with over half of those in health care. Similarly, the retention rate is higher for employers who offer good jobs—more than half of those who were in good jobs in 2003 were in the workforce in 1992.

Of course, since this chapter is about employer dynamics and job volatility, it is of great interest to examine the industry-specific relationship between job retention and employer entry and exit.

A comparison of job retention rates with the contribution of employer entry to net job change in table 5.1 reveals several interesting patterns. Industries like accommodations and food services, retail trade, and administrative and support services, which contribute large amounts to total job growth through employer entry, have lower workforce retention rates than industries that do not (such as information, finance, and health care). This picture is more nuanced for good jobs, however; one of the industries that contributes the greatest amount to job growth through employer entry—health care—has quite high levels of industry workforce retention, while the same is not true for manufacturing. All of this is consistent with the industry patterns of job changing that we saw in chapter 3.

Examining the relationship between employer exit and retention rates paints a similar picture if manufacturing is excluded. The industries that contribute large amounts of job destruction—like hotel and food, retail trade, and support services—also have low rates of job retention. In sum, the churn in employers in industries tends to churn workers. The complementary analysis for good jobs is illuminating. By comparison with all jobs, the contribution of employer exit to net job change is much lower. And the relationship between employer exit and worker retention goes, if anything, in the opposite direction. This seems to suggest that the worker and employer dynamics associated with good jobs are fundamentally different from all jobs—and that even when employers exit the industry, workers are able to find jobs with the entering employers. This is very consistent with what has been suggested in earlier chapters.

The dynamics of the manufacturing sector deserve discussion in their own right, given the importance of manufacturing in the policy debate. The striking feature is the importance of both employer entry and exit in the manufacturing sector. The entry of employers contributed more than one out of two net new jobs, and more than four out of five net new good jobs, between 1992 and 2003. This is also very consistent with the findings of chapter 3, which showed that most displaced manufacturing workers found subsequent new employment in that same broad sector.

For the rest of the chapter, using the lens of differences in metropolitan areas, we focus on these results in more detail, especially on the role of firm entry.

EXAMINING FIRM ENTRY AND DIFFERENCES
ACROSS METROPOLITAN AREAS

Chapter 4 identified important differences in employment outcomes across metropolitan areas in the 1990s and early 2000s. Both employment and earnings grew more rapidly in the largest MSAs in the 1990s, but earnings grew the most for workers with the highest skills. Smaller MSAs were more cyclical and experienced less dramatic polarization but also lower growth in the boom, and they were more dependent on growth in retail trade and health care to replace the lost jobs in manufacturing.

The patterns of employer entry and exit confirm the individual analysis. Our data tabulations show that, in the large metropolitan areas, there were more than 2.4 million additional workers in 2003 relative to the 1992 level—a 16 percent increase in employment. However, only one in three jobs came from employers that existed in both periods. Most of the action came from firms entering and exiting: 7.5 million jobs were lost to employer exit, but 9.2 million jobs were gained from employer entry. By contrast, the much smaller MSAs grew less in both absolute and relative terms: they gained a quarter of a million workers (a 12 percent increase over 1992 levels). But fewer than one in ten jobs in smaller MSAs came from employers that existed in 1992; 1.2 million jobs were created by entering employers, and 986,000 were lost by employers exiting.

An examination of table 5.2 shows that much of the employment growth, particularly in small MSAs, came from the retail and health care sectors. Again, employer entry was by far the most important driver. The net growth in jobs in the retail trade sector was 65,000, but nearly 214,000 jobs were created by entering employers. To put this in perspective, it is worth noting that entering employers in retail trade created almost as many jobs as the entire growth in the economy of small MSAs in this time period. Of course, almost as many jobs were destroyed by exiting employers—about 160,000. These figures are so dramatic because the retail trade industry is one of the most turbulent of all industries. Yet employer dynamics are also very important in the much more stable health care industry. The net increase of just over 93,000 jobs in this sector resulted from many more being created by entering firms (132,000) and almost as many being destroyed by exiting firms (86,000).

Another way of looking at this turbulence is depicted in figure 5.2. In small MSAs, nearly two-thirds of employment in 2003 in retail trade was

Table 5.2 Firm Entry and Firm Exit, 1992 to 2003

The Contribution of Firm Entry and Exit to Net Employment Change

	Large MSAs				Small MSAs			
	Exit	Entry	Continuing	Net Change	Exit	Entry	Continuing	Net Change
Construction	-9.8%	15.9%	4.3%	10.4%	-9.5%	15.7%	3.3%	9.5%
Manufacturing	-63.4	45.7	-8.5	-26.3	-136.4	110.0	-27.1	-53.5
Wholesale	-19.4	18.2	1.5	0.2	-20.6	22.2	2.5	4.1
Retail	-40.4	46.0	13.1	18.7	-68.1	91.0	4.8	27.7
Transportation	-11.9	14.9	0.1	3.1	-15.1	17.5	3.1	5.5
Information	-11.6	19.7	0.1	8.2	-12.9	15.9	1.2	4.2
Finance	-22.9	23.5	2.1	2.6	-22.8	25.6	3.9	6.8
Professional	-19.9	27.3	2.2	9.5	-11.1	16.3	0.7	5.9
Support	-23.4	43.3	2.9	22.8	-20.7	46.8	-2.6	23.5
Health care	-32.4	42.5	11.1	21.2	-36.7	56.0	20.3	39.6
Entertainment	-4.6	10.2	1.3	6.8	-2.7	5.5	1.2	4.1
Hotels and food	-27.2	39.1	0.5	12.4	-40.5	55.8	0.9	16.3
Other services	-6.9	7.9	1.7	2.8	-6.1	8.8	1.4	4.1
Other industries	-12.9	22.0	-1.5	7.6	-16.3	23.1	-4.5	2.2
Total	-306.7	376.0	30.7	100.0	-419.4	510.3	9.1	100.0

Source: Authors' tabulations using microdata from U.S. Bureau of the Census (1992–2003).

Figure 5.2   The Contribution of Firm Entry to 2003 Employment in Key Industries by MSA Size

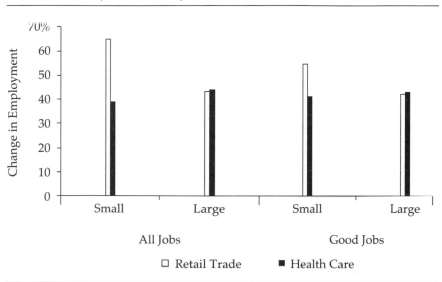

Source: Authors' tabulations using microdata from U.S. Bureau of the Census (1992–2003).

accounted for by employers that did not exist in 1992. Even in the stable health care industry, almost two-fifths of 2003 employment was accounted for by new employers. Even for good jobs, entering firms accounted for over half of jobs in retail trade and about two-fifths of all jobs in health care in small MSAs.

In all, more than half of all employment in 2003 for small MSAs came from new employers, and the values for specific industries ranged from about two in five jobs in health care to almost nine in ten jobs in management of companies and enterprises. Even for the larger MSAs, over half of employment derived from new businesses, and the only industry in which this number fell below two in five was utilities. The picture is only slightly less dramatic for good jobs: in smaller MSAs, more than half of good jobs came from new employers.

Workforce retention also differed by MSA size and industry, ranging in major industries from 4 percent lower for large MSAs in health care to 10 percent higher for large MSAs in construction. Workforce retention was much higher for good jobs: nearly every combination of industry and MSA group had higher retention for good jobs.

In general, the proportion of the 1992 workforce retained was greater for good jobs relative to all jobs. In addition, firm entry contributed more to net job change for small MSAs than for large ones, and for good jobs relative to all jobs. Finally, the positive relationship between a dynamic industry and the ability to retain workers is particularly evident in good jobs and large MSAs, where the sorting and matching of jobs and workers is most pronounced.

At the end of this chapter, and then again in chapter 6, we consider the implications of this work for policy. Many of the policy approaches that we cite as being effective require intensive interactions with firms. Therefore, firms with good jobs have to be identified in order to determine what occupational skills are needed; these can then be provided to lower-wage workers with customized training. Similar identification of such firms is needed for efforts that help place workers with firms that have good jobs.

Although the difficulty of identifying the firms might seem overwhelming at first blush, our earlier work (Andersson, Holzer, and Lane 2005) showed that most hiring of low-wage workers is done by a small fraction of all firms. Indeed, we found that in some industries, such as health care, more than 40 percent of such hiring was done by ten or fewer firms. The policy challenge is to find those firms, build long-term relationships with them, and expand the base by working with entering firms that are just starting to form their human resource policies.

Table 5.3 gives some sense of how many firms might be in play. The total number of firms offering good jobs in health care, for example, in all small MSAs is just under 1,000, and many fewer in each individual MSA. Even in the large MSAs, the total number is not much over 5,000.

CONCLUSION

This chapter has focused on examining the pervasive change and economic turbulence in the labor market in more detail. The results shown here suggest that the important contribution of firm entry to employment offers policymakers a valuable opportunity to affect labor market outcomes. Previous research has shown that each firm, and each industry, is different in some ways. Each firm chooses a different business model with very different levels of workforce quality and worker turnover rates. Some employers compete by following a "low road" of paying low wages and having low prices. Others compete by following a "high road" by attracting, retaining, and motivating good workers at all skill levels. Firms that get their labor strategies wrong are more likely to exit; in the United States the most competitive firms are more likely to be high-road firms than low-road firms.

Table 5.3   Number of "Good" Firms in 2003

	Small		Large	
	Total	Entering	Total	Entering
Construction	815	427	7,470	3,953
Manufacturing	2,404	1,284	11,713	5,669
Wholesale	1,276	853	8,114	4,503
Retail	1,273	812	6,828	3,662
Transportation	471	307	2,596	1,460
Information	434	349	3,173	2,426
Finance	1,251	883	6,033	3,536
Professional	802	542	9,838	6,301
Support	499	378	3,781	2,766
Health care	982	629	5,242	3,207
Entertainment	50	25	632	414
Hotels and food	275	212	2,206	1,625
Other services	275	182	2,090	1,107
Other industries	689	510	4,500	2,991
Total	11,496	7,393	74,216	43,620

Source: Authors' tabulations using microdata from U.S. Bureau of the Census (1992–2003).

There is also ample room here for policy interventions aimed at firms. Since firm pay and turnover behavior are not only heterogeneous but also persistent, and since most hiring of low-wage workers is done by very few firms, one implication of our findings is the possibility of working with the larger new firms that are likely to hire less-skilled workers and provide them with technical assistance for creating better jobs. Perhaps the new human resource behaviors of such firms will expand to other and similar firms. This might involve encouraging state and local governments to combine economic and workforce development approaches, as we discuss later.

Though we explore policy implications more fully in chapter 6, a few implications for differences across countries are worth noting here. For instance, differences in the way that countries treat firm volatility in entry and exit provide some insights. The European Union (EU), which has a very different labor market policy environment than the United States, protects jobs through employment protection legislation (EPL). Yet detailed studies of longitudinal firm-level data in both the EU and the United States suggest that the U.S. approach fosters relatively greater economic growth, while the EU's stronger EPL leads to a misallocation of labor, reduces firm value, and discourages the entry of new firms and the exit of low-productivity firms (Bartelsman, Haltiwanger, and Scarpetta 2009; Foster, Haltiwanger, and Krizan 2001; Poschke forthcoming[a]).

All of this suggests that trying to hold on to existing good jobs in existing firms might not be appropriate. Instead, we need to encourage more flexibility—by, for instance, reducing administrative entry costs to foster new firm entry, exempting exiting firms from firing costs to speed up their exit, and facilitating technology transfer (O'Mahony and van Ark 2003; Poschke, forthcoming[b]; van Ark, O'Mahony, and Timmer 2008). Of course, the short-term and long-term costs borne by displaced workers must be addressed—through a range of policies that provide them with cash assistance for a limited time and help them find new jobs.

Indeed, in the United States efforts to reduce the turnover borne by low-wage workers accept the sorting and matching that occurs here between good workers and good jobs. Some approaches have focused on first providing low-wage workers with the customized training and credentialing for occupations needed by a subset of employers in key industries—such as health care—and then creating direct links between workers and firms. Examples of this "sectoral" approach, which we discuss in more depth in chapter 6, include the Massachusetts Extended Care Career Ladder Initiative (1999 to the present) and Kentucky Career Pathways (2004 to the present).

Another quite promising approach that recognizes the importance of both demand- and supply-side strategies is the Work Advancement and Support Center Demonstration, which focuses on job retention and advancement services aimed at both meeting employer needs and enabling low-wage workers to find better-paying jobs (see Anderson et al. 2006). Other initiatives, such as the "Jobs-Plus" demonstration, have been designed to reduce turnover by better matching workers and firms. The Jobs-Plus initiative combines financial incentives with a mix of other factors—individualized job coaching, help with transportation costs, referrals for other education or training or social services, and sometimes just ongoing informal encouragement and support from the program.

We discuss all of these approaches more fully in chapter 6.

Chapter 6 | Conclusion and Policy Implications

WHAT HAVE WE LEARNED about long-term trends in job quality and volatility in the previous chapters, and what do these findings imply for trends in inequality and insecurity among workers in the United States? What kinds of good jobs are growing in this country, and who is getting them? What happens to workers who lose good jobs, especially if they are less educated? What kinds of firms generate new good jobs? How do these trends play out in metropolitan areas, large and small? And what does all of this mean for policy—especially in the aftermath of the Great Recession and our slow recovery from it?

In the previous chapters, we have explored these issues with a unique and enormous administrative data set from the U.S. Census Bureau, focused on twelve states in the period of 1992 to 2003. Here we review the main findings of these chapters, and then we discuss their implications for economic and labor market policy at the federal, state, and local levels.

A REVIEW OF OUR PREVIOUS FINDINGS

We began in chapter 2 with an analysis of the kinds of firms and jobs that pay relatively high wages, controlling for worker skills, and the kinds of workers who get these jobs. Our primary measure of job quality was the firm fixed effect, which measures how well the firm and job pay any particular workers after controlling for their personal skills. The skills themselves are mostly measured by the person fixed effect, which we showed is quite highly correlated with a worker's educational attainment but also is likely to capture a broader range of skills that are rewarded in the labor market.

We calculated firm and person effects separately for each firm and each worker over the periods of 1992 to 1995, 1996 to 1999, and 2000 to 2003, as well as the entire period. We then measured the extent of employment growth for jobs of different quality levels, where these jobs were located (by industry), and the extent to which the skill levels of workers filling jobs of different quality were themselves changing over time.

Our findings indicate that high-quality jobs are more likely to be found in certain kinds of firms (especially larger ones) and certain industries—including construction, durable manufacturing, and wholesale trade, but also professional services and finance. Less-educated workers are more likely to obtain good jobs in the former industries, and more-educated workers in the latter. Over time, jobs in both the highest and lowest quality categories have grown a bit more rapidly than those in the middle categories of quality, consistent with the notion of growing labor market polarization, but the differences in growth rates across quality categories are relatively small, and substantial growth has occurred in the middle categories as well.

Perhaps more importantly, the nature and locations of good jobs changed over the twelve-year period that we studied, with many fewer good jobs found in manufacturing over time and more in the professional services and finance. Middle-quality jobs were also more likely to be found in construction, health care, public administration, or retail trade. And consistent with these changes, the ability of less-educated workers (or those with lower person effects) to obtain high-quality jobs seemed to diminish somewhat over time. This suggests that *good worker skills and education are increasingly becoming preconditions for obtaining high-quality jobs, with worker quality and job quality increasingly becoming complements to rather than substitutes for one another*. It also implies rising economic inequality, unless the skills of the workers at the bottom to middle of the distribution begin to rise.

In chapter 3, we analyzed rates of job changing, including a measure (admittedly imperfect) of involuntary job displacement. We measured trends across job quality categories over time in rates of job changing and displacement—especially for workers with some minimal level of job seniority (or "tenure"), who tend to sacrifice the wage gains associated with such tenure when they leave or lose jobs, even if they move to better ones. Then we analyzed the extent to which job-leavers and job-losers found jobs of higher or lower quality over time, and how changes in job quality over time were related to earnings changes for these workers. We also estimated these effects separately for each of our three subperiods—1992 to 1995, 1996 to 1999, and 2000 to 2003, which correspond to periods of recovery, boom, and recession in our national labor market—in order to gauge the effects of overall labor market conditions.

The results indicate mildly increasing rates of involuntary job change during the 1990s, even before the recession of 2001 occurred. Workers with at least three years of job tenure who lose jobs involuntarily often tend to suffer some earnings loss. But the *earnings changes associated with job changes and dislocations are strongly correlated with changes in the quality of new jobs obtained by these workers*. Those who manage to get jobs of comparable or better quality than the ones they held originally generally find their earnings improving after a job change, even after losing job tenure, while those whose new jobs are of lower quality often suffer earnings losses over time.

Thus, a diminishing availability of good jobs for less-skilled workers over time implies potentially greater earnings losses associated with job changing, especially involuntary job displacement, for that group. We also found that the earnings changes associated with job changing vary heavily with overall job market conditions. Specifically, earnings changes were most positive in the boom period of the late 1990s for any change in job quality, while they were most negative in the recessionary environment between 2000 and 2003. This suggests that the costs of permenent job loss in the next several years, after the Great Recession and during a period of slow recovery, might be quite severe for many workers.

In chapter 4, we switched our focus to local labor markets, measured at the metropolitan level. For the twelve states in our sample, we identified two groups of metropolitan areas according to population size, where the larger ones had populations of 1 million or more residents. Importantly, we used all of the larger MSAs in our sample but limited the smaller ones to a group that had also lost large quantities of manufacturing jobs in the 1990s and experienced restructuring difficulties over time. We then studied the rates of employment and earnings growth over time in both groups of MSAs, both overall and at different levels of job and worker quality. We also analyzed the correlates of earnings growth across MSAs, both larger and smaller, as well as the effects of job displacement for individual workers within each.

Our findings indicate that average earnings were mostly higher in the larger MSAs than in the smaller ones that we studied, and also that the larger MSAs enjoyed greater employment and earnings growth over time (though there was very substantial variation within each group of MSAs). Job growth was greatest at both the highest and lowest levels of job quality within the larger MSAs—apparently reflecting the greater growth of higher-quality professional service jobs and also low-paying jobs (often filled by immigrants) in these areas. Not surprisingly (given the sample of smaller MSAs that we chose), the loss of manufacturing jobs was greater in the smaller MSAs, and their labor markets were more cyclically sensitive. These areas had more difficulty replacing the high-quality jobs they lost, while relying more heavily on a few traditional sectors (like health care and retail trade) to shore up new job creation in the middle of the quality spectrum.

Across MSAs, earnings growth for workers at all levels of skill tended to be correlated with overall job growth, especially growth at the highest level of job quality. Apparently, the growth of employment and earnings that provides great benefits to young and educated professionals in the largest MSAs also seems to provide benefits to workers at all levels of skill and in all job categories, including the lowest. And earnings losses for individual workers associated with displacement from good jobs—especially in manufacturing—were greatest in the smaller and heavily restructuring metro areas, where these workers had more difficulty replacing their lost jobs with others of comparable quality. Thus, the smaller MSAs that lost large quantities of relatively high-quality manufacturing jobs in the 1990s were more challenging labor market environments for workers who chose to remain there after displacement, and will especially be so for several years after the Great Recession.

In chapter 5, we took a closer look at firms that produce good jobs and the dynamics of job creation at the firm (or establishment) level. First we established the enormous rates of churning that exist in jobs and the extent to which firm entry and exit account for large parts of that. We then analyzed the relationships between good job creation and the births and deaths of firms, as well as the growth and decline of ongoing firms over time. Our results show that large new firms account for large fractions of local net job creation, including good job creation, and especially in smaller MSAs. Though no particular industry accounts for most of this growth, the results suggest that supports for new firms and establishments that create good jobs should be an important part of our local economic development strategies.

Overall, these findings suggest that, beside our need for more jobs overall in the aftermath of the Great Recession, job quality matters importantly for long-term trends over time in worker inequality and insecurity in the United States. In particular:

- Relatively high-quality jobs continue to be generated in the United States, but not in the same sectors as before, and they require higher levels of education and skill than those of more traditional industries in the past.

- The old bifurcation between "good workers" and "good jobs" is thus breaking down, and a sensible policy approach must focus on improving the quality of both.

- Since good jobs increasingly require good skills, and since good jobs are important for the prospects of displaced workers as well as others, improving the skills of the disadvantaged and the displaced should be done with an eye toward improving their access to good jobs.

- Economic strategies for smaller MSAs in regions especially hard hit by economic restructuring should focus on their ability to generate, attract, and retain both good workers and good jobs, especially in new establishments and firms.

IMPLICATIONS FOR POLICY

What do all of these findings imply for economic and labor market policy, at both the federal level and the state and local levels?

Broadly speaking, we often hear arguments for at least two kinds of approaches to helping more workers find and keep good jobs: (1) improve the education and skill levels of Americans so that more of them can fill the kinds of good jobs that are becoming available, or (2) directly create more good jobs for less-skilled workers. And for those workers who will not gain better skills and will suffer the loss of good jobs or persistently low earnings over time, another option might be necessary: (3) expand the set of earnings supplements and supports available to the unemployed and to low earners.

Of course, these three approaches are not mutually exclusive, and we believe strongly that some versions of all three need to be pursued simultaneously. But in each area, what do we know about the costs and relative effectiveness of different approaches? How can we make sure that the different parts of these strategies fit together so that the skill enhancement we pursue will enable workers to fill the good jobs that exist today and that are likely to be created tomorrow? Do the most promising options differ across different parts of the U.S. workforce? What should the federal government do in this regard, and which policies can states and localities implement to help workers in the smaller metro areas that have suffered greatly from economic restructuring over the past few decades? Finally, how might the labor market and relevant policy options be affected by the Great Recession of 2008 and its aftermath—especially in light of the evidence already available of a possibly growing mismatch between the unemployed (especially those suffering long-term joblessness) and the skills sought by employers to fill vacant jobs?

THE FIRST APPROACH: IMPROVE SKILLS TO ENABLE WORKERS TO FILL AVAILABLE GOOD JOBS

What kinds of skills would help American workers get better jobs? And might a better-trained American workforce make it easier for employers to create more such jobs?

At one level, the answer to the latter question is probably "yes." Any increase in the supply of well-educated workers should, all else being equal, cause employers to create more jobs that they can fill, and at a somewhat lower "price" (or wage) than would otherwise be needed to attract them. This has been especially true in recent years, when technology and globalization have increased employer demand for workers with higher education and better cognitive and analytical skills and the supply of workers with these skills has failed to keep pace, thus creating a strong labor market premium for those who have them (Autor and Dorn 2009; Goldin and Katz 2008).

But the quality of the jobs created is not driven exclusively by worker quality, because it reflects other forces (both market and institutional) that also operate somewhat independently of worker skills. So we focus here on jobs that pay well independently of, or perhaps in addition to, the skills embodied directly in workers. The evidence on "high-road" firms mostly suggests that they are more profitable and more successful—and their workers more productive—than those paying low wages (Abowd, McKinney, and Vilhuber 2009), even if the same workers are not necessarily as productive and highly paid on other jobs.[1] In some cases, the organization of the workplace and the nature of the work elicit greater output in these firms than would be observed from the same workers in other settings. In other cases, the workers probably have sector-specific skills that they have not had the chance to use elsewhere, and the human resource policies at these firms often contribute to the development of these skills. Indeed, the various case studies of high-wage firms in Appelbaum, Bernhardt, and Murnane (2003) suggest that all of these factors contribute to better worker performance at high-wage firms.

But if the skills of workers tend to be more highly correlated over time with the wage premium paid by firms, how might we enhance the skills of the workers in ways that will induce employers to generate more high-paying jobs? Both the statistical and case study evidence suggest that employers will invest in more on-the-job training when they are convinced that their workers are "trainable" in terms of strong literacy and numeracy, good communication and problem-solving skills, and helpful noncognitive skills like attitude and work ethic (Appelbaum, Bernhardt, and Murnane 2003; Heckman 2008; Partnership for Twenty-First-Century Skills 2010). As we noted earlier, the well-paid jobs that remain available in health care, construction, and retail trade today require more arithmetic, science, or communication skills than did the good jobs of the past, and this is probably true of good jobs in other sectors as well.

Thus, anything that improves the general academic and applied skills on which employers can build is likely to be helpful in this regard. But investments in key sector-specific skills outside of the workplace might also make employers in these sectors more likely to hire certain workers, especially where various market failures (like imperfect information, imperfect capital markets, or wage rigidities) deter employers from directly investing in training these workers on their own (Lerman, McKernan, and Riegg 2004). Thus, state and local policymakers must decide in which specific sectors and skills to invest, based on local labor market data. Given the general strength of demand in the middle-skill jobs of our economy (Holzer and Lerman 2007), some sectors—like health and elder care, construction (after the recession), and certain parts of manufacturing—are good bets anywhere, while others require more analysis of local or national labor market data on trends in employment growth.[2] And of course, workers need to have a base of good general skills so that they can adapt to inevitable labor market demand shifts over time and be able to find new (good) jobs elsewhere.

So what kinds of policies would lead to workers having more of the relevant skills needed to more easily fill well-paid middle- and high-skill jobs? Any such policies would, of course, start with reforms in the education system in the K through 12 years to strengthen the academic and applied skills of many Americans; they would also make early childhood and prekindergarten programs available to provide children who are beginning school with adequate preparation for learning. Indeed, a very wide research literature is available on these topics, and new policy efforts by states and the federal government abound in this area.[3] For instance, many states are now adopting "common core standards" for English and math in grades K through 12 that significantly increase the desired levels of competency in each area, though how these standards will be administered and assessed, and with what kinds of accountability for states and individuals who fail to achieve them, are questions that remain largely unanswered.

Our discussion here focuses on policies and programs for youth in high school and beyond—as well as for adults who seek additional training—that prepare them more directly for good jobs in the labor market. The adults in this group include displaced workers and others seeking additional skills so that they can find good new jobs after either losing a good job or becoming at risk of doing so. We primarily focus on individuals in the lower to middle part of the income spectrum; these workers have the greatest difficulties finding well-paid jobs and experience the most insecurity when the labor market restructures.

Our review of workforce development programs that have been rigorously evaluated and that generate cost-effective impacts on the earnings of youths and adults (Holzer 2008, 2009) suggests that what works, especially for disadvantaged populations but even more broadly, is some combination of the following:

- Attainment of appropriate secondary and postsecondary credentials;

- Targeting (at least partly) education and employment services to sectors and firms that provide well-paid jobs and engaging the relevant employers during the education and training process;

- Providing a range of support services and supplements to earnings that assist workers as they train for new employment and motivate them to take and keep available jobs, sometimes at relatively low pay.

In many cases, the services of *intermediary* individuals or organizations can pull together the three elements of this approach and ensure that students and workers have access to the schools, employers, and publicly provided supports they need to find and keep good jobs.

Of course, in education and workforce policy, the cliché that "one size does not fit all" is certainly true. What works for youth in terms of generating skills that enable them to fill good jobs may not work for adults. Guiding those who are still in school to the appropriate education and services (at the secondary and postsecondary levels) requires different strategies from what is needed to reconnect those who have already dropped out and disconnected from both school and the labor market (Edelman, Holzer, and Offner 2006). Among adults, the "working poor" often require different assistance than the "hard-to-employ"; the disadvantaged in general require more than those in the middle class, and those at risk of displacement (or already displaced) need a different package of assistance than these other groups. And of course, within each demographic group, some will manage to get the appropriate skills and good jobs while others will not, and policy options must be developed for the latter group as well.

Beyond this insight, some programs and policies have been rigorously evaluated and can be considered *proven* approaches, while others await such evaluation but meanwhile remain *promising* (in terms of outcomes achieved for the treated population). What has proven to work for one group in one location, however, can sometimes be difficult to scale up and replicate elsewhere.[4]

In this chapter, we consider how each of these groups can be best served by policies to improve their education and ultimately their ability to obtain well-paid jobs. Focusing here on efforts to improve workers' skills and access to good jobs outside of the firms that provide these jobs, we also consider efforts to improve skill-building within high-road firms.

Youth: In High School and Out

At a minimum, our education and employment strategy for youth requires that we improve not only their academic and applied (problem-solving and communication) skills but also high school graduation and readiness for postsecondary education, as well as both the general and sector-specific skills that the labor market will reward with their attainment of good jobs.

Though there remains some controversy about how to measure it, the rate of high school graduation in the United States remains roughly 75 percent (Heckman and Lafontaine 2007). High school dropouts subsequently do very poorly—in terms of employment and earnings, as well as other outcomes[5]—and among those who graduate, attendance and completion rates in postsecondary programs are often low, while employment and earnings are limited among those who are not in school. Thus, for young people in general (and especially those from disadvantaged backgrounds), the first priority must be making high school graduation as nearly universal as possible and ensuring that students are prepared for the transition to postsecondary education or the labor market (or some combination of the two).

The evidence on what works at improving high school graduation rates is not very strong, whether in terms of programs for individuals or for entire schools. Some evidence suggests positive effects of individual counseling and intensive case management, with early identification of at-risk students so that they can be referred for academic or other services as soon as possible (Kemple and Rouse 2009). The creation of special interventions for those who are well below grade level in literacy and numeracy skills and the development of "multiple pathways" to graduation for those at risk of dropping out are being explored in some areas, and the broader restructuring of large high schools into smaller learning communities has also shown some promise.[6]

There is one approach that does tend to improve graduation rates and labor market earnings for at-risk youth: high-quality career and technical education (CTE). Unlike traditional "vocational education," newer and better versions of CTE combine more rigorous academic curricula with occupational training and work experience that generate better labor market possibilities and access to good jobs right after high school, but that also preserve postsecondary options for students.

For instance, the Career Academies are specialty CTE programs within comprehensive high schools that provide occupational training and work experience in specific economic sectors—especially those where employment is growing and good jobs are widely available to workers without a bachelor's degree—while students continue to take other courses in the broader academic curriculum. A random-assignment evaluation of students in Career Academies shows strong earnings gains for at-risk youth, especially young males, for as long as eight years after graduation (Kemple 2008). High school dropout rates were also improved for this group within the first few years. And fears that CTE programs "track" lower-income students away from postsecondary education are not well founded in this case: Career Academy students attended college at the same rates as those in the control group.

Among the other versions of high-quality CTE in high schools that promote postsecondary education and access to good jobs is the Tech-Prep program, which combines career education in the last two years of high school with two more years in a community college. Stephanie Cellini (2006) has shown that attending Tech-Prep raises high school graduation and attendance at two-year colleges, though there is some small decline in attendance at four-year schools for participants. And Robert Lerman (2007) has documented the potential of apprenticeship programs to improve educational credentials and access to good jobs for both high school students and community college students. More broadly, programs that tie paid work experience to different kinds of schooling interventions seem to improve the willingness of youth to participate in these efforts and therefore the success of the program (Bloom 2010).

Of course, attempts to improve CTE options should not be made at the expense of other efforts to improve high school students' access to four-year colleges and universities. Haskins, Holzer, and Lerman (2009) note that weak academic preparation tends to limit college attendance among lower- to middle-income students, as does more limited information about and awareness of the requirements for college attendance and completion. They note a range of programs—like Achievement Via Individual Determination (AVID) and the federal government's TRIO programs—that seek to strengthen preparation in high school students, along with several mentoring programs designed to improve information and awareness of college requirements and financial aid possibilities.[7] Dual enrollment programs, an increasingly popular option in many states, also offer high school students a chance to enroll directly in college courses. While many of these have provided greater benefits to date to upper-income students and schools, some impressive efforts have also reached more disadvantaged populations in a number of areas.

What about students who have already dropped out of school and are disconnected from the labor market? Programs that stress paid service employment plus schooling, such as YouthBuild and the Youth Service and Conservation Corps, have generated positive outcomes and some short-term impacts in rigorous evaluation, respectively.[8] The skills that youth receive related to housing and construction in YouthBuild might well improve their ability to gain good jobs in that sector. The federal Job Corps program—which provides job training and other services in a residential setting—also generates improvements in earnings for dropouts, though its positive effects tend to fade over time.[9]

Other efforts simply try to reconnect dropouts to secondary or postsecondary schools. The most successful such effort to date in generating general equivalence degrees (GEDs) or high school diplomas for this population has been the National Guard's ChalleNGe program, a highly structured residential effort that uses a military model to impose discipline and focus on students (Millenky, Bloom, and Dillon 2010). Also promising are the Gateways programs, which began in Portland, Oregon, and have now spread to other parts of the country; Gateways seeks to get dropouts a high school degree and quickly transition them into community college.

Finally, it seems important to create not only isolated programs but also more *systemic* efforts to improve youth education and access to employers and good jobs, especially in poor neighborhoods, where outcomes for youth tend to lag badly behind the national average. The Youth Opportunities (YO) grants to thirty-six low-income communities in 2000 generated positive impacts on both educational and employment outcomes for young residents through partnerships between schools, employers, and other local institutions.[10] On a larger scale, the Philadelphia Youth Network and the San Francisco Youth Council have coordinated programs and created a comprehensive range of interventions for youth in two of our largest cities.

Though many questions remain about the cost-effectiveness of these different interventions, we have at least some clear evidence on what works to improve the skills of disadvantaged youth and ultimately their access to good jobs.

Community (or Proprietary) College and Youth

A great deal of attention is now being paid to community college as a mechanism for providing postsecondary credentials and access to good jobs for a wide range of youth (as well as adults). But it is also well known that community college dropout rates are extremely high: over half of all students fail to achieve any kind of credential within six years of enrolling (Bailey, Leinbach, and Jenkins 2005). Many states have therefore launched efforts to reform their curricula and to improve a range of supports for students at their community colleges to improve completion rates. Several major foundations, such as Mott, Gates, and Lumina, have funded such efforts on a national scale (Holzer and Nightingale 2009).[11]

But rigorous evidence on what works in this regard remains fairly thin, since most of these projects have not yet been carefully evaluated. So far, MDRC's evaluation of the Opening Doors programs at community colleges in New York, Louisiana, Ohio, and California provides the clearest evidence to date on what works in community colleges for disadvantaged students. Taken together, the evidence shows that performance-based financial aid, the creation of "learning communities" of students who take their classes together, and certain mandatory support services can all improve academic performance and retention at community colleges.

Financial aid seems to matter enormously to low-income students at community colleges, and Pell grants have recently been made much more generous by the Obama administration. Yet the evidence on whether Pell grants generate higher educational attainment has been mixed (Turner 2007), with somewhat stronger evidence so far for greater academic success among adults than among youth. Susan Dynarski (2007) has argued persuasively that the complexity of financial aid forms and requirements might undercut their effectiveness, and she has recommended some simplifications to remedy these problems (Dynarski and Scott-Clayton 2006).

It is also well known that weak academic preparation tends to undercut the performance of disadvantaged students in this setting. Many students get stuck in remedial (or "developmental") classes from which they frequently drop out before advancing to for-credit training. Some advocates therefore stress the need to provide "bridge" programs for students before they arrive and to better integrate developmental and occupational education at community colleges from the beginning of the period of study, including efforts to improve general academic skills as well as the more specific occupational skills needed for good jobs. The best-known effort to do so to date has been the Integrated Basic Education and Sectoral Training (I-BEST) program in the state of Washington. The evidence so far suggests positive outcomes in terms of credit attainment (Jenkins, Zeidenberg, and Kienzl 2009), though more rigorous evaluation is in order.

Although all of these efforts look very promising, there remains a need to better connect students at community colleges with real employers and good jobs in the labor market. As noted earlier, the payoffs associated with community college certificates and degrees vary enormously across fields of study. In many cases, students seem unaware of which labor market credentials offer high payoffs or how to find the well-paid jobs associated with the credentials they obtain. And many analysts argue that community colleges have little incentive to build instructional capacity in the high-return areas of study, where equipment or instructional costs are often higher than in other fields of study but reimbursements from the states per student are not.

The importance of information about and linkages to good jobs in the labor market is apparent in James Rosenbaum's (2006) recent work on proprietary occupational colleges. He argues that these institutions are often more successful than community colleges in counseling students about good job opportunities in their areas of study and then helping students obtain these jobs.

These arguments imply the need to integrate community colleges more fully into local workforce development systems, where data on relative labor market rewards and good jobs are more available. Counselors at community colleges should be better able to advise students on the more lucrative fields of study (within their ability ranges) and better-paying jobs in the local area. Better administrative data need to be made available on labor market opportunities and good jobs in local areas, and career counseling should be provided through links to local workforce development systems. In addition, states need to reform their methods of reimbursement to local colleges so that colleges have stronger incentives to invest in areas of study where instructional capacity may be more expensive for them (as in nursing, for example) but where well-paid jobs will more often be available to graduates.

Adults: The Disadvantaged, the Displaced, and the "Lifelong Learners"

Community colleges have become a primary source of occupational training for available good jobs, not only for youth coming out of high school but also for adults returning to school either part-time or full-time to obtain new academic credentials that will strengthen their ability to get a good job. Some of these adults are low-income workers who want to upgrade their skills; some are displaced workers who have lost good jobs and now need new credentials to pursue other jobs; and some are simply returning for a chance to improve their skills and access to available good jobs, whether in their current sector of employment or elsewhere.

A variety of new instructional innovations are being developed around the country to make it easier for adults to access community college education for workforce development. These include modular courses, various kinds of online instruction, and "stackable credentials" (Holzer and Nightingale 2009). More evidence is needed on the extent to which these innovations make it easier for adults to complete their courses of study and get good jobs in the labor market afterwards.

But what courses of study generate payoffs for these workers? Louis Jacobson, Robert Lalonde, and Daniel Sullivan (2003) have shown that community college training for displaced workers can have high payoffs in certain high-demand fields (such as health care) or technical areas. For the disadvantaged, some of the most successful training efforts are *sectoral* in nature—the training and associated work experience are clearly targeted to specific economic sectors that provide well-paid jobs (Maguire et al. 2009). Similarly, *career pathway* programs have been developed in many states that provide combinations of coursework and on-the-job experience in specific high-growth and well-paid occupations or sectors for workers who begin with limited basic skills and credentials (Alssid 2002; Holzer and Martinson 2008). All of these approaches target good jobs for those who lack a four-year college degree in particular occupations and sectors of the economy and try to provide them with the skills needed to obtain these jobs.

Of course, job placement assistance and other services from trained labor market *intermediaries*—either in not-for-profit agencies that focus on particular industries or demographic groups (like the Paraprofessional Health Institute or the Center for Employment Opportunity in New York) or in for-profit temporary help agencies (Andersson et al. 2009)—can help ensure that workers obtain well-paid jobs in the appropriate sectors when they finish training by locating employers with such jobs and helping make the case for their clients.[12] Intermediaries also can provide important support services during and after the training period, including post-employment services to improve job retention and even means of transportation to better jobs. They can also help trainees find good jobs, regardless of where they are located, by following data on employment opportunities anywhere in their metropolitan area and perhaps even beyond it.

Getting There: Enhancing Skills for Good Jobs After the Great Recession

So far we have discussed a range of programs—some promising, others proven through rigorous evaluation—that help workers at different ages, in different circumstances, and of different skill levels obtain new educational credentials and ultimately good jobs. How can we replicate the successful programs and bring them to scale so that many more workers benefit from them? And how can we develop even more knowledge about what works in this area and for whom?

A number of policy vehicles are available for enhancing state and local efforts to improve worker skills and access to good jobs. Through the federal Workforce Investment Act (WIA), the U.S. Department of Labor provides funding to state and local workforce investment boards (WIBs) for job training and other employment services for youth, adults, and displaced workers (Holzer 2008). Improving the link between worker skills and the job needs of local employers is an explicit goal of these programs. Evaluation efforts show that these efforts are modestly effective, with small positive impacts on participant earnings achieved at relatively low cost.[13]

But WIA is poorly funded, with federal support having declined by as much as 90 percent over the past three decades; moreover, its services are frequently fragmented across institutions (for example, community colleges provide training in some areas, while "one-stop" offices provide employment services elsewhere) as well as across geographic boundaries (for example, central-city versus suburban locations). Incentives for local program operators to improve performance are also weakened by a set of performance measures that encourage "cream-skimming" and other forms of gaming (Barnow and Smith 2004).

Other efforts work directly through the U.S. Department of Education and in local school systems. The Obama administration's new American Graduation Initiative (AGI) will provide new but very limited funds to community college systems for innovative efforts that improve completion rates and ultimately labor market success for disadvantaged students. Pell grants have also been made much more generous, paid for by reforms in the programs that fund student loans to all colleges and universities.[14] And the federal Perkins Act provides modest assistance to state and local CTE programs, including Career Academies and Tech-Prep.

So how can we encourage more skill-building for good jobs within these policy vehicles? Wherever possible, these programs should encourage states and localities to use data to identify local labor market opportunities in high-growing sectors with good jobs for workers who do not have a four-year college degree. States and localities should develop a range of sectoral programs and career pathways for potential students of different ages, backgrounds, and circumstances, and they should work with skill providers, employers, and other intermediaries to get as many students as possible trained for these good jobs. Local college systems must also provide students with better information about such opportunities and better access to job placement services, both nearby (within the metro area) and beyond, and states must reform these colleges' incentives to provide the training. A range of support services must also be developed to assist students while they pursue better training and jobs.

If anything, the need to ensure that the skills that we build among workers are relevant for the good jobs we are creating seems to be growing more urgent. Even before we entered the Great Recession, the fraction of the unemployed who had been out of work for six months or longer—the long-term unemployed—had been rising for some time. And the ratio of unemployed workers to vacant jobs had been rising as well (Elsby, Hobijn, and Sahin 2010). Both phenomena have become even more prevalent with the severe downturn of the past few years. While most of today's unemployment remains cyclical, there may be a greater mismatch between the skills of workers and those sought by employers than in the past, especially in well-paid jobs, and this mismatch may be related to rapid structural changes at workplaces owing to globalization and the introduction of new technologies.

In this environment, our education and employment policies must generate better matches between workers and well-paid jobs. Increased funding for WIA and Perkins would improve the capacity of these programs to generate positive impacts on skills acquisition tied to available good jobs. But increased formula funds within these programs cannot be justified without better measures of performance (in the case of WIA) and better connections to strong programs like Career Academies, Tech-Prep, and apprenticeships (in the case of Perkins).[15]

The proposed competitive grants within WIA ("innovation funds") and AGI can play an important role in giving WIBs and community colleges in metropolitan areas and states incentives to generate comprehensive strategies for improving worker skills and linking them to opportunities for good jobs. The SECTORS Act, recently passed by the U.S. House of Representatives, also would provide competitive grants to training efforts aimed at sectors that provide good jobs. Active partnerships between local educational systems, workforce systems, and employers should be encouraged. The federal government should provide technical assistance to the key intermediaries at these levels and help them develop better data to serve these purposes.[16] Rigorous evaluation should accompany the provision of grants wherever possible. And where performance measures indicate that sustained long-term improvements in outcomes have been generated, such grants should be renewable so as to sustain system building.

All of these steps would help generate education and workforce systems at the metropolitan and state levels that create better-trained workers who are more appropriately equipped to fill the many well-paid jobs that will be created as we emerge (albeit slowly) from the Great Recession.

THE SECOND APPROACH: CREATING MORE GOOD JOBS

Turning away now from the issue of enhancing worker skills to fill available good jobs, how can public policy encourage the creation of more such jobs—especially for workers who lack postsecondary credentials?[17] Can and should we encourage more firms to take the "high road," with compensation policies that generate and reward more productive employees?

The easiest way for the federal and state governments to improve job quality is simply to mandate higher wages and/or benefits. For instance, raising the statutory minimum wage (assuming enforcement) by definition raises the earnings from such jobs relative to skill requirements. And mandating the provision of health, pension, or other benefits similarly improves job quality along these dimensions.

Mandates Versus Inducements and Assistance (or Sticks Versus Carrots)

Of course, economists have long argued that mandating wage increases without matching productivity improvements might reduce employment levels for the affected workers and that mandating benefits might reduce wages or employment levels in these jobs.[18] Employers that choose to take the "high road" on compensation often do so because they believe that it enhances productivity and competitiveness—even though such a choice probably reduces their demand for employees whom they regard as having low skills and productive potential. But employers that are forced to take this road might well reduce employment by even more, especially among low-skill workers or over the long term, as they develop and adopt more technologies to replace workers or outsource more work overseas.

What does the empirical evidence show in this regard? The most recent summaries of the research on the effects of minimum wages on employment (see, for example, Neumark and Wascher 2009) suggest modest negative impacts of the minimum wage on employment: employment may be reduced about one percentage point among youth or unskilled adults for every 10 percent increase in the minimum. Other studies (for example, Card and Krueger 1995) have found less evidence of employment loss, though this research is by now a bit dated. Studies of mandated benefits generally find evidence of small declines in earnings and/or employment in many cases (see, for example, Houseman 1998).

On net, we believe that moderate increases in the minimum wage over time generate very modest employment losses; thus, we support periodic increases in the statutory federal minimum wage to keep it from falling well below its historical average (relative to median wages in the economy). Modest mandates on contributions to health benefits or parental leave likewise generate little employment loss and might be worth doing as well.

On the other hand, to the extent that markets for labor (as well as capital and products) have become more competitive, demand might be more "elastic" (responsive to changes in the price) than in earlier periods. Thus, we would be reluctant to embrace proposals that set statutory minimum wages at their historic peaks (such as 50 percent of median wages), especially if these are then indexed to inflation or median wages.[19] Indeed, indexing might well generate long-term employment losses well beyond what we have observed in the literature to date, since employers would have more incentive to economize on labor costs if these costs did not erode with inflation over time.

What about enabling more workers to join trade unions and bargain collectively? The economics literature leaves little doubt that unions have raised the earnings of less-educated workers and that their disappearance in the private sector over the past fifty years has contributed to declining earnings of less-educated workers and growing inequality in the labor market (Freeman 2007b). We also believe that, all else being equal, employer opposition (both legal and illegal) has made it more difficult for workers to choose to bargain collectively.

Accordingly, we support efforts to make it easier for workers to join unions, such as the Employee Free Choice Act (EFCA). On the other hand, we also believe that the growing competitiveness of input and product markets that we mentioned earlier limits the ability of unions to raise compensation, absent offsetting productivity growth, without reducing employment. Indeed, Hirsch (2008) argues that competitive pressures have probably contributed to declining union representation over time, and we tend to agree.

Funding and Assistance for the Creation of Good Jobs

Can federal and state governments use "carrots" to improve job quality rather than "sticks"? And how might such policies relate to the other economic development strategies targeting the demand side of the labor market that are often used by state and local governments to increase job availability in economically depressed areas?

One set of federal policies and programs might explicitly try to encourage the formation of good jobs for less-educated workers, wherever they appear geographically. Federal grants and technical assistance from the U.S. Commerce and Labor Departments could be used to reward employers who provide good wages and benefits or upward promotion paths for frontline incumbent employees who have lower levels of education and who start at lower wages. Our research reported in chapter 5 suggests that these policies might be particularly potent if they target *large new employers*, which often provide important numbers of good jobs and whose human resource policies may be open to influence.

Indeed, during the early years of the Clinton administration, Secretary of Labor Robert Reich proposed a set of subsidies and taxes for high-road employers. But he was roundly (and correctly) criticized for proposing that we tax firms with high rates of layoffs—such layoffs are an important adjustment mechanism for the U.S. labor market.[20]

Other versions of this idea can be found in various federal and state programs, and these might be built upon and expanded. One such effort is the federal Manufacturing Extension Program, which provides federal assistance to individual firms within the high-wage manufacturing sector to improve productivity. Of course, even if effective, there is no guarantee that such higher productivity would be attained through increased (or even maintained) employment of less-educated workers, whom these firms might replace with more capital and better technology.

Alternatively, there are many state programs that provide grants or tax credits for *incumbent worker training* (Hollenbeck 2008), which does more to ensure that the gains of higher productivity are broadly shared with frontline employees. The evidence cited by Kevin Hollenbeck, though not very rigorous, supports the notion that these expenditures by states are cost-effective and might be built into broader programs of skill upgrading and support for high-road firms.[21] "Customized" training for workers in particular firms has also been supported in many states, though such programs are harder to scale up; they also raise questions about whether the firms in question are "free-riding" by gaining very specifically trained workers for their own benefit at taxpayer expense.

Another approach is to require a broader range of government contractors to pay higher wages or to provide good jobs to their workers, since they are benefiting from contracts that are often quite lucrative. Requirements that contractors pay "prevailing wages," which appear in the federal Davis-Bacon Act for construction workers and in the McNamara O'Hara Service Contracts Act for service workers, are one version of this approach. Similar laws at the local level require the payment of "living wages" to local government contractors or to any firms receiving financial assistance from the local government (Neumark and Adams 2005). Whether prevailing or living wage laws are mandates that lead to restrictions in employment opportunities has been debated by economists, with mixed results (Azari-Rad and Philips 2003; Holzer 2009).

Alternatively, state and local governments sometimes require contractors to include "community benefit agreements" in their development plans, which are usually provisions to ensure that such lucrative contracts provide at least some benefits to disadvantaged populations in the local community—often through the provision of well-paid jobs or direct services to workers from the community. "First source" agreements, in which employers agree to recruit lower-income workers through the local job training system, are another example (Bartik 2001). The flexibility in how these benefits are provided and their link to very desirable contracts for firms make them somewhat less likely to reduce employment or impose any other kinds of major inefficiencies. Thus, we encourage further application and experimentation with this approach in local contracting; specifically, we would apply this principle to infrastructure and "green job" projects funded across the country with funds from the American Recovery and Reconstruction Act (ARRA) over the next few years.

State and Local Economic Development

State and local economic development programs and policies usually differ from the programs and policies we have been describing here. The goal of most such economic development programs is to stimulate the creation of more jobs—often in depressed metropolitan areas or in areas that have experienced painful restructuring and often with a focus on growing sectors with strong demand for highly educated workers. New proposals in this area are particularly intended to help medium-sized metropolitan areas that have lost large quantities of manufacturing jobs (see chapter 4).

For instance, various papers in McGahey and Vey (2008) argue that state and local governments, with assistance from the federal government, should undertake a range of efforts to encourage technological innovation in local firms (through better access to capital markets, assistance with technology transfer, education in entrepreneurship, and so on), which presumably will lead to employment growth, especially in well-paid jobs, in competitive sectors of the national or global economy. These authors usually want to ensure that the "human capital" needs of such sectors are met through a range of policies that align education and training with the needs of growing "sectors" or industry "clusters," similar to what we discussed in the previous section. The Center On Wisconsin Strategy (COWS) is one prominent example of a state effort to encourage high-road economic development combined with appropriate job training through the Wisconsin Regional Training Partnership (WRTP).[22]

These analysts also recognize the importance of attracting to these regions, and retaining, highly educated young people from outside—consistent with our finding in chapter 4 (and in the research literature by Edward Glaeser and others) that all workers in metropolitan labor markets seem to benefit from the presence and growth of earnings and employment for highly educated workers. This research points to the need to provide the urban amenities valued by these populations and to invest in neighborhood stabilization efforts, and it also emphasizes the importance of providing local and regional infrastructure to enhance the competitiveness of local economies. Indeed, providing assistance to new structures of "regional governance," such as metropolitan planning organizations (MPOs), is often considered critical to the effort to attract well-educated workers.[23]

The economist Timothy Bartik (2004, 2009) has similarly endorsed a range of state and local economic development policies in which both the demand side (firms and jobs) and the supply side (workers' skills) of the labor market are targeted for assistance. Bartik argues for grants, lower "marginal" taxes (tax supports for new and expanding rather than existing employment), and technical assistance to be carefully targeted to firms and sectors of the local economy that "export" goods and services to other states and countries; that might see their productivity enhanced through such assistance; that make very marginal location decisions; or that serve underutilized forms of labor (such as disadvantaged populations) or occupy underutilized land (such as urban brownfields). His emphasis on policies that help start up, attract, and retain businesses that meet these criteria is broadly consistent with our results reported in chapter 5—large numbers of jobs, especially good jobs, are found in new and growing firms.

It is important to note that all of these authors reject the more traditional forms of economic development in which states compete for a small number of large employers by engaging in bidding wars to lower taxes or subsidize operations for these firms. Such activities generate enormous financial windfalls for recipient companies and generate zero-sum games in which one state's gain is another's loss. Instead, these authors argue for forms of assistance that will provide net value-added to the overall economy, with new skills generated for well-paid jobs that otherwise would not exist or would not be available to underserved areas and groups. Similarly, most authors reject "enterprise zones," in which local businesses get large subsidies or tax breaks for locating in a depressed area with no obvious benefits provided to the local communities.[24]

Despite their appeal, we have a number of concerns about these suggestions for state and local development. For starters, the rigorous evidence on what is cost-effective remains quite thin. Indeed, even what constitutes "rigorous evidence" in this context is somewhat unclear, since random-assignment techniques are not appropriate to any regional effort in which no one can be excluded from the services provided and therefore no one constitutes a real "control group." But putting aside issues of measurement, it is clear that the potential for large windfalls to firms or groups that do not change their behaviors in a meaningful way is quite large.

Furthermore, most of these proposals call for careful targeting of development resources to specific local sectors. Doing so invariably involves making judgments about which sectors merit assistance and which do not—a process quite reminiscent of the debates on "industrial policy" in the 1980s. When states and localities around the country all decide that the same sectors—like biotechnology—deserve support, we end up with duplicative and competitive processes that are not unlike the bidding wars on tax breaks that we often see with regard to large employers. And unless we believe that certain key sectors provide large positive technological or economic externalities to the rest of the local economy, none of these sectors will be large enough to generate broadly shared benefits to the region. The arguments for why narrowly defined industries, as opposed to larger populations of highly educated workers, would provide such externalities outside of their own "clusters" are less than apparent.

Perhaps the best way to move forward on these proposals is for the federal government to fund a series of competitive grant programs designed to support statewide or metropolitan-wide growth, with attention paid to skill formation, job formation, and job quality. Rigorous evaluation should be required of all grant recipients so that we develop a greater understanding over time of what seems to work and what does not in this area.

It is also important to note that, as the economy struggles in the aftermath of the Great Recession for the next several years, public-sector inducements to job creation more broadly may be appropriate as temporary countercyclical (rather than secular) policy. Whether these inducements should take the form of additional tax credits for net new job creation (as advocated by Bartik [2010] and others) or targeted public service employment for the disadvantaged (Holzer and Lerman 2009) can be debated, though the need for some such policies may remain for some time to come.

THE THIRD APPROACH: PUBLICLY FUNDED SUPPORTS AND SERVICES

All of the approaches discussed so far in this chapter suggest that we seek to improve the quality of workers' skills (so we can better match them to existing good jobs) and improve the quantities and qualities of the jobs available in heavily restructuring metro areas or in the aggregate.

No matter which of these policies we embrace, however, there can be little doubt that the economic processes of new technology and globalization will cause our labor markets to generate large numbers of low-wage, low-quality jobs for many years to come. Realistically, there may be no way to require or motivate employers to improve the wages or benefits they provide (above whatever floor is provided by federal and state statutory minimum wage levels) without causing jobs to disappear in large numbers.

A sensible set of additional policies, then, would have the public sector provide a range of financial supports and services for workers who accept these jobs. For *disadvantaged* or very unskilled workers, one set of supports is appropriate; another set might be appropriate for *displaced* workers who held a good job but lost it and now cannot replace it with another of comparable quality.

For instance, disadvantaged workers can benefit from tax credits, like the Earned Income Tax Credit (EITC) or the Child Tax Credit (CTC), which are progressive and at least partially or fully refundable for those with no federal tax liabilities. The current federal EITC is very generous for single parents with custody of two or more children and earnings of $15,000 a year or less; the research evidence suggests that the credit raises employment among low-income female heads of household while providing important income support to their families (Scholz 2007). The CTC is somewhat less generous and is less refundable, so its benefits to low-income families are more meager. Both provide very little benefit to some groups, like low-income childless adults (especially noncustodial parents paying child support), whose earnings and labor force participation have declined quite substantially in recent years. A number of proposals to expand the EITC and better integrate it with the CTC have been developed and deserve serious consideration (Edelman et al. 2009; Holt and Maag 2009).

Assistance with child care and transportation is critical for ensuring that low-income populations continue to work (Greenberg 2007; Waller 2005). Beyond that, making sure that health insurance is available to low-income workers and their children is also critical; we hope that the recent enactment of health care reform legislation will provide something close to universal availability of affordable coverage, if not universal coverage per se. In addition, the federal government needs to help states provide a range of other benefits that make it easier for low-income workers to maintain their jobs while providing very important benefits to families with children, such as paid family and sick leave (Waldfogel 2007).

For workers who are displaced from good jobs (rather than being disadvantaged), a different set of supports is appropriate—some temporary and others perhaps more permanent. For instance, trade adjustment assistance (TAA) provides generous temporary income support—above and beyond what is available through unemployment insurance (UI)—as well as job training for workers displaced by imports. Whether the income support induces workers not to look for other work is a reasonable question; another major question is why only those workers who have been displaced by international trade receive such assistance, and not those displaced by other forces, like technology and workplace reorganizations (Baicker and Rehavi 2002).

Although UI is more universally available to those who lose a job involuntarily and not for cause, even here program coverage during nonrecessionary periods has fallen very low. Most displaced employees who worked full-time and accumulated more than minimal job experience will continue to be covered. But coverage is usually exhausted after twenty-six weeks— often before new employment has been found—and replacement rates (relative to previous earnings) tend to fall below 50 percent for those who previously had a well-paid job. UI also is not available in many states for those who do not seek new full-time employment (Simms and Kuehn 2008). Although states and the federal government are reluctant to extend the regular period of coverage beyond twenty-six weeks for fear of giving workers an incentive to refrain from seeking new jobs, extending coverage to those seeking (or even accepting) part-time employment seems reasonable.

Recently, the American Recovery and Reconstruction Act included subsidies to states that were willing to extend coverage to those seeking part-time employment and other groups; enacting these subsidies more broadly would be sensible.[25] And efforts to implement "short-time compensation," as well as partial UI payments, to those who become employed part-time involuntarily should be considered as well.[26]

More broadly, workers need longer-term insurance against the growing risks of displacement and earnings declines from the loss of good jobs. Again, displaced workers must be able to get *affordable health insurance coverage* when they lose jobs in which employers provided such coverage in the past; we hope that the new reform legislation enables most displaced workers to do so, if they choose.

Additionally, *wage insurance* could help cushion the blow to earnings caused by the loss of good jobs, at least for a few years. Most wage insurance schemes propose that involuntarily displaced workers receive publicly funded payments for a percentage (for example, 50 percent) of their earnings loss when they accept new employment for up to two years (see, for example, Kling 2006). Such insurance would provide not only equitable compensation for those hurt by new technology and globalization (while benefits are generated for consumers and more-skilled workers) but also incentives for such workers to more quickly accept newer jobs that are perhaps less appealing than the ones they lost.[27] Currently, TAA provides for such payments, but only to small populations of older workers who lose manufacturing jobs owing to global trade. We suggest a broader use of wage insurance for the larger populations of workers at risk of losing good jobs in a volatile economy.

Two issues naturally arise in any discussion of expanding benefits to disadvantaged or displaced workers. One is the cost of such public benefits in a time of growing fiscal imbalance. Very simply, we do not support mandating the private provision of most such benefits, unless they are modest in magnitude, because such benefits ultimately are paid for at least partly through reduced employment or earnings of the workers themselves (as noted earlier). But if these benefits are publicly funded, there must be some mechanisms in place to generate the tax revenue required to pay for them. Such mechanisms have been put in place in California, New Jersey, and elsewhere, and they could serve as models for federal or state provision more broadly.

A second issue is whether public funds should be used to subsidize private low-paying jobs—such subsidies make it easier for employers to attract and retain workers at low wages and benefits. Indeed, rightly or wrongly, this criticism of Wal-Mart and other lower-wage employers has appeared in a variety of contexts.

In fact, the research evidence shows that some EITC benefits, for example, accrue to employers that lower their wage payments rather than to the workers who directly receive the benefits (Rothstein 2008). On the other hand, the groups that receive the predominant share of benefits are the recipients themselves. And in a world where relatively low wages in many kinds of jobs are unavoidable, we think that the benefits that accrue to these recipients far outweigh the costs of assisting employers who pay even less to their workers.

AS ALWAYS, AN ONGOING NEED FOR MORE RESEARCH

Although a great deal of data have been analyzed and presented here regarding job quality and its trends in America, a good deal more research remains to be done on this issue.

Perhaps the greatest remaining need is for research on job quality and its effects to be updated beyond the year 2003. Since that time, the U.S. labor market has undergone another full cycle: recovering and peaking in 2007 and then entering into the Great Recession of 2008 and beyond. Of course, the boom that ended in 2007 was much less robust than we enjoyed between 1999 to 2000, while the subsequent decline has been far more severe than the one observed between 2001 to 2003. It is likely to take several more years for the labor market to fully recover from the effects of this downturn, and the overall *quantity* of available jobs (and of overall earnings growth) will be a major concern in the interim, as well as the distribution and quality of available jobs.

Many of the patterns of job growth and its effects that we observed between 1992 and 2003 are likely to remain with us over time. For instance, declining employment in manufacturing and rising employment in healthcare have clearly occurred since 2003 and will no doubt continue. But it is also likely that these patterns will be changed to some extent by more recent labor market developments. For instance, the good jobs created in the recovery period of 2003 to 2007 were almost certainly more heavily concentrated in construction and finance than was true earlier, given the subsequent bubbles in the housing and financial markets. But the distribution of good jobs going forward beyond the Great Recession is likely to be somewhat less concentrated in these sectors.

Moreover, if the current economic episode results in a major restructuring of labor markets, the long-term implications for trends in job quality would only become apparent after a number of years. And separately from the Great Recession, ongoing patterns of technological change and globalization will no doubt have important effects on the future distribution of good jobs, perhaps somewhat differently than in the past. Although, as noted earlier, we have some evidence of growing mismatches between unemployed workers and vacant jobs (such as longer durations of unemployment), we do not understand much about how and why this is occurring. And in addition to extending the time period, it would be useful at some point to analyze broader samples of both larger and smaller MSAs in a fuller set of U.S. states than the ones to which we were limited in this work.

Beyond these more recent trends, we need to know a good deal more about other dimensions of job quality besides cash earnings and about the range of skills required to attain these jobs. Among the most important noncash benefits of employment until now has been employer-provided health insurance, which has always been quite positively correlated with observed earnings levels (Hamermesh 1998). Perhaps the recent passage of health care reform legislation will make this particular job-related benefit somewhat less important than before. But if employer provision of this benefit continues to diminish over time, the pattern of its decline—and the implications for the distribution of wages—will need more attention. Trends in other important dimensions of job quality—such as the employer provision of pension benefits in 401(k) plans and paid family or medical leave—remain very important and need further study as well.

Given our apparent finding that skill requirements for good jobs are growing, we need to know a good deal more about the kinds of skills and credentials that are needed, and for which jobs. The economist David Autor, among others, has argued that as a range of analytical and interactive skills become increasingly important in labor markets, routine skills that can be more easily replaced by computerized technology will continue to diminish in importance (Autor and Dorn 2009). Michael Handel's (2006) survey research on worker skills used on jobs and how they are rewarded has also shed important light on this process.

What do all of these trends imply for the kinds of skills needed to do the good jobs of the future, and the credentials that signal their attainment? Even today, the work of Louis Jacobson (Jacobson and Mokher 2009) (using Florida administrative data) and others shows high variation in the rewards to community college certificates and degrees, as well as those of four-year institutions—more technical certification and those in rapidly growing fields (most obviously health care) generate the strongest rewards. More study and elucidation are needed to understand the exact pattern of skills and certifications that get rewarded in good labor market jobs, and how this pattern evolves over time.

Finally, we need to know much more about the cost-effectiveness of the full range of policies aimed at increasing the worker skills needed for good jobs and the availability of the jobs themselves. Of the many education and training policies described here, rigorous evidence on their cost-effectiveness remains limited; exactly what works, and for whom, is still uncertain. This is especially true of the sectoral and career pathway efforts that explicitly try to prepare more-disadvantaged workers for the good jobs that appear to be growing in various local labor markets.

Even less is known about the cost-effectiveness of the economic development policies described here and of public efforts to reward good job creation more broadly. In all of these areas, the need for rigorous research and evaluation to accompany experimentation with policy remains paramount. Furthermore, as administrative data on educational attainment and certification as well as jobs and earnings become more available across many states, our ability to enhance the kinds of research done here on job quality and its relationship to worker skills should certainly grow.

Notes

CHAPTER 1

1. See, for instance, Anderson and Gascon (2007). Louis Uchitelle (2006) also documents the severe economic and psychological costs associated with permanent layoffs from work and how these might feed popular anxiety.
2. Analyses of trends in real wages over time are quite sensitive to how we adjust for inflation. Given that the consumer price index (CPI) tends to overstate inflation, computations of real earnings growth over several decades might understate such growth. See Eckstein and Nagypál (2004) for a balanced discussion of these issues. For evidence on the extent to which productivity growth has mostly benefited those with very high earnings over the past few decades, see Piketty and Saez (2003) and Dew-Becker and Gordon (2005).
3. On this issue, see, for instance, the congressional testimony of Peter Orszag (2007) when he was director of the Congressional Budget Office.
4. Eckstein and Nagypál, 2004.
5. See Brown, Haltiwanger, and Lane (2006) for evidence of strong labor market gains by many workers in a volatile labor market.
6. See Levy and Murnane (2004); Autor, Katz, and Kearney (2006); and Goldin and Katz (2008) for further discussion of these issues.
7. See Levy and Temin (2007) and Card and DiNardo (2006) for discussions that emphasize institutional as well as market determinants of rising inequality.
8. See Krueger and Summers (1987) for industry effects on wages, and Brown, Hamilton, and Medoff (1990) for an analysis of the effects of firm size.
9. See Katz (1986) for a discussion of the research on "efficiency wages," and Appelbaum, Bernhardt, and Murnane (2003) for a broader discussion of how firms choose their compensation levels and practices in a variety of major sectors.
10. See Abowd and Kramarz (1999); Andersson, Holzer, and Lane (2005); and Holzer (1996).

11. See Dobbs and Myers (2004), for instance.
12. See Freeman (2007a) and Blinder (2007).
13. See Goldin and Katz (2008).
14. See Thomas Friedman's (2009) discussion in the *New York Times*, especially the quote from Lawrence Katz.
15. Among men, the drop in employment in durable manufacturing has been sharper.
16. See Freeman (2007b) and Hirsch (2008).
17. See Economic Policy Institute (2008).
18. See Levy and Murnane (2004).
19. Although some of the forces generating greater competition in the product market—like an undervalued Chinese renminbi—may not reflect true underlying competitive forces, they nonetheless have the effect of generating more competitive pressure in that market.
20. See Reich (2007) for a broad description of how product and capital markets have become more competitive over time. Since harnessing economic forces such as new technologies and globalization is somewhat costly for firms, it makes sense that firms are more likely to incur such costs when those forces could reduce employment more among higher-wage than lower-wage employees, thereby making labor demand more elastic.
21. Barry Hirsch (2008) argues that one source of difficulty for unions in the past few decades has been their inability to offset higher wages with rising productivity in more competitive labor markets.
22. For instance, in contrast to the claim that Costco can compete successfully with Wal-Mart despite its more generous compensation packages, Robert Reich (2007) argues that Costco's customers have, on average, much higher incomes than Wal-Mart's customers and that Costco has had more difficulty in the capital markets in the past few years.
23. See Levy and Murnane (2004) and Autor, Katz, and Kearny (2006).
24. See Holzer and Lerman (2007, 2008) for broad descriptions of the kinds of middle-skill jobs that have remained in high demand over the past two decades and will continue to be in high demand over the next decade. See also Council of Economic Advisers (2009) for a report that predicts some recovery in demand for moderately skilled labor in industries such as construction and manufacturing.
25. See Andersson, Holzer, and Lane (2005).
26. Some recent research also suggests that displaced workers can suffer from deteriorating health and rising mortality, while their children endure educational setbacks and long-term earnings losses; see Oreopoulos, Page, and Stevens (2008) and von Wachter (2010).
27. See Jacobson et al. (1993); Kletzer and Fairlie (2003); and Farber (2007).
28. Most educational policy in the United States is determined by state and local

school agencies, while most federal job training dollars (from the Workforce Investment Act) are distributed locally as well by workforce investment boards (WIBs). We discuss these issues in greater detail in chapter 6.

29. See Holzer and Stoll (2007) for evidence of the growth of both employment and residential locations in the suburbs. Growth of employment has been greater in higher-income suburbs, while growth of residences, especially among minorities, has been greater in lower-income suburban areas.

30. For instance, unemployment rates in Michigan had gone over 17 percent as of September 2009. In the city of Detroit, the unemployment rate recently stood at nearly 30 percent.

31. Labor market outcomes are also affected by a wide range of policies in other markets, such as health care reform, financial market regulation, and foreign exchange policy. These important policy areas are beyond the scope of this book.

32. The Current Population Survey (CPS) and the American Community Survey (ACS), as well as the major longitudinal data sources like the National Longitudinal Surveys (NLS) and the Panel Study on Income Dynamics (PSID), generally do not contain any data on employers and their characteristics. Although the CPS and ACS have very large sample sizes, neither is longitudinal; the NLS and PSID are panel data sets, but both are too small in size to study detailed local areas.

33. The LEHD data are used by the Census Bureau to compute the quarterly workforce indicators (QWIs) that appear for local areas as part of the Local Employment Dynamics (LED) program at the Census Bureau. Other longitudinal data sets on firms, such as the Business Dynamics Survey (BDS) and Longitudinal Business Datasets (LBD) (discussed in chapter 3), also provide valuable microdata on firms, though not with the detailed microdata on workers that appear in the LEHD data.

34. As we note later, the large MSAs are a complete set of the largest ones in these states, while the smaller ones are somewhat nonrandomly chosen—though they are of great substantive interest to us and our funders. In chapter 4, we consider some demographic and economic characteristics of smaller MSAs from the same states not included in this sample, and we conclude that those on which we focus are not terribly unrepresentative of the broader group of smaller MSAs.

CHAPTER 2

1. The approach is described in Abowd and Vilhuber (2005).
2. See Abowd, Lengermann, and McKinney (2003).
3. Though Jacob Mincer's (1974) classic work suggests a trade-off between starting wage levels and wage growth for any given firm, Fredrik Andersson and

his colleagues (2005) find that wage levels and wage growth are correlated positively across firms. Daniel Hamermesh (1998) also shows that inequality in benefits and other job attributes (like safety) tends to exacerbate inequality based on wages only.

4. We explored a variety of methods for calculating person and firm effects, as described in the appendix to this chapter. Details are available from the authors. The correlations across the estimates generated by these methods were high—roughly 0.8 to 0.9 across methods and time periods. Estimated patterns across industry and firm size groups for the different firm effects, as well as patterns across demographic groups for the person effects, were quite consistent across estimation methods and generally were consistent with what we have seen in previous literature. This robustness across methods further strengthens our confidence in the validity of our estimation procedures.

5. The methods we use to annualize earnings are exactly the ones used in all previous LEHD work by John Abowd, John Haltiwanger, Julia Lane, and many others. It is described in the appendix to this chapter as well.

6. On the other hand, the lower levels of earnings of those who work part-time (or fewer hours) per time period are accurately reflected in the data. Workers who choose part-time work voluntarily—especially married women with small children—cannot be distinguished from those whose choices are constrained by their lower earnings potential in any year. But the higher earnings capacity of those who work part-time for just a short period of time is captured by their person fixed-effects estimates.

7. By imposing a zero mean on firm effects for each period, we do not allow real wage growth over time to affect job quality measures, but this makes it harder to observe job quality growth. Since we focus on job quality as distinct from worker quality, it is not clear how the mean of an absolute measure of job quality would have trended over time, had we been able to estimate it.

8. Beginning in this section and continuing throughout the book, we describe summary measures of earnings outcomes—especially means and medians—and differences in those measures across categories of firms and workers without explicit references to the standard errors on these estimates. Given the enormous sample sizes used here, most computed standard errors on estimated means are very small. But we have considered them when measuring mean differences in our work. It can therefore be assumed that any differences in summary measures of earnings that we highlight are statistically significant by conventional standards. Discussions of regression coefficients in chapters 3 and 4 do explicitly include t-values based on estimated standard errors.

9. Since we adjust for inflation over time with the consumer price index for urban workers (CPI-U), our adjustments are mildly overstated, and real wage

growth understated. But this bias is constant across all of the job and worker categories we consider and thus does not affect our results.

10.   We have omitted firms with fewer than twenty-five workers from our analysis because employment estimates for firms that small tend to be more unstable and more prone to error in measurement.

11.   The notion that on-the-job training and earnings growth over time should discourage job turnover has been emphasized by Boyan Jovanovic (1979a) and Edward Lazear (1979), among others.

12.   Derek Neal and William Johnson (1996) show that racial gaps in earnings are greatly reduced, though not fully eliminated, when one controls for cognitive achievement as measured by test scores. Jane Waldfogel (1998) shows that the male-female wage gap has mostly disappeared for young women and men but remains for older cohorts and appears to be related to maternity. George Borjas and Lawrence Katz (2005) and Stephen Trejo (1997) show that immigrant-native earnings disparities, especially for Mexican Americans, mostly reflect differences in educational attainment and language ability.

13.   Glenn Loury (2003) has argued that racial stigmas affect incentives among minorities to invest in human capital. Muriel Niederle and Lise Vesterlund (2007) show experimental evidence that women, compared to men, tend to shy away from competitive situations. The persistence of discrimination in hiring has been demonstrated in a series of audit studies comparing matched pairs of whites and blacks (Darity and Mason 1998; Pager 2003), though James Heckman (1998) has cautioned against inferring too much about marketwide discrimination from these studies.

14.   For recent evidence on how the labor market increasingly rewards cognitive and interactive skills, see Levy and Murnane (2004) and Autor and Dorn (2009). The fact that similar skills are rewarded differently in different firms and sectors of the economy has recently been emphasized by Lazear (2009).

15.   The greater concentration of workers at the top and bottom diagonal elements, relative to those in the middle, occurs at least partly because there are no more adjacent categories above and below the former elements, respectively.

16.   Details are available from the authors. The estimated negative effects of being female, minority, or foreign-born, controlling for person effects, were just one percentage point or so in each case, while the coefficient on the person-effects coefficient was roughly .3. Surprisingly, the estimated effects of being black were small but positive, a result that probably reflects the greater tendency of blacks to be employed at large firms (Holzer 1998) and of so many unskilled blacks to be absent from the workforce altogether.

17.   See Holzer (1996) for a broader discussion of how access to different kinds of firms and jobs varies by race-ethnicity and gender. Andersson and his colleagues (2005) also present evidence that high-wage jobs are concentrated

geographically near higher-income residential areas, further limiting access for lower-income and minority groups.

18. As noted earlier, changes in measured job quality are primarily relative in nature, since the means of firm fixed effects are set at zero in each period by our estimation procedure.

19. The trough of that recession occurred in 2002 when measured by payroll employment, and in 2003 when measured by unemployment rates. The latter often continue to rise, even after employment levels at firms have bottomed out, until employment growth is strong enough to absorb new labor force entrants.

20. See Autor, Katz, and Kearney (2006).

21. By definition, no such category exists for those in the top quintile of person effects.

22. See, for instance, Holzer (1996); Handel (2006); and Holzer and Lerman (2007).

23. In other words, pay gaps widen over time within firms between those at fixed percentiles of the person fixed-effects distribution.

24. The empirical basis for these assumptions regarding durations of employment per quarter are presented in Abowd, Lengermann, and McKinney (2003).

25. Computing limitations forced us to use a smaller number of firms in a few cases with the largest data sets.

26. This is done using the "absorb" procedure in SAS, which allows a linear model to "control" for a set of variables without actually including them as regressors with estimated coefficients. Details of this procedure can be found at: http://support.sas.com/documentation/cdl/en/statug/63347/HTML/default/viewer.htm#/documentation/cdl/en/statug/63347/HTML/default/statug_glm_sect009.htm (accessed July 20, 2010).

CHAPTER 3

1. Economists generally believe that workers mostly "pay" for their benefits in the form of lower wages. In this case, a loss of such benefits might not amount to a clear loss of compensation for these workers. But this is not how most workers perceive their coverage. Whether they would be able to buy such insurance at similar premia on their own has indeed been uncertain for most workers—especially in the period preceding federal health care reform.

2. Earnings volatility can reflect reduced wages or hours worked as well as a loss of employment, whether for voluntary or involuntary reasons. And income volatility at the household level can reflect volatility in the earnings of a worker's spouse as well as potential changes in his or her own income.

3. Davis and his coauthors analyze flows of workers into and out of jobs in the

census LBD and BDS data, described in chapter 1, note 33. The declines in both job creation and job destruction and associated drops in flows of workers into new spells of unemployment (Elsby, Hobijn, and Sahin 2010) help account for the rise in the average duration of unemployment spells in the United States, even before the recession began in 2008.

4. Responses to these survey questions do not enable researchers to perfectly distinguish among these sources of leaving or losing employment. For one thing, they are all based on self-reports, which might be subject to error. Employers might induce quits among those whom they want to discharge or lay off, especially in order to avoid having to pay higher unemployment insurance taxes (because of experience-rating) in the latter case. And the quality of those workers who are laid off or discharged might be lower than the quality of those displaced in ways that are not observable in the data (Gibbons and Katz 1991).

5. The 30 percent threshold is used to define "mass layoffs" by the Bureau of Labor Statistics.

6. On the one hand, some of those who leave at this time could be quits or discharges. Some employees might be choosing to leave voluntarily when they expect a downsizing to occur. On the other hand, some workers might be displaced, even if overall employment levels are not declining, if a large group of incumbent employees is replaced by another large group of new hires during a workplace reorganization.

7. For a theoretical basis for this argument, see Jovanovic (1979b). For evidence that job separations diminish with job tenure, see Farber (1999).

8. For a discussion, see, for instance, Ehrenberg and Schwartz (1987).

9. See also Holzer and Lalonde (2000) for evidence on person and firm characteristics that determine job turnover among young workers.

10. If individual worker productivity is not completely observable to the employer at any point in time, then the employer might want to defer some of the worker's compensation until later, to create incentives for the employee to stay with the employer and perform well on the job (see Lazear 1979).

11. Immigrants, especially if they are undocumented, might have lower reservation wages for employment and perhaps are less likely to leave their jobs, but their employers might well invest less in the maintenance of the employment relationship over time. Empirical evidence has shown that black employees are more likely to be discharged and more likely to quit, though the latter is not true after controlling for wage levels (Blau and Kahn 1981; Jackson and Montgomery 1986; Holzer and Lalonde 2000).

12. Because we need to observe the worker's employer one year subsequent to the initial separation in order to identify it, our measures of separation begin in 1992 but end in 2002—one year short of the last year we observe in the data.

13. A few anomalies appear in the data for which we have no explanations. For

instance, a spike in displacements occurs in the first quintile of firms in 1995, driven mostly by durable goods manufacturing in California and Pennsylvania and information industries in California and Pennsylvania.

14. See the arguments on "layoffs and lemons" by Robert Gibbons and Lawrence Katz (1991).

15. This argument probably applies not only to the recession period of the early 2000s but, to some extent, to the entire decade that followed, during which time employment growth remained modest and employers faced little pressure to translate high productivity growth into wage growth. Indeed, median real earnings growth was virtually nonexistent over the entire decade (Mishel, Bernstein, and Shierholz 2009). With data mostly covering just one full business cycle over twelve years, however, it might be difficult to separate out business cycle effects from other forces in effect during this time period.

16. Given the questions about the extent to which we successfully disentangle worker from firm effects in chapter 2, it is possible that firm effects are spuriously correlated with those of the workers whom they hire. Controlling for the level of person effects in these equations at least partially addresses this issue.

CHAPTER 4

1. Specifically, these smaller MSAs had at least 100,000 jobs in 2005, at least 5 percent greater shares of manufacturing employment than the average MSA in 1990, and significant losses in these shares over time.

2. The Ford and MacArthur Foundations, which funded this project, were both interested in labor and economic development issues in metropolitan areas that were undergoing major restructuring, and the sample chosen here matched others used in work funded by MacArthur in particular. See Wial (2008) for a fuller description of these areas, how they were chosen, and the reasons they were chosen.

3. There are thirty-two MSAs that we do not use with populations in the same range (between 200,000 and 1 million in 2000) as those in our sample of smaller ones. Average earnings are very comparable across the two groups, and earnings growth averaged just a bit higher in the excluded areas over the twelve years (at 14.6 versus 12.3 percent). Employment growth was considerably higher in the excluded MSAs (at 27.2 versus 12.4 percent), though at least part of that difference was probably supply-driven by a high concentration of the excluded MSAs in Washington, Idaho, Oregon, California, Colorado, and North Carolina (twenty-five of thirty-two MSAs, compared to seven of eighteen for the sample we used)—states that experienced higher population and economic growth in this period.

4. The large MSAs are Baltimore, Charlotte, Chicago, Denver, Kansas City, Los Angeles, Milwaukee, Philadelphia, Pittsburgh, Portland, Riverside, Sacramento, San Diego, San Francisco, San Jose, St. Louis, and Seattle. The smaller ones are Allentown, Appleton, Asheville, Boulder, Erie, Fort Collins, Greensboro, Hagerstown, Hickory, Lancaster, Modesto, Peoria, Reading, Rockford, Scranton, Wichita, Winston-Salem, and York.

5. All means in these tables and those that follow, as well as the correlations presented later, are employment-weighted across MSAs; as a result, larger MSAs within each group receive proportionately more weight in our calculations.

6. The shares of workers in the bottom quintiles of the person-effects distribution who were women or immigrants in the larger MSAs were, respectively, 0.534 and 0.213 in 1992 and 0.533 and 0.252 in 2003. Comparable shares in the smaller MSAs were 0.640 and 0.061 in 1992 and 0.606 and 0.081 in 2003.

7. We include some data on employment shares of industries and their changes, as well as on growth rates, because small changes in the latter can look quite large when the employment base on which changes are calculated is small. The levels of shares and their changes give a more accurate indication of the relevant magnitudes of employment across industries and how they have changed over time.

8. The online appendix can be found at www.russellsage.org/sites/all/files/holzeretal_onlineappendix.pdf. Quintile shares of total employment often exceed or fall be low 20 percent within specific groups of MSAs, since the quintiles are defined on the basis of cutoffs for the total group of MSAs.

9. See, for instance, the first few chapters of Ehrenberg and Smith (2009).

10. The fact that employment growth in all quintiles of the person-effects distribution is correlated with growth in the same industrial categories partly reflects the fact that employment growth rates across the quintiles are also quite highly correlated with one another.

11. See, for instance, Ottaviano, Paolo, and Peri (2007) and Card (2009). Almost all empirical results on the impacts of immigration on earnings for native-born workers suggest that the least-skilled immigrants are complementary with higher-skill workers and partially substitutable for the lowest-skilled workers, especially those in earlier cohorts of their own immigrant group. Whether the complementarity between native-born workers and immigrants occurs mostly through the workplace (in establishments that require both kinds of workers) or through the product market (with highly paid professionals demanding more low-wage services) is unclear from this work.

12. As in chapter 3, displacement rates cannot be calculated beyond 2002, since our definition requires that workers have not returned to these firms in the subsequent years. Also, displacements for those with at least three years of

job tenure cannot be observed before 1995, since this is the earliest point at which such lengths of tenure can be observed in our data.

13. Displacements occur in the first year of the period, and workers are subsequently observed in the last period. The samples of workers observed here are also limited to those who remained in the same MSA and subsequently became reemployed there after displacement.

14. The percentages of younger and older workers who left the MSA labor force after a displacement in 1996 were 36.9 and 63.1 percent, respectively. We presume that younger workers more frequently migrated to other MSAs (Bound and Holzer 2000), and that older workers more frequently retired.

CHAPTER 5

1. In examining the impact of employer dynamics, it is worth revisiting how job flows are measured. An important concept is net job change at the employer level—between 1992 and 2003, employers exited, entered, created, or destroyed jobs. The measures that we use reflect these concepts. Job creation is defined as the employment gains (including those from firm births) from one point in time to another, and job destruction is defined as the employment losses (including those from firm deaths) between 1992 and 2003. Job reallocation is the sum of job creation and destruction and as such is a summary measure of all job flows. In the text, we often discuss net job change, which is defined as the average of job creation and destruction in the period; by definition, this magnitude is bounded by −2 (for firms that exit) and 2 (for firms that enter).

2. Although there is some recent evidence of a decline in firm and establishment entry and exit rates over time in the United States (Davis et al. 2010), these levels of births and deaths and the associated rates of job market turbulence remain very high by almost any international standard.

3. For a good discussion of this issue, see Benedetto et al. (2007).

4. "Good jobs" are defined in this case as those with employers in the top two quintiles of the firm fixed-effects distribution in 1992.

5. These aggregate figures actually understate the amount of job reallocation during the period, for two reasons. First, many more firms entered and exited during the period, but do not show up in either 1992 or 2003. Second, there was job reallocation across continuing firms, since many continuing firms expanded (creating jobs) while others shrank (destroying jobs).

6. The sum of the three columns is 100 percent—net job change is, by definition, the sum across industries of jobs contributed by entering employers less jobs lost by exiting employers plus net job change from continuing employers.

7. More details on these calculations can be obtained from the authors.

CHAPTER 6

1. In other words, a positive firm fixed effect implies that, on average, the same workers at this particular firm are paid more highly than elsewhere. If the higher wages paid when the firm effect is positive also reflect higher productivity, it implies that their productivity was not as high at other jobs held before or even afterward.

2. Because of the elimination of the housing bubble in the current downturn, and also because of ongoing changes in workplace technologies and globalization, construction and manufacturing employment may not be areas that will see significant job growth anytime soon. Still, most economists expect that employment in both sectors will recover somewhat with the broader economic recovery, with public investments in infrastructure and "green" jobs helping both sectors and exports contributing to some recovery in manufacturing; see the Council of Economic Advisers (2009) report.

3. See Jacob and Ludwig (2009) and Figlio (2009) for reviews of this literature and recommendations for policy.

4. Proven programs are those that have undergone rigorous evaluation based on methods like random-assignment studies or "natural experiments," and those we consider promising programs have shown improvements in participant outcomes over time that are greater in magnitude than those observed for observationally similar populations. Even proven interventions, however, have not always been replicated or taken to scale.

5. See Swanson (2004) and Mishel and Roy (2006) for a debate on how to measure high school graduation and the different results achieved from survey versus administrative data. See also Hill, Holzer, and Chen (2009) for evidence on the extent to which high school dropouts, especially African Americans, have high rates of unwed childbirth and incarceration.

6. For promising efforts aimed at youth with very poor literacy and numeracy, see Youth Development Institute (2009) or Sturgis (2008). For high school reform proposals, see Haskins and Kemple (2009). An overall discussion of youth issues can be found in Heinrich and Holzer (2010).

7. The federal TRIO programs include Upward Bound, Talent Search, and the Educational Opportunity Programs. Haskins and his colleagues (2009) review the evaluation evidence on these programs.

8. A random-assignment evaluation of the Youth Service and Conservation Corps (Jastrzab et al. 1997) showed very positive short-term effects on a range of outcomes in a few sites; a longer-term evaluation of a larger number of sites is now under way. Outcomes for YouthBuild have been analyzed by Mark Cohen and Alex Piquero (2008), using a variety of comparison groups. A random-assignment evaluation of YouthBuild is also now under way.

9. See Schochet, Burghardt, and McConnell (2008) for evidence from a rigorous evaluation of the Job Corps over a thirty-month period. At the end of the period, impacts for those age twenty to twenty-four were still considered cost-beneficial, while those for teens had diminished to below this level.

10. See Decision Information Resources (2008).

11. For instance, Achieving the Dream, a project funded by the Lumina Foundation to design curricular changes and supports for disadvantaged students, now involves more than one hundred participating community colleges. Breaking Through is another such attempt, funded by the Ford, Gates, and Mott Foundations. Shifting Gears, funded by the Joyce Foundation, focuses on midwestern states.

12. See the volume edited by Robert Giloth (2004).

13. See Bloom et al. (1997) and Heinrich et al. (2009).

14. Pell grant expansions and student loan reforms were ultimately included in the health care reform legislation passed by Congress and signed by President Obama in 2010. Although AGI, in its initial form, was ultimately not funded by the student loan reforms, some very limited funding was provided from available funds in the Trade Adjustment Assistance program for the next few years.

15. At the moment, the Perkins Act provides just over $1 billion in funding that is widely dispersed to state and local vocational education programs. See Holzer (2008) and Brand (2003) for proposed reforms in WIA and Perkins, respectively.

16. For instance, the Local Employment Dynamics (LED) program at the U.S. Census Bureau provides very detailed data on recent employment and earnings trends by industry and demographic group at the county or subcounty level in participating states. Also, the National Labor Exchange database run by Job Central and the National Association of State Workforce Agencies currently collects data on about 2 million job vacancies on a daily basis (Vollman and Carnevale 2009).

17. This entire discussion sets aside the issue of how to create a greater *quantity* of jobs—in order to speed recovery from the current recession—and focuses only on increasing the *quality* of the jobs we create.

18. Economists note that, if workers value any mandated nonwage benefits, they will accept lower wages in return. Indeed, if they value these benefits at the full cost to firms of producing them, their wages will fall by the full cost of the mandated benefits. In this case, employment will not decline, but workers will bear the full cost of benefit provision. If workers value the benefits by less than the full cost of producing them, however, or if wage rigidities inhibit wage adjustment, both employment levels and wages could be reduced. See Summers (1989) and Houseman (1998) for more discussion of these issues.

19. The statutory federal minimum wage was often set at half the national me-

dian wage whenever it was increased during the 1960s and 1970s, and then it would erode in real and relative terms afterwards. But it reached a low of about 30 percent in 2006, before being increased by Congress, and was increased to a level over 40 percent in 2008.

20. The unemployment insurance (UI) system already taxes firms to some extent based on their layoff history. But such "experience rating" is incomplete, since the tax rate varies only within a particular range of layoff rates, and the system does not extend to other dimensions of employer human resources behavior.

21. For additional evidence on the impacts of state-level training supports to firms for incumbent worker training, see also Holzer et al. (1993); Moore et al. (2003); and Ahlstrand, Bassi, and McMurrer (2003).

22. See Center on Wisconsin Strategy (COWS), "Economic and Workforce Development," available at: http://www.cows.org/hr_economic_dev.asp (accessed March 8, 2010). WRTP is one of the sites evaluated in the Public/Private Ventures (PPV) study of sectoral strategies; it was found to be highly cost-effective (see Maguire et al. 2009).

23. See Pastore and Turner (2010) for a discussion of the Sustainable Development Grants that the Obama administration has proposed for economic development at the metropolitan level.

24. See Pastore and Turner (2010) for a recent review of evidence on enterprise zones.

25. Provisions in ARRA to extend UI coverage were based on proposals included in the UI Modernization Act that had been earlier proposed by Rep. James McDermott of Washington. States received federal subsidies if they agreed to at least some of a range of efforts to extend coverage, including the use of alternative base periods for measuring eligibility, coverage of part-time job-seekers, and coverage for maternity of domestic abuse victims. See "Unemployment Insurance Provisions in the American Recovery and Reinvestment Act of 2009," Congressional Research Reports for the People, March 4, available at: http://opencrs.com/document/R40368/ (accessed March 8, 2010). Of course, extensions of UI eligibility would also increase financial pressures on the system, which would best be met by inducing states to expand the currently limited wage bases on which taxes are paid to finance these benefits (see Vroman 2009).

26. For some discussion of recent state-level efforts to encourage work-sharing, see Steven Greenhouse, "Work-Sharing May Help Companies Avoid Layoffs," New York Times, June 15, 2009, available at: http://www.nytimes.com/2009/06/16/business/economy/16workshare.html (accessed March 8, 2010). For a discussion of short-time compensation, see Abraham and Houseman (2008).

27. Jeffrey Kling's proposals (2006) call for a system of private accounts from

which unemployment or wage insurance would be paid to account owners to replace the current UI system. Even absent such a far-reaching proposal, a wage insurance scheme would improve the incentives of displaced workers to accept jobs that pay less than those they held earlier, especially if their UI or TAA payments have expired.

References

Abowd, John M., and Francis Kramarz. 1999. "The Analysis of Labor Markets Using Matched Employer-Employee Data." In *Handbook of Labor Economics*, edited by Orley Ashenfelter and David Card. Amsterdam: North Holland.

Abowd, John M., Paul Lengermann, and Kevin L. McKinney. 2002. "The Measurement of Human Capital in the U.S. Economy." LEHD technical paper no. TP-2002-09, 2002. Washington: U.S. Bureau of the Census.

Abowd, John M., Kevin L. McKinney, and Lars Vilhuber. 2009. "The Link Between Human Capital, Mass Layoffs, and Firm Deaths." In *Producer Dynamics: New Evidence from Micro Data*, edited by Timothy Dunne, J. Bradford Jensen, and Mark J. Roberts. Chicago: University of Chicago Press for the National Bureau of Economic Research.

Abowd, John M., Bryce E. Stephens, Lars Vilhuber, Fredrik Andersson, Kevin L. McKinney, Marc Roemer, and Simon Woodcock. 2006. "The LEHD Infrastructure Files and the Creation of the Quarterly Workforce Indicators." LEHD technical paper TP-2006-01. Washington: U.S. Bureau of the Census.

Abowd, John M., and Lars Vilhuber. 2005. "The Sensitivity of Economic Statistics to Coding Errors in Personal Identifiers." *Journal of Business and Economics Statistics* 23(2): 133–52.

———. 2010. "National Estimates of Gross Employment and Job Flows from the Quarterly Workforce Indicators with Demographic and Industry Detail." Center for Economic Studies working paper 10-11. Washington: U.S. Bureau of the Census.

Abraham, Katharine, and Susan N. Houseman. 2008. "Removing Barriers to Work for Older Americans." In *A Future of Good Jobs? America's Challenge in the Global Economy*, edited by Timothy Bartik and Susan Houseman. Kalamazoo, Mich.: W. E. Upjohn Institute for Employment Research.

Ahlstrand, Amanda, Laurie Bassi, and Daniel McMurrer. 2003. *Workplace Education for Low-Wage Workers*. Kalamazoo, Mich.: W. E. Upjohn Institute for Employment Research.

185

Alssid, Julian. 2002. "Building a Career Pathways System." New York: Workforce Strategies Center.

Anderson, Jacquelyn, Linda Yuriko Kato, and James A. Riccio, with Susan Blank. 2006. "A New Approach to Low-Wage Workers and Employers: Launching the Work Advancement and Support Center Demonstration." New York: MDRC (March).

Anderson, Patricia, and Bruce Meyer. 1994. "The Effects of Unemployment Insurance Taxes and Benefits on Layoffs Using Firm and Individual Data." National Bureau of Economic Research working paper no. 4960. Washington, D.C.: NBER.

Anderson, Richard, and Charles Gascon. 2007. "The Perils of Globalization: Off-shoring and Economic Insecurity of the American Worker." Working paper 2007-004A (February). Available at: http://research.stlouisfed.org/wp/2007/2007-004.pdf (accessed February 14, 2008).

Andersson, Fredrik, Harry J. Holzer, and Julia I. Lane. 2005. *Moving Up or Moving On: Who Advances in the Low-Wage Labor Market?* New York: Russell Sage Foundation.

————. 2009. "Temporary Help Agencies and the Advancement Prospects of Low Earners." In *Studies of Labor Market Intermediation*, edited by David Autor. Chicago: University of Chicago Press.

Appelbaum, Eileen, Annette Bernhardt, and Richard Murnane. 2003. *Low-Wage America: How Employers Are Reshaping Opportunity in the Workplace.* New York: Russell Sage Foundation.

Autor, David, and David Dorn. 2009. "This Job Is 'Getting Old': Measuring Changes in Job Opportunities Using Occupational Age Structure." *American Economic Association Papers and Proceedings* 94(2): 45–51.

Autor, David H., Lawrence F. Katz, and Melissa S. Kearney. 2006. "The Polarization of the U.S. Labor Market." *American Economic Review: Papers and Proceedings* 96(2): 189–94.

Azari-Rad, Hamid, and Peter Philips. 2003. "Race and Prevailing Wage Laws in the Construction Industry: Comment on Thieblot." *Journal of Labor Research* 24(1): 161–68.

Baicker, Katherine, and M. Marit Rehavi. 2002. "Trade Adjustment Assistance." *Journal of Economic Perspectives* 18(2): 239–56.

Bailey, Thomas, D. Timothy Leinbach, and Davis Jenkins. 2005. "Graduation Rates, Student Goals, and Measuring Community College Effectiveness." Brief 28. New York: Columbia University, Teachers College, Community College Research Center (CCRC).

Barnow, Burt, and Jeffrey Smith. 2004. "Performance Management of U.S. Job Training Programs." In *Job Training Policy in the United States*, edited by Christopher J. O'Leary, Robert A. Straits, and Stephen A. Wandner. Kalamazoo, Mich.: W. E. Upjohn Institute for Employment Research.

Bartel, Ann P., and George J. Borjas. 1981. "Wage Growth and Job Turnover: An

Empirical Analysis." In *Studies in Labor Markets*, edited by Sherwin Rosen. Cambridge, Mass. National Bureau of Economic Research.

Bartelsman, Eric J., John C. Haltiwanger, and Stefano Scarpetta. 2009. "Cross-Country Differences in Productivity: The Role of Allocation and Selection." Working paper 4578. Bonn, Ger.: Institute for the Study of Labor (IZA).

Bartik, Timothy. 2001. *Jobs for the Poor: Can Labor Demand Policies Help?* New York: Russell Sage Foundation.

———. 2004. "Economic Development." In *Management Policies in Local Government Finance*, edited by J. Richard Aronson and Eli Schwartz. Washington, D.C.: International City/County Management Association.

———. 2009. "The Revitalization of Older Industrial Cities: A Review Essay of *Retooling for Growth.*" *Growth and Change* 40(1): 1.

———. 2010. "Not All Job Creation Tax Credits Are Created Equal." Washington, D.C.: Economic Policy Institute (February 12).

Bebchuk, Lucian, and Jesse Fried. 2004. *Pay Without Performance: The Unfulfilled Promise of Executive Compensation.* Cambridge, Mass.: Harvard University Press.

Benedetto, Gary, John Haltiwanger, Julia Lane, and Kevin McKinney. 2007. "Using Worker Flows in the Analysis of the Firm." *Journal of Business and Economic Statistics* 25(3): 299–313.

Blanchard, Olivier Jean, and Lawrence F. Katz. 1992. "Regional Evolutions." *Brookings Papers on Economic Activity* 23(1): 1–76.

Blau, Francine D., and Lawrence M. Kahn. 1981. "Race and Sex Difference in Quits by Young Workers." *Industrial and Labor Relations Review* 34(4): 563–77.

Blinder, Alan S. 2007. "How Many U.S. Jobs Might Be Offshorable?" Working paper 142. Princeton, N.J.: Princeton University, Center for Economic Policy Studies.

Bloom, Dan. 2010. "Programs and Policies to Assist High School Dropouts in the Transition to Adulthood." *The Future of Children* 20(1): 89–108.

Bloom, Howard S., Larry L. Orr, Stephen H. Bell, George Cave, Fred Doolittle, Winston Lin, and Johannes M. Bos. 1997. "The Benefits and Costs of Title II-A Programs." *Journal of Human Resources* 32(3): 549–76.

Borjas, George J., and Lawrence F. Katz. 2005. "The Evolution of the Mexican-Born Workforce in the United States." Working paper 11281. Cambridge, Mass.: National Bureau of Economic Research.

Bound, John, and Harry J. Holzer. 1993. "Industrial Shifts, Skill Levels, and the Labor Market for White and Black Males." *Review of Economics and Statistics* 75(3): 387–96.

———. 2000. "Demand Shifts, Population Adjustments, and Labor Market Outcomes During the 1980s." *Journal of Labor Economics* 18(1): 20–54.

Brand, Betsy. 2003. "Rigor and Relevance: A New Vision for Career and Technical Education." Washington, D.C.: American Youth Policy Forum.

Brown, Charles, James Hamilton, and James L. Medoff. 1990. *Employers Large and Small.* Cambridge, Mass.: Harvard University Press.

Brown, Clair, John Haltiwanger, and Julia Lane. 2006. *Economic Turbulence: Is a Volatile Economy Good for America?* Chicago: University of Chicago Press.

Bureau of Labor Statistics (BLS). 1997. *Handbook of Methods*. Washington: U.S. Government Printing Office.

Burgess, Simon, Julia Lane, and Kevin McKinney. 2009. "Matching, Reallocation, and Changes in Earnings Dispersion." *Oxford Bulletin of Economics and Statistics* 71(1): 91–110.

Burtless, Gary. 2007. "Income Supports for Workers and Their Families: Earnings Supplements and Health Insurance." In *Reshaping the American Workforce for a Changing Economy*, edited by Harry J. Holzer and Demetra Smith Nightingale. Washington, D.C.: Urban Institute Press.

Card, David. 2009. "Immigration and Inequality." *American Economic Association Papers and Proceedings* 99(2): 1–21.

Card, David, and Jonathan DiNardo. 2006. "The Impact of Technological Change on Low-Wage Workers: A Review." In *Working and Poor*, edited by Rebecca M. Blank, Sheldon H. Danziger, and Robert F. Schoeni. New York: Russell Sage Foundation.

Card, David, and Alan Krueger. 1995. *Myth and Measurement*. Princeton, N.J.: Princeton University Press.

Cellini, Stephanie. 2006. "Smoothing the Transition to College? The Effect of Tech-Prep Programs on Educational Attainment." *Economics of Education Review* 25(4): 394–411.

Cohen, Mark A., and Alex R. Piquero. 2008. "Costs and Benefits of a Targeted Intervention Program for Youth Offenders: The YouthBuild USA Offender Program." Boston: Jobs for the Future.

Couch, Kenneth A., and Dana Placzek. 2010. "Earnings Impacts of Job Displacement Revisited." *American Economic Review* 100(1): 1.

Council of Economic Advisers. 2009. *Preparing the Workers of Today for the Jobs of Tomorrow*. Washington: U.S. Government Printing Office (July 13).

Dahl, Molly, Thomas DeLeire, and Jonathan Schwabish. 2008. "Year-to-Year Variability in Worker Earnings and in Household Incomes: Estimates from Administrative Data." Washington: Congressional Budget Office.

Darity, William L., Jr., and Patrick L. Mason. 1998. "Evidence on Discrimination in Employment: Codes of Color, Codes of Gender." *Journal of Economic Perspectives* 12(2): 63–90.

Davis, Steven. 2008. "The Decline of Job Loss and Why It Matters." *American Economic Review Papers and Proceedings* 98(2): 263–67.

Davis, Steven, Jason Faberman, John Haltiwanger, Ron Jarmin, and Javier Miranda. 2010. "Business Volatility, Job Destruction, and Unemployment." *American Economic Journal: Macroeconomics* 2(2): 259–87.

Davis, Steven, John Haltiwanger, and Scott Schuh. 1998. *Job Creation and Destruction*. Cambridge, Mass.: MIT Press.

Decision Information Resources. 2008. "Evaluation of Youth Opportunities Program." Report to U.S. Department of Labor, Employment and Training Administration. Houston: Decision Information Resources.

Dew-Becker, Ian, and Robert Gordon. 2005. "Where Did the Productivity Growth Go? Inflation Dynamics and the Distribution of Income." Working paper 11842. Cambridge, Mass.: National Bureau of Economic Research.

Dickens, William T., and Lawrence F. Katz. 1987. "Interindustry Wage Differences and Industry Characteristics." Working paper 2014. Cambridge, Mass.: National Bureau of Economic Research.

Dobbs, Lou, and Joann Myers. 2004. *Exporting America: Why Corporate Greed Is Shipping American Jobs Overseas*. New York: Warner Business Books.

Dynan, Karen, Douglas Elmendorf, and Daniel Sichel. 2008. "The Evolution of Household Income Volatility." Washington, D.C.: Brookings Institution.

Dynarski, Susan. 2007. "Financial Aid on a Postcard." Washington, D.C.: Brookings Institution, Hamilton Project.

Dynarski, Susan, and Judith Scott-Clayton. 2006. "The Cost of Complexity in Student Aid: Lessons from Behavioral Economics and Optimal Tax Theory." Working paper 12227. Cambridge, Mass.: National Bureau of Economic Research.

Eckstein, Zvi, and Éva Nagypál. 2004. "The Evolution of U.S. Earnings Inequality: 1961–2002." Federal Reserve Bank of Minneapolis *Quarterly Review* (December): 10–29.

Edelman, Peter B., Mark Greenberg, Steve Holt, and Harry J. Holzer. 2009. "Expanding the EITC to Help More Low-Wage Workers." Policy brief. Washington, D.C.: Georgetown University, Center on Poverty, Inequality, and Public Policy.

Edelman, Peter B., Harry J. Holzer, and Paul Offner. 2006. *Reconnecting Disadvantaged Young Men*. Washington: Urban Institute Press.

Economic Policy Institute. 2008. *Minimum Wage: Facts at a Glance*. Available at: http://www.epi.org/content.cfm/issueguides_minwage_minwagefacts.

Ehrenberg, Ronald, and Joshua Schwartz. 1987. "Public Sector Labor Markets." Working paper 1179. Cambridge, Mass.: National Bureau of Economic Research.

Ehrenberg, Ronald, and Robert Smith. 2009. *Modern Labor Economics*. Reading, Mass.: Pearson–Addison Wesley.

Elsby, Michael, Bart Hobijn, and Aysegul Sahin. 2010. "The Labor Market in the Great Recession." Working paper 15979. Cambridge, Mass.: National Bureau of Economic Research.

Farber, Henry. 1999. "Mobility and Stability: The Dynamics of Job Change in Labor Markets." In *The Handbook of Labor Economics*, edited by Orley Ashenfelter and David Card. Amsterdam: North Holland.

———. 2005. "What Do We Know About Job Loss in the United States? Evidence from the Displaced Workers Survey, 1981–2004." Federal Reserve Bank of Chicago *Economic Perspectives*: 13–28.

Farber, Henry. 2007. "Job Loss and the Decline in Job Security in the United States." Working paper 520. Princeton, N.J.: Princeton University, Industrial Relations Section.

Figlio, David. 2009. "School Reforms and Improved Life Outcomes for Disadvantaged Children." In *Making the Work-Based Safety Net Work Better*, edited by Carolyn J. Heinrich and John Karl Scholz. New York: Russell Sage Foundation.

Florida, Richard. 2004. *Cities and the Creative Class*. New York: Routledge.

———. 2008. *Who's Your City?: How the Creative Economy is Making Where to Live the Most Important Decision of Your Life*. New York: Basic Books.

Foster, Lucia, John Haltiwanger, and C. J. Krizan. 2001. "Aggregate Productivity Growth: Lessons from Microeconomic Evidence." In *New Developments in Productivity Analysis*, edited by Charles R. Hulten, Edwin R. Dean, and Michael Harper. Chicago: University of Chicago Press.

———. 2006. "Market Selection, Reallocation, and Restructuring in the U.S. Retail Trade Sector in the 1990s." *Review of Economics and Statistics* 88(4): 748–58.

Freeman, Richard. 2007a. "Is a Great Labor Shortage Coming? Replacement Demand in a Global Economy." In *Reshaping Workforce Policies for a Changing Economy*, edited by Harry J. Holzer and Demetra Smith Nightingale. Washington, D.C.: Urban Institute Press.

———. 2007b. *America Works: The Exceptional Labor Market*. New York: Russell Sage Foundation.

Freeman, Richard, and William Rodgers. 2000. "Area Economic Conditions and the Crime of Young Men in the 1990s Expansion." Paper presented to the meetings of the Association for Public Policy and Management. Washington, D.C. (October 31–November 2).

Friedman, Thomas. 2009. "Being Average Is Not Good Enough." *New York Times*, October 22.

Gabler, Alain, and Omar Licandro. 2006. "Endogenous Growth Through Firm Entry, Exit, and Imitation." *Meeting Papers of the Society for Economic Dynamics* 532.

Gibbons, Robert, and Lawrence Katz. 1991. "Layoffs and Lemons." *Journal of Labor Economics* 9(4): 351–80.

Giloth, Robert, ed. 2004. *Workforce Intermediaries for the Twenty-First Century*. Philadelphia: Temple University Press.

Glaeser, Edward L., and Joshua D. Gottlieb. 2009. "The Wealth of Cities: Agglomeration Economies and Spatial Equilibrium in the United States." *Journal of Economic Literature* 47(4): 983–1028.

Golan, Amos, Julia Lane, and Erika McEntarfer. 2007. "The Dynamics of Worker Reallocation: A Markov Approach." *Economica* 74(293): 1–20.

Goldin, Claudia, and Lawrence F. Katz. 2008. *The Race Between Education and Technology*. Cambridge, Mass.: Belknap Press of Harvard University Press.

Gosselin, Peter. 2008. *High Wire: The Precarious Financial Lives of American Families*. New York: Basic Books.

Gottschalk, Peter, and Robert Moffitt. 2009. "The Rising Instability of U.S. Earnings." *Journal of Economic Perspectives* 23(4): 3–24.

Greenberg, Mark. 2007. "Next Steps for Federal Child Care Policy." *The Future of Children* 17(2): 73–96.

Hacker, Jacob. 2006. *The Great Risk Shift: The New Economic Insecurity and the Decline of the American Dream.* New York: Oxford University Press.

Hallock, Kevin. 2009. "Job Loss and the Fraying of the Implicit Employment Contract." *Journal of Economic Perspectives* 23(4): 69–93.

Haltiwanger, John C., Julia I. Lane, and James R. Spletzer. 2007. "Wages, Productivity, and the Dynamic Interaction of Businesses and Workers." *Labor Economics* 14(3): 575–602.

Hamermesh, Daniel. 1998. "Changing Inequality in Markets for Workplace Amenities." *Quarterly Journal of Economics* 114(4): 1085–1123.

Handel, Michael. 2006. *Worker Skills and Job Requirements: Is There a Mismatch?* Washington, D.C.: Economic Policy Institute.

Haskins, Ron, Harry J. Holzer, and Robert Lerman. 2009. "Promoting Economic Mobility by Increasing Postsecondary Education." Washington, D.C.: Pew Charitable Trusts, Economic Mobility Project.

Haskins, Ron, and James Kemple. 2009. "A New Goal for America's High Schools: College Preparation for All." Policy brief. *The Future of Children* (May 14).

Heckman, James. 1998. "Detecting Discrimination." *Journal of Economic Perspectives* 12(2): 100–114.

———. 2008. "Schools, Skills and Synapses." Working paper 14064. Cambridge, Mass.: National Bureau of Economic Research.

Heckman, James, and Paul Lafontaine. 2007. "The American High School Graduation Rate: Trends and Levels." Discussion paper. Bonn, Ger.: Institute for the Study of Labor (IZA).

Heinrich, Carolyn, and Harry Holzer. 2010. "Improving Education and Employment for Disadvantaged Young Men: Proven and Promising Strategies." Discussion paper 1374-10. Madison: University of Wisconsin, Institute for Research on Poverty (IRP).

Heinrich, Carolyn, Peter Mueser, Kyung-Seong Jeon, Daver Kahvecioglu, and Kenneth Troske. 2009. "New Estimates of Public Employment and Training Programs Net Impacts: A Nonexperimental Evaluation of the Workforce Investment Act Programs." IZA discussion paper no. 4569 (November).

Hill, Carolyn J., Harry J. Holzer , and Henry Chen. 2009. *Against the Tide: Household Structure, Opportunities, and Outcomes Among White and Minority Youth.* Kalamazoo, Mich.: W. E. Upjohn Institute for Employment Research.

Hirsch, Barry. 2008. "Sluggish Institutions in a Dynamic World: Can Unions and Industrial Competition Coexist?" *Journal of Economic Perspectives* 22(1): 153–76.

Hirsch, Barry, and David McPherson. 2003. "Wages, Sorting on Skill, and the Racial Composition of Jobs." IZA discussion paper 741.

Hollenbeck, Kevin. 2008. "Is There a Role for Public Support in Incumbent Worker On-the-Job Training?" Working paper no. 138. Kalamazoo, Mich.: W. E. Upjohn Institute for Employment Research.

Holt, Steve, and Elaine Maag. 2009. "Considerations in Efforts to Restructure Refundable Tax Credits." Unpublished paper, Georgetown Center on Poverty, Inequality, and Public Policy. Washington, D.C.: Georgetown University.

Holzer, Harry. 1991. "The Spatial Mismatch Hypothesis: What Has the Evidence Shown?" *Urban Studies* 28(1): 105–22.

———. 1996. *What Employers Want: Job Prospects for Less-Educated Workers.* New York: Russell Sage Foundation.

———. 1998. "Why Do Small Establishments Hire Fewer Blacks Than Larger Ones?" *Journal of Human Resource* 33(4): 896–914.

———. 2004. "Advancement for Low-Wage Workers: A Different Approach." Brief 30. Washington, D.C.: Brookings Institution, Center on Children and Families (May).

———. 2008. "Workforce Policy and the Disadvantaged: The Workforce Investment Act in 2009 and Beyond." Washington, D.C.: Urban Institute.

———. 2009. "Living Wage Laws: How Much Do (Can) They Matter?" In *Urban and Regional Policy and Its Effects*, vol. 2, edited by Nancy Pindus, Howard Wial, and Harold Wolman. Washington, D.C.: Brookings Institution Press.

Holzer, Harry J., Richard N. Block, Marcus Cheatham, and Jack H. Knott. 1993. "Are Training Subsidies for Firms Effective? The Michigan Experience." *Industrial and Labor Relations Review* 46(4): 625–36.

Holzer, Harry J., and Robert J. Lalonde. 2000. "Employment and Job Stability Among Less-Skilled Workers." In *Finding Jobs: Work and Welfare Reform*, edited by Rebecca Blank and David Card. New York: Russell Sage Foundation.

Holzer, Harry J., and Robert Lerman. 2007. *America's Forgotten Middle-Skill Jobs: Education and Training Requirements in the Next Decade and Beyond.* Washington, D.C.: Workforce Alliance.

———. 2008. *The Future of Middle-Skill Jobs.* Washington, D.C.: Brookings Institution.

———. 2009. "Time for a Federal Jobs Program." *Cleveland Plain Dealer.* November 23.

Holzer, Harry J., and Karin Martinson. 2008. *Helping Poor Working Parents Get Ahead: Federal Funds for New State Strategies and Systems.* Paper 4. Washington, D.C.: Urban Institute, New Safety Net.

Holzer, Harry J., and Demetra Smith Nightingale. 2009. *Strong Students, Strong Workers: Models for Student Success Through Workforce Development and Community College Partnerships.* Washington, D.C.: Center for American Progress.

Holzer, Harry J., Steven Raphael, and Michael A. Stoll. 2006. "Employers in the Boom: How Did the Hiring of Unskilled Workers Change in the 1990s?" *Review of Economics and Statistics* 88(2): 283–99.

Holzer, Harry J., and Michael Stoll. 2007. *Where Workers Go, Do Jobs Follow? Metropolitan Labor Markets in the United States, 1990–2000.* Metropolitan Economy Initiative 4. Washington, D.C.: Brookings Institution, Metropolitan Policy Program.

Houseman, Susan. 1998. "The Effects of Employer Mandates." In *Generating Jobs: How to Increase Demand for Less-Skilled Workers,* edited by Richard B. Freeman and Peter Gottschalk. New York: Russell Sage Foundation.

Hoynes, Hilary. 2000. "The Employment and Earnings of Less-Skilled Workers over the Business Cycle." In *Finding Jobs: Work and Welfare Reform,* edited by David Card and Rebecca Blank. New York: Russell Sage Foundation.

Ihlanfeldt, Keith, and David Sjoquist. 1998. "The Spatial Mismatch Hypothesis: A Review of Recent Evidence and Their Implications for Welfare Reform." *Housing Policy Debate* 9(4): 849–92.

Jackson, Peter, and Edward Montgomery. 1986. "Layoffs, Discharges, and Youth Unemployment." In *The Black Youth Employment Crisis,* edited by Richard B. Freeman and Harry J. Holzer. Chicago: University of Chicago Press.

Jacob, Brian, and Jens Ludwig. 2009. "Improving Educational Outcomes for Poor Children." In *Changing Poverty, Changing Policies,* edited by Maria Cancian and Sheldon Danziger. New York: Russell Sage Foundation.

Jacobson, Louis S., Robert J. Lalonde, and Daniel G. Sullivan. 1993. "Earnings Losses of Displaced Workers." *American Economic Review* 83(4): 685–709.

———. 2003. "Should We Teach Old Dogs New Tricks? The Impact of Community College Retraining on Older Workers." Working paper. Bonn, Ger.: Institute for the Study of Labor (IZA).

Jacobson, Louis, and Christine Mukher. 2009. "Pathways to Boosting the Earnings of Low-Income Students by Increasing Their Educational Attainment." Arlington, Va.: CNA.

Jastrzab, Joann, John Blomquist, Julie Musker, and Larry Orr. 1997. *Youth Corps: Promising Strategies for Young People and Their Communities.* Washington, D.C.: Abt Associates.

Jenkins, Davis, Matthew Zeidenberg, and Gregory Kienzl. 2009. "Building Bridges to Postsecondary Training for Low-Skill Adults: Outcomes of Washington State's I-BEST Program." Brief 42. New York: Columbia University, Community College Research Center (CCRC).

Jovanovic, Boyan. 1979a. "Firm-Specific Capital and Turnover." *Journal of Political Economy* 87(6): 1246–60.

———. 1979b. "Job Matching and the Theory of Turnover." *Journal of Political Economy* 87(5): 972–90.

Kain, John. 1992. "The Spatial Mismatch Hypothesis: Three Decades Later." *Housing Policy Debate* 3(2): 371–460.

Kasarda, John. 1995. "Industrial Restructuring and the Changing Location of Jobs." In *State of the Union: America in the 1990s,* edited by Reynolds Farley. New York: Russell Sage Foundation.

Katz, Lawrence. 1986. "Efficiency Wage Theories: A Partial Evaluation." *National Bureau of Economic Research Macroeconomics Annual* 1: 235–90.

Kemple, James. 2008. *Career Academies: Long-Term Impacts on Labor Market Outcomes, Educational Attainment, and Transitions to Adulthood.* New York: MDRC.

Kemple, James, and Cecelia Rouse. 2009. "America's High Schools: Introducing the Issue." *The Future of Children* 19(1): 3–15.

Kletzer, Lori G., and Robert W. Fairlie. 2003. "The Long-Term Costs of Job Displacement for Young Adult Workers." *Industrial and Labor Relations Review* 56(4): 682–98.

Kling, Jeffrey. 2006. "Fundamental Restructuring of Unemployment Insurance: Wage-Loss Insurance and Earnings Accounts." Washington, D.C.: Brookings Institution, Hamilton Project.

Kotkin, Joel. 2000. *The New Geography: How the Digital Revolution Is Reshaping the American Landscape.* New York: Random House.

Krueger, Alan B., and Lawrence H. Summers. 1987. "Reflections on the Inter-Industry Wage Structure." In *Unemployment and the Structure of Labor Markets,* edited by Kevin Lang and Jonathan S. Leonard. London: Basil Blackwell Press.

Krugman, Paul. 1991. "First Nature, Second Nature, and Metropolitan Location." Working paper 3740. Cambridge, Mass.: National Bureau of Economic Research.

Lane, Julia. 2009. "Inequality and the Labor Market: Employers." In *The Oxford Handbook of Economic Inequality,* edited by Wiemer Salverda, Brian Nolan, and Timothy M. Smeeding. Oxford: Oxford University Press.

Lazear, Edward P. 1979. "Why Is There Mandatory Retirement?" *Journal of Political Economy* 87(6): 1261–84.

———. 2009. "Firm-Specific Human Capital: A Skills-Weighted Approach." *Journal of Political Economy* 117(5): 914–40.

Lerman, Robert. 2007. "Career-Focused Education and Training for Youth." In *Reshaping the American Workforce in a Changing Economy,* edited by Harry Holzer and Demetra Nightingale. Washington, D.C.: The Urban Institute.

Lerman, Robert, Signe-Mary McKernan, and Stephanie Riegg. 2004. "The Scope of Employer-Provided Training in the United States: Who, What, Where, and How Much?" In *Job Training Policy in the United States,* edited by Christopher J. O'Leary, Robert A. Straits, and Stephen A. Wandner. Kalamazoo, Mich.: W. E. Upjohn Institute for Employment Research.

Levy, Frank, and Richard Murnane. 2004. *The New Division of Labor: How Computers are Creating the Next Job Market.* New York: Russell Sage Foundation.

Levy, Frank, and Peter Temin. 2007. "Inequality and Institutions in Twentieth-Century America." Working paper 07-17. Cambridge, Mass.: Massachusetts Institute of Technology, Department of Economics.

Loury, Glenn. 2003. "Racial Stigma: Toward a New Paradigm for Discrimination Theory." *American Economic Review* 93(2): 334–37.

Maguire, Sheila, Joshua Freely, Carol Clymer, and Maureen Conway. 2009. *Job Training That Works. Findings from the Sectoral Employment Impact Study.* Philadelphia: Public/Private Ventures (PPV).

Mann, Catherine. 2006. *Accelerating Globalization: The Role of Information Technology.* Washington, D.C.: Institute for International Economics.

McGahey, Richard, and Jennifer Vey. 2008. *Retooling for Growth.* Washington, D.C.: Brookings Institution Press.

Meyerson, Harold. 2009. "One Word: Factories." *Washington Post,* August 12.

Millenky, Megan, Dan Bloom, and Colleen Dillon. 2010. *Making the Transition: Interim Results of the National Guard Youth ChalleNGe Evaluation.* New York: MDRC.

Mincer, Jacob. 1974. *Schooling, Experience, and Earnings.* New York: Columbia University Press and National Bureau of Economic Research.

Mishel, Lawrence, Jared Bernstein, and Heidi Shierholz. 2009. *State of Working America 2008–2009.* Ithaca, N.Y.: Cornell University Press.

Mishel, Lawrence, and Joydeep Roy. 2006. *Rethinking High School Graduation Rates and Trends.* Washington, D.C.: Economic Policy Institute.

Moore, Richard W., Daniel R. Blake, G. Michael Phillips, and Daniel McConaughy. 2003. *Training That Works: Lessons from California's Employment Training Panel Program.* Kalamazoo, Mich.: W. E. Upjohn Institute for Employment Research.

Neal, Derek A., and William R. Johnson. 1996. "The Role of Premarket Factors in Black-White Wage Differences." *Journal of Political Economy* 104(5): 869–95.

Neumark, David, and Scott Adams. 2005. "The Effects of Living Wage Laws: Evidence from Failed and Derailed Living Wage Campaigns." Working paper 11342. Cambridge, Mass.: National Bureau of Economic Research.

Neumark, David, and William L. Wascher. 2009. *Minimum Wages.* Cambridge, Mass.: MIT Press.

Niederle, Muriel, and Lise Vesterlund. 2007. "Do Women Shy Away from Competition? Do Men Compete Too Much?" *Quarterly Journal of Economics* 122(3): 1067–1101.

O'Mahony, Mary, and Bart van Ark. 2003. "EU Productivity and Competitiveness: An Industry Perspective—Can Europe Resume the Catching-Up Process?" Luxembourg: Office for Official Publications of the European Communities.

Oreopoulos, Philip, Marianne Page, and Ann Huff Stevens. 2008. "The Intergenerational Effects of Worker Displacement." *Journal of Labor Economics* 26(3): 455–83.

Orszag, Peter R. 2007. "CBO Testimony." Statement before the House Ways and Means Committee hearing on economic volatility, January 31, 2007. Available at: http://www.cbo.gov/ftpdocs/77xx/doc7777/01-31-Volatility.pdf (accessed March 14, 2007).

Ottaviano, Gianmarco, Ireo Paolo, and Giovanni Peri. 2007. "The Effects of Immigration on WS Wages and Rents: A General Equilibrium Approach." Discussion paper 6551. London: Centre for Economic Policy Research.

Pager, Devah. 2003. "The Mark of a Criminal Record." *American Journal of Sociology* 108(5): 937–75.

Parsons, Donald O. 1987. "The Employment Relationship: Job Attachment, Work Effort, and the Nature of Contracts." In *Handbook of Labor Economics*, edited by Orley Ashenfelter and Richard Layard, vol. 2. Amsterdam: North Holland.

Partnership for Twenty-First-Century Skills. 2010. *Twenty-First-Century Readiness for Every Child: A Guide to the Reauthorization of the Elementary and Secondary Education Act*. Washington, D.C.: Partnership for Twenty-First-Century Skills.

Pastore, Manuel, and Marjorie Turner. 2010. "Reducing Poverty and Economic Distress After ARRA: Potential Roles for Place-Conscious Strategies." Washington, D.C.: Urban Institute.

Piketty, Thomas, and Emmanuel Saez. 2003. "Income Inequality in the United States, 1913–1998." *Quarterly Journal of Economics* 118(1): 1–39.

Poschke, Markus. Forthcoming(a). "Employment Protection, Firm Selection, and Growth." *Journal of Monetary Economics*.

———. Forthcoming(b). "The Regulation of Entry and Aggregate Productivity." *Economic Journal*.

Reich, Robert. 2007. *Supercapitalism: The Transformation of Business, Democracy, and Everyday Life*. New York: Alfred A. Knopf.

Rosenbaum, James. 2006. *After Admission: From College Access to College Success*. New York: Russell Sage Foundation.

Rothstein, Jesse. 2008. "The Unintended Consequences of Encouraging Work: Tax Incidence and the EITC." Working paper. Princeton, N.J.: Princeton University.

Roubini, Nouriel, and Steve Mimh. 2010. *Crisis Economics: A Crash Course in the Future of Finance*. New York: Penguin.

Schochet, Peter Z., John Burghardt, and Sheena McConnell. 2008. "Does Job Corps Work? Impacts from the National Job Corps Study." *American Economic Review* 98(5): 1864–86.

Scholz, J. Karl. 2007. "Employment-Based Tax Credits for Low-Skilled Workers." Washington, D.C.: Brookings Institution, Hamilton Project.

Shin, Donggyun, and Gary Solon. 2008. "Trends in Men's Earnings Volatility: What Does the Panel Study of Income Dynamics Show?" Working paper 14075. Cambridge, Mass.: National Bureau of Economic Research.

Simms, Margaret, and Daniel Kuehn. 2008. "Unemployment Insurance During a Recession." Policy brief. Washington, D.C.: Urban Institute.

Spletzer, James R. 2000. "The Contribution of Establishment Births and Deaths to Employment Growth." *Journal of Business and Economic Statistics* 18(1): 113–26.

Stoll, Michael, Harry J. Holzer, and Keith Ihlanfeldt. 2000. "Within Cities and Suburbs: Racial Residential Concentration and the Spatial Distribution of Employment Opportunities Across Sub-Metropolitan Areas." *Journal of Policy Analysis and Management* 19(2): 207–31.

Sturgis, Chris. 2008. "Stemming the Tide: Accelerating the Adoption of the Multiple Pathways Framework to Graduation Through Coordinated Grantmaking and Leadership." Report. New York: Youth Transitions Funders Group.

Summers, Lawrence. 1989. "Some Simple Economics of Mandated Benefits." *American Economic Review* 79(2): 177–83.

Swanson, Chris. 2004. "Who Graduates? Who Doesn't? A Statistical Portrait of Public High School Graduation." Washington, D.C.: Urban Institute.

Topel, Robert H., and Michael P. Ward. 1992. "Job Mobility and the Careers of Young Men." *Quarterly Journal of Economics* 107(4): 441–79.

Trejo, Stephen J. 1997. "Why Do Mexican Americans Earn Low Wages?" *Journal of Political Economy* 105(6): 1235–68.

Turner, Sarah. 2007. "Higher Education Policies Generating the Twenty-First-Century Workforce." In *Reshaping the American Workforce in a Changing Economy*, edited by Harry J. Holzer and Demetra Smith Nightingale. Washington, D.C.: Urban Institute Press.

Uchitelle, Louis. 2006. *The Disposable American: Layoffs and Their Consequences.* New York: Vintage Books.

U.S. Bureau of the Census. 1992–2003. LEHD Program [unpublished and confidential microdata on workers and their firms]. Available at: http://lehd.did.cens us.gov/led/about-us-FAQ.html#lehd (accessed September 30, 2010).

van Ark, Bart, Mary O'Mahony, and Marcel P. Timmer. 2008. "The Productivity Gap Between Europe and the United States: Trends and Causes." *Journal of Economic Perspectives* 22(1): 25–44.

Vollman, James, and Anthony Carnevale. 2009. "Jobs Agenda." Unpublished paper. Washington, D.C.: Georgetown University, Center on Education and the Workforce.

von Wachter, Till. 2010. Testimony before the Joint Economic Committee of Congress, May 26.

Vroman, Wayne. 2009. "Unemployment Insurance: Current Situation and Potential Reforms." Washington, D.C.: Urban Institute.

Waldfogel, Jane. 1998. "The Family Gap for Young Women in the United States and Britain: Can Maternity Leave Make a Difference?" *Journal of Labor Economics* 16(3): 505–45.

———. 2007. "Work-Family Policies." In *Workforce Policies for a Changing Economy*, edited by Harry J. Holzer and Demetra Smith Nightingale. Washington, D.C.: Urban Institute Press.

Waller, Margy. 2005. "High Cost or High Opportunity Cost? Transportation and Family Economic Success." Policy brief. Washington, D.C.: Brookings Institution.

Wial, Howard. 2008. "Rebuilding America's Industrial Regions: The Changing Industrial Composition of Manufacturing-Based Regions, 1980–2005." Paper presented to the sixtieth annual meeting of the Labor and Employment Relations Association. New Orleans (January 4–6).

Youth Development Institute. 2009. "Tailor-Made: Attracting, Engaging, and Retaining Hard-to-Reach Youth." New York: Youth Development Institute.

Index

Boldface numbers refer to figures and tables.